FROM FLOWCHART TO PROGRAM

No. 1862
$19.95

FROM FLOWCHART TO PROGRAM

RICHARD G. TODD

To Bob

FIRST EDITION

FIRST PRINTING

Library of Congress Cataloging in Publication Data

Todd, Richard G.
From flowchart to a program.

Bibliography: p.
Includes index.
1. Electronic digital computers—Programming.
I. Title.
QA76.6.T618 1985 001.64'2 85-8093
ISBN 0-8306-0862-1
ISBN 0-8306-1862-7 (pbk.)

Contents

PART 3 OTHER USES OF FLOWCHARTING

Introduction

This book was originally conceived as a simple guide to flowcharting. As it evolved, it became obvious that it is difficult, and unwise, to separate flowcharting from the principles of program design. Flowcharts can be created by an individual with no knowledge of these principles, but they will be of little value. Thus, this book became a synthesis of flowcharting and program design principles.

Because this book is a flowcharting guide, program design often takes a back seat. Many examples do not show the "best" way to solve a particular problem. The examples are meant to show how a flowchart can be used to represent a program or process. You are encouraged to improve on any example by using your new understanding of program design.

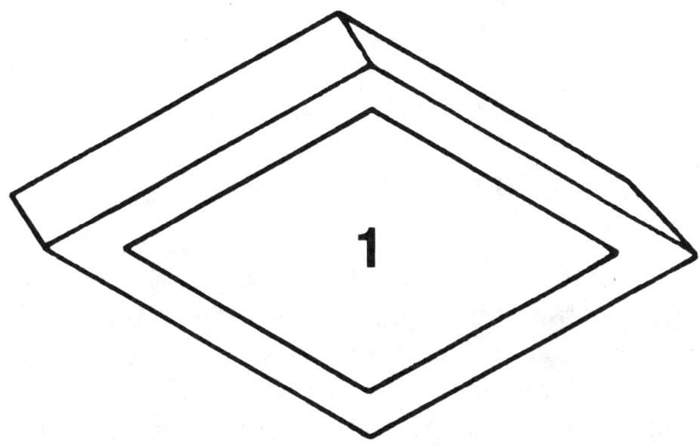

Getting Started

Everyone wants to be successful at what they do. Programmers are no exception. But every year, the thousands of people who set out to learn how to program a computer find they are slaves to syntax errors and program bugs.

Successful programming in not impossible. There are three things necessary to be a successful programmer:

☐ **Equipment.** Programming requires practice. Almost any computer will do, although pocket computers and some portable computers, because of their small display, may make it harder for you. You should also have a cassette or floppy disk system to store the programs you write.

☐ **Motivation**. Like any other skill, programming requires motivation to learn well. You must be willing to spend some serious time learning the concepts presented in this book.

☐ **Instruction**. This book explains the principles of problem solving and programming techniques. Don't overlook other sources; programming courses, other programmers, and book and magazine articles can be most useful, especially for help with special problems.

Your progress will depend on your current status as a computer user and member of the user's community. Assess your status: What type of computer are you going to use? How well do you know how to use it? Who do you know who can help you with problems? How much time do you have and are willing to spend learning this material? The better you know your computer, the more experienced programmers you know and the more time you can devote to practicing programming techniques, the faster you will produce satisfactory programs. Now we will look at the mechanics of computer operation. It is not necessary to understand all the inner workings of a computer—many programmers don't—but generally knowing how a computer functions will help you understand why a program does what it does. You'll find that many BASIC instructions will make sense when you know what the computer does with them.

THE BINARY SYSTEM: USING 0 AND 1

An important function of a computer is its ability to store data. The earliest computers used mechanical switches to do this. The switches, called *relays,* were either on or off. They were switched, or *toggled,* electronically. The proper electrical signal would make a switched-off relay switch on, and vice versa.

Relays have two states, on or off; the binary number system was perfectly suited to use to store data. Binary numbers use the digits 0 and 1. If a relay was off, it represented a 0. If it was switched on, it represented a 1. By stringing relays together, entire numbers could be represented. Figure 1-1 shows how the binary number 0110 could be stored. The lights connected to each relay indicate whether the relay is on.

Modern technology has eliminated relays in modern computers. Solid-state devices, sometimes called *flip-flops,* are to today's computer what relays were to the computers of yesterday. Although they have no moving parts, they respond in an off-on fashion, and can still be thought of as little switches; thus modern computer technology still uses the binary system.

Before we look at binary numbers, let's take a close look at the decimal numbers with which we are all familiar, and see how they function.

The decimal number system uses 10 digits (*deci-* means 10). Nine represent quantity: 1, 2, 3, 4, 5, 6, 7, 8, and 9. The tenth digit, 0, is used as a place holder; it doesn't represent a quantity, but takes up space in the representation of a number.

Let's take a look at an ordinary number and see what it really is. The number 139 can be thought of as 100 + 30 + 9. Each of these figures uses a digit (1-9) which may

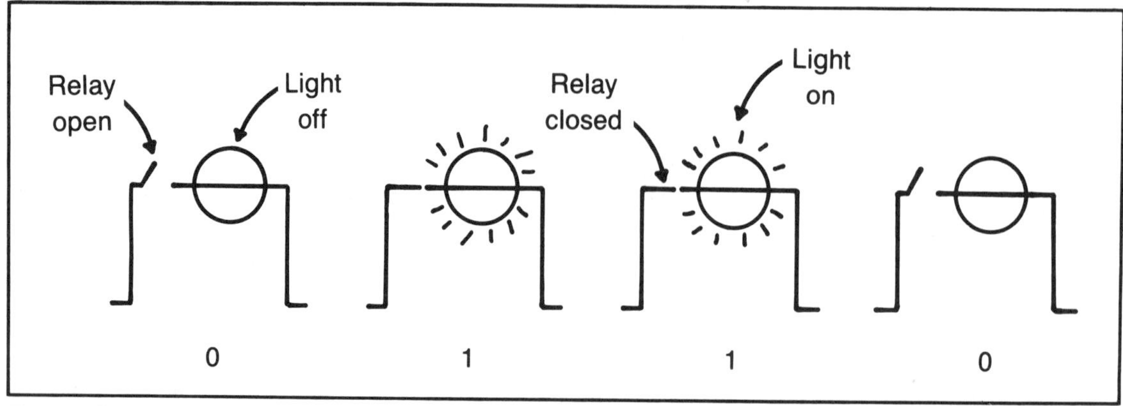

Fig. 1-1. Representing 0110 with relays.

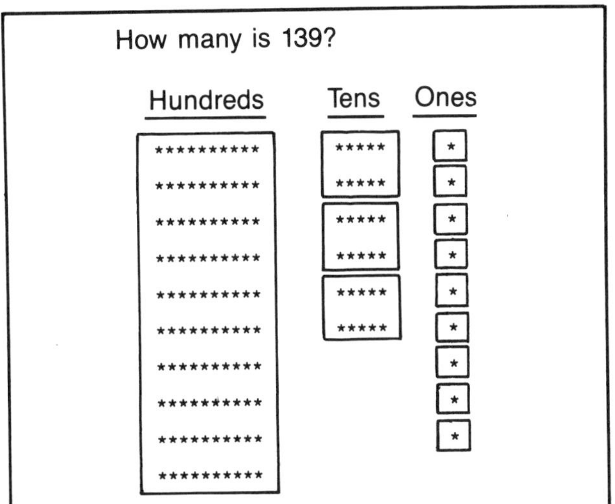

Fig. 1-2. Grouping 139 by ones, tens, and hundreds.

or may not be followed by zeroes. The rightmost digit, 9, is in the *units* column of the number 139; the 9 represents nine things. The middle number, 3, is in the *tens* column; it represents three groups of ten. The last number, 1, is in the *hundreds* place, representing one group of 100. This fact is shown pictorially in Fig. 1-2. Another way to picture the grouping is: if you were to pick up 139 things, you could do so by first picking up 100 items once, 10 items three times, and 9 items one at a time.

We can generalize this by showing that each column in a decimal number is worth a power of ten. That is, the second column is worth 10, the third is worth 10 × 10, or 100, the fourth is worth 10 × 10 × 10, or 1000, and so on. The first column is worth 1, as it is in any number system. The values can be represented by exponents. An *exponent* indicates how many times you multiply a number by itself. A number with an exponent of 5 would mean multiply the number by itself five times. If the exponent is negative, the inverse of the number is taken. A number with an exponent of −3 means multiply the number by itself three times and then take the reciprocal. A table of decimal exponents is shown in Table 1-1.

Table 1-1. Powers of Ten.

Column	Value	
1	2^0	= 1
2	2^1	= 2
3	2^2	= 4
		= 2 × 2
4	2^3	= 8
		= 2 × 2 × 2
5	2^4	= 16
		= 2 × 2 × 2 × 2
6	2^5	= 32
		= 2 × 2 × 2 × 2 × 2
7	2^6	= 64
		= 2 × 2 × 2 × 2 × 2 × 2
8	2^7	= 128
		= 2 × 2 × 2 × 2 × 2 × 2 × 2

Column	Value
1	10^0 = 1
2	10^1 = 10
3	10^2 = 100
	= 10 × 10
4	10^3 = 1,000
	= 10 × 10 × 10
5	10^4 = 10,000
	= 10 × 10 × 10 × 10
6	10^5 = 100,000
	= 10 × 10 × 10 × 10 × 10
7	10^6 = 1,000,000
	= 10 × 10 × 10 × 10 × 10 × 10
8	10^7 = 10,000,000
	= 10 × 10 × 10 × 10 × 10 × 10 × 10

Table 1-2. Powers of Two.

The binary number system uses only two digits: 0 and 1 (*bi-* means two). Unlike the decimal system, each column in a binary number is worth a power of 2 rather than a power of 10: 1, 2, 4, 8, 16 and so on. Table 1-2 lists the powers of two and their values. As in any number system, 0 is used as a place holder. In binary, this leaves us with only the digit 1 to represent a value.

In the decimal number system, the digits 2-9 represented multiples of the worth of the digit in each column. Remember, the 3 in the tens column represented three groups of ten. However, because the only digit that can represent a quantity in the binary number system is 1, we never have to deal with multiples. If a one is in a particular column of a binary number, we simply add the value of that column to the entire value of the number. Thus, the value of a binary number 1101 would be 1 (the value of the right-most column), plus 4 (the value of the third column), plus 8 (the value of the fourth column): 1 + 4 + 8 is 13, so the value of 1101 is 13.

You can convert from a binary number to a decimal number easily once you realize we have been using the decimal number system to represent the values of the different columns in a binary number. To calculate the decimal value of a binary number, add together the values of the columns with 1s in them; this process is shown in Fig. 1-3.

The binary number 101101_2 is what decimal number?

Column number:	6	5	4	3	2	1
Contents:	1	0	1	1	0	1

Since positions 6, 4, 3, and 1 have 1s in them, we will add up their values.

Column 1 is worth	1
Column 3 is worth	4
Column 4 is worth	8
Column 6 is worth	+ 32
Total	45

The decimal equivalent of 101101_2 is 45_{10}.

Fig. 1-3. Converting from binary to decimal.

The binary number 11101_2 is what decimal number?

Column number:	5	4	3	2	1
Contents:	[ ]	[ ]	[ ]	[ ]	[ ]

Since positions [ ], [ ], [ ], and [ ] have 1's in them, we will add up their values.

Column [ ] is worth	[ ]
Column [ ] is worth	[ ]
Column [ ] is worth	[ ]
Column [ ] is worth	+ [ ]
Total	[ ]

Therefore, the decimal equivalent of 11101_2 is $[\ \ ]_{10}$.

Fig. 1-4. An exercise in converting from binary to decimal.

Practice converting binary to decimal with the problem shown in Fig. 1-4.

Converting from decimal to binary requires a little more effort. Start by finding the largest power of two (1, 2, 4, 8, 16, . . .) that is less than or equal to our decimal number. For example, if our number were 10, we would pick eight. The binary number will have a 1 in the column representing the value we picked. In this example, place it in column 4. Then subtract the power of two from the original number and repeat the process with the difference, in this case 2 (10 − 8), until the difference is zero. Figure 1-5 is an example of how this is done. Try the problem in Fig. 1-6 for practice converting from decimal to binary.

The decimal number 27_{10} is what binary number?

27		
−16	⟶	Value of column 5
11		
− 8	⟶	Value of column 4
3		
− 2	⟶	Value of column 2
1		
− 1	⟶	Value of column 1
0	⟶	Conversion is complete

We know our binary number has 1's in columns 1, 2, 4, and 5.

Column number:	5	4	3	2	1
Contents:	1	1	0	1	1

Therefore, the binary equivalent of 27_{10} is 11011_2.

Fig. 1-5. Converting from decimal to binary.

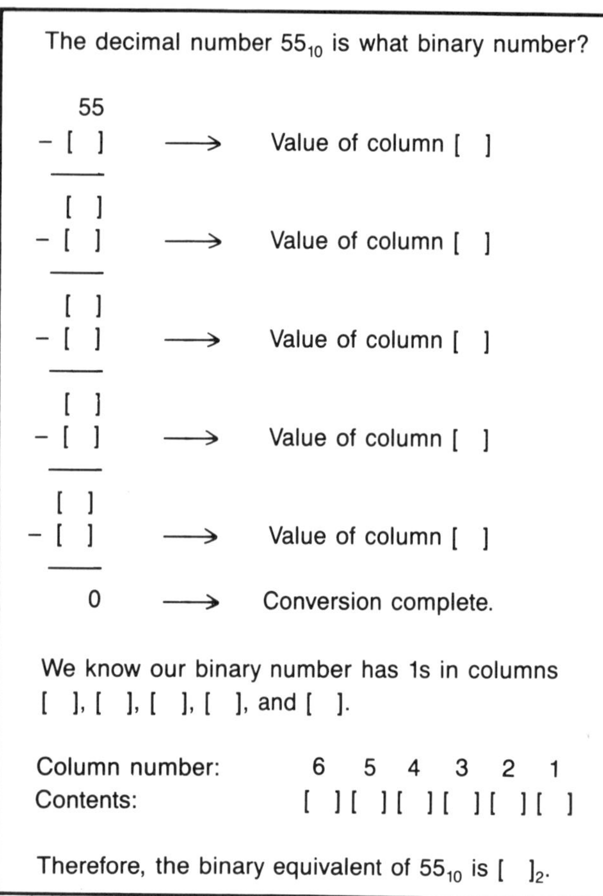

Fig. 1-6. An exercise in converting from decimal to binary.

You may have found this discussion of binary and decimal numbers confusing because it is difficult to distinguish a decimal number from a binary number. For example, look at Fig. 1-7 and count the number of crosses. How many are there—1110 or 14? Both, you may say, because the binary number 1110 and the decimal number 14 are equivalent. Knowing what number system the number is written in is necessary to interpreting its correct value. To show what number system a number uses, its *base*

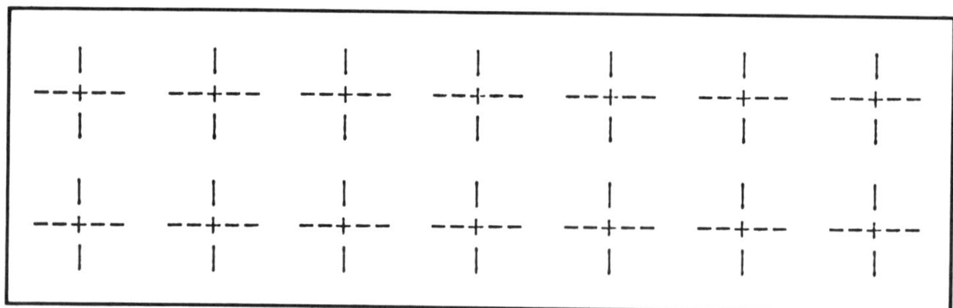

Fig. 1-7. A number of crosses.

is written as a subscript after the number. Binary is base 2, and decimal is base 10. Thus, the two numbers mentioned above would be written as 1110_2 and 14_{10}. This prevents misunderstandings.

BITS, BYTES, AND WORDS

Computers store binary numbers by storing separately each one and zero in the number. Each digit is called a *bit.* Bit is an abbreviation for Binary digIT. Because it is inefficient to store and retrieve single bits, they are grouped together to form *bytes,* a binary number. Bytes are composed of eight bits. Especially with reference to larger computers, you may find references to *words.* Words are groups of bytes—for instance, a 4-byte word. When we say a personal computer has 32K bytes of memory, we mean a computer can store 32 × 1024 (1024 is one K) 8-digit binary numbers.

A SIMPLE COMPUTER

Figure 1-8 shows a computer system. Let's take a close look at the parts that comprise it.

In the center of things is the *central processing unit,* or CPU. The CPU is usually a single integrated circuit chip (IC). Although it is small compared to the entire computer system, the CPU does all the computation and control. The CPU often has support hardware, usually on ICs located next to the CPU, that regulates information flowing into and out from the CPU and generates signals affecting the system.

Connected to the CPU is *memory.* Memory can be thought of as a set of boxes where bytes of information are stored. Each box has a label called an *address.* Memory can be written or read from. When writing to memory, the address where the information

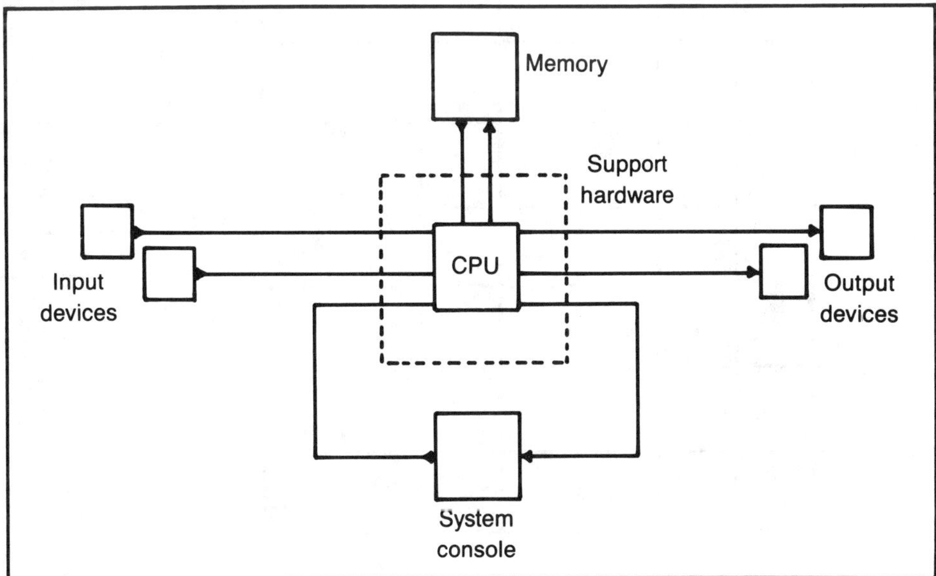

Fig. 1-8. A simple computer system.

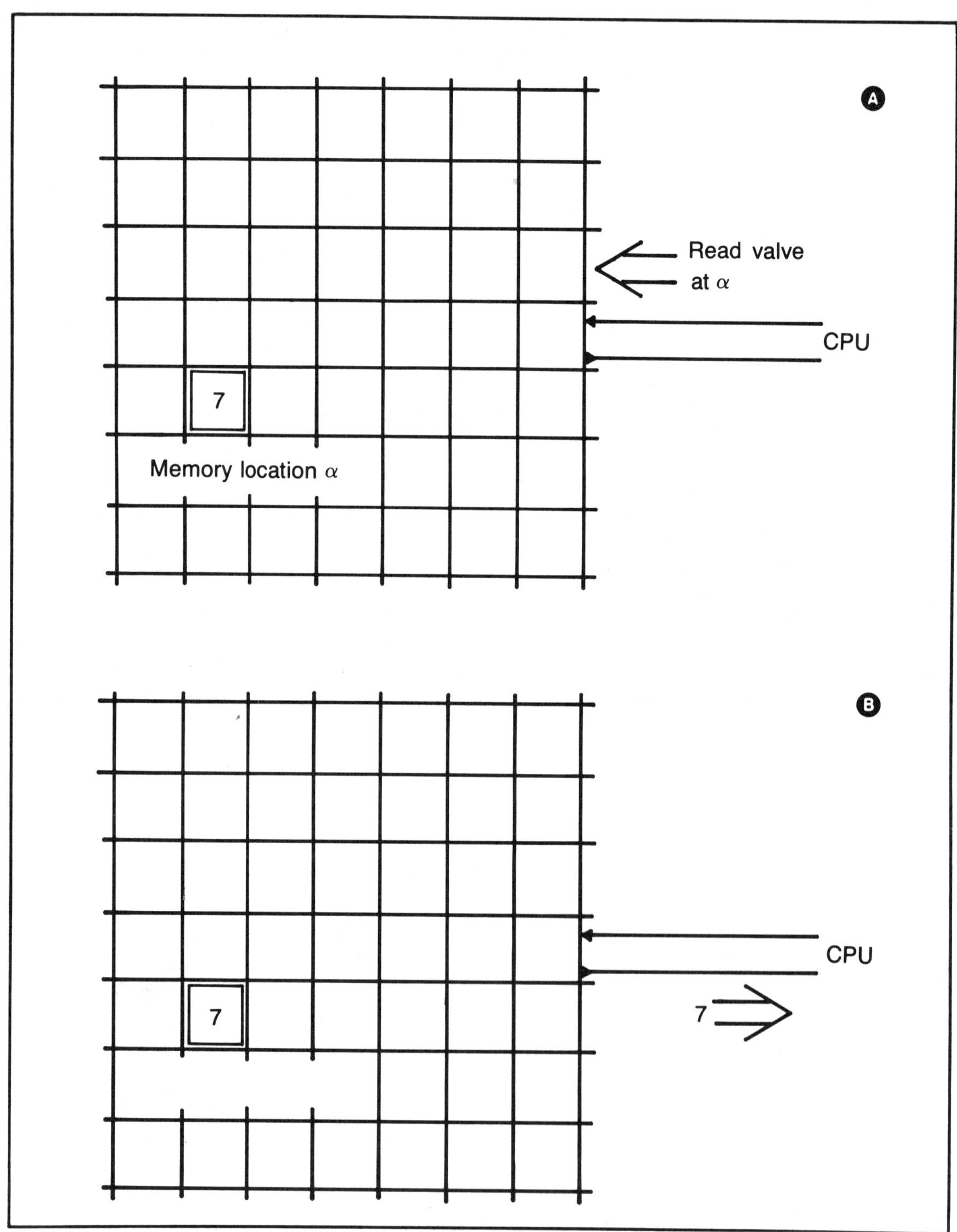

Fig. 1-9. How memory is used: (A) Reading—before (B) Reading—after.

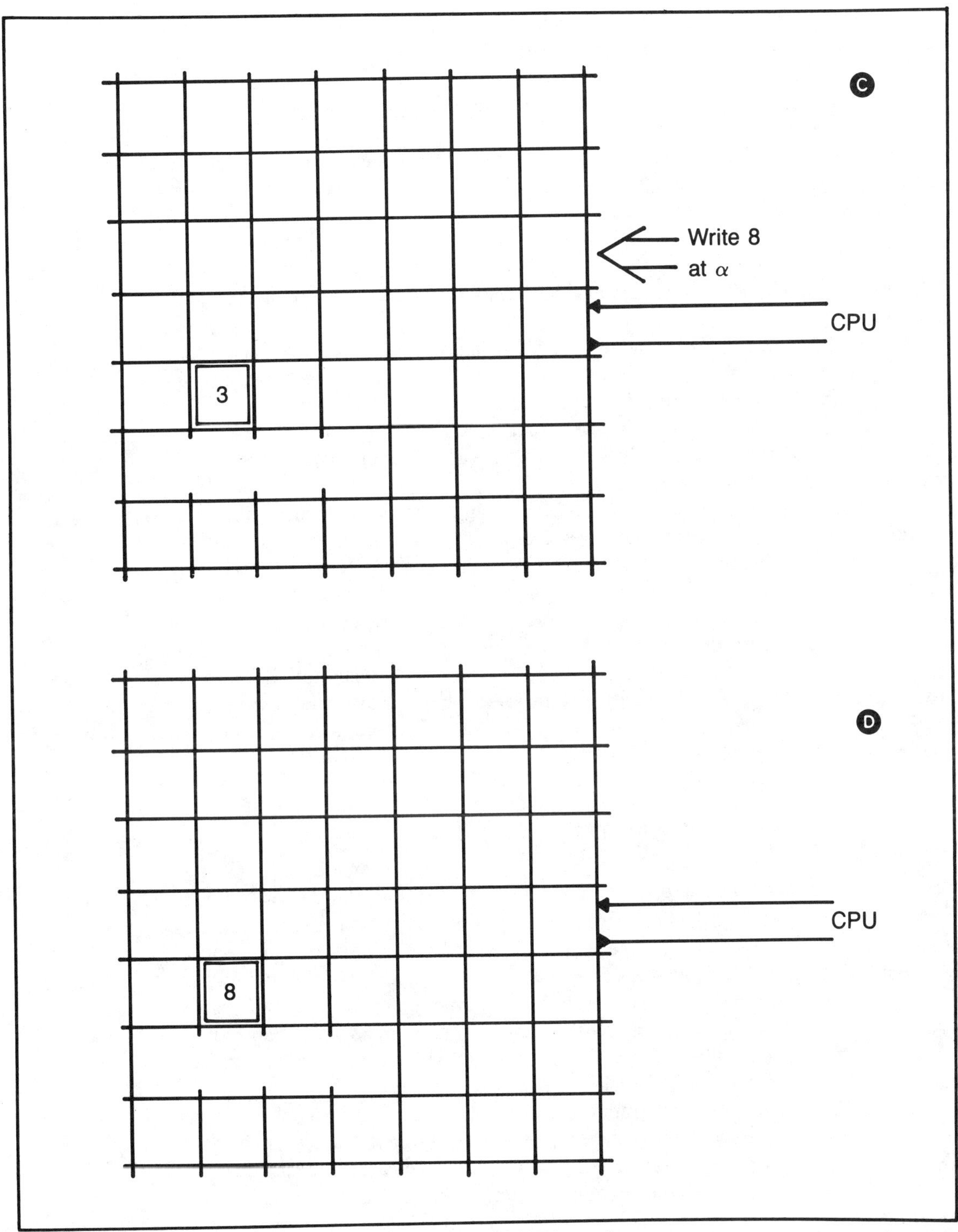

Fig. 1-9. (cont.) How memory is used: (C) Writing—before (D) Writing—after.

is to be placed, as well as the information itself, is sent to memory. Memory then places the information in the proper box, which destroys any information previously stored there.

When reading from memory, the CPU sends the address of the requested information to memory. Memory returns a copy of the contents of that address, without destroying the contents to the CPU. These processes are shown pictorially in Fig. 1-9. The type of memory just described is *random access memory* or *RAM*. RAM is used to store the programs we will soon be writing.

Most computers have another type of memory, called *ROM*. ROM stands for read-only memory. ROM can be read from just like RAM, but we cannot store information there. ROMs are manufactured containing information the CPU uses: for instance, the BASIC language.

Flowing into the CPU from the left are input lines with input devices connected to them. Input devices are used to send data to the CPU. Examples of input devices include keyboards and cassette recorders.

Leaving the CPU from the right are output lines with output devices connected to them. Output devices read data flowing from the CPU. Examples of output devices are printers and video displays.

The system console, at the bottom of the diagram, represents a special pair of input and output devices a programmer uses to communicate to the CPU. The input device is usually a keyboard, and the output device a video display or printer. The CPU is also connected to a device that stores the programs a programmer writes and later reads them back to the CPU, such as a cassette tape recorder or disk drive. These devices are often referred to as *mass storage devices*, they can hold larger quantities of information than can be stored in the computer's memory at one time. Because the device can perform input and output, it is also referred to as an input/output or *I/O* device. The system console is often considered an I/O device because the input device and output device operate as one.

COMPUTER FUNCTIONS

Computers execute programs. A *program* is a set of instructions that tell the computer how to perform a certain task. The program that the CPU executes is a series of binary numbers called *machine code*. Machine code is stored in memory cells with consecutive addresses. When the CPU executes a program, it reads and performs the first instruction in memory. Then the CPU reads in the next instruction at the next address and executes it, etc. If an instruction tells the computer to jump to a certain address, the next instruction the computer reads will be the address indicated in the jump instruction. The process repeats until the CPU is instructed to halt.

It would be hard to write a program composed of a series of binary numbers. That's why BASIC, as well as many other computer languages, was developed to make it easier. Computer languages are themselves programs written in machine code, that take English-like instructions from a computer user and change them into machine code for the computer.

SUMMARY

Computers use numbers written in the binary system. Each column in a binary number represents a power of two; in the decimal system, each column represents a power of ten.

A computer system is composed of a CPU, support hardware, memory, input devices, and output devices. There are usually two I/O devices: the system console and a mass storage device.

The purpose of a computer is to execute programs. A program is a series of binary numbers (machine code) stored in memory. Languages such as BASIC automatically translate English-like commands into machine code.

EXERCISES

1. Convert the following binary numbers to decimal.

a) 101101	d) 1101011
b) 100101	e) 1101110
c) 110100	*f) 110110101 hint: What is 2^8?)

2. Convert the following decimal numbers to binary.

a) 5	d) 100
b) 13	e) 231
c) 41	f) 429

3. Fill in the blanks.

   a) 10110100 is a ______ bit byte.
   b) 101101010101 is a ______ bit byte.
   c) 101100110101 is a ______ byte word (assuming each byte is 4 bits long).

4. Fill in the blanks of the computer system diagram at the bottom of this page.

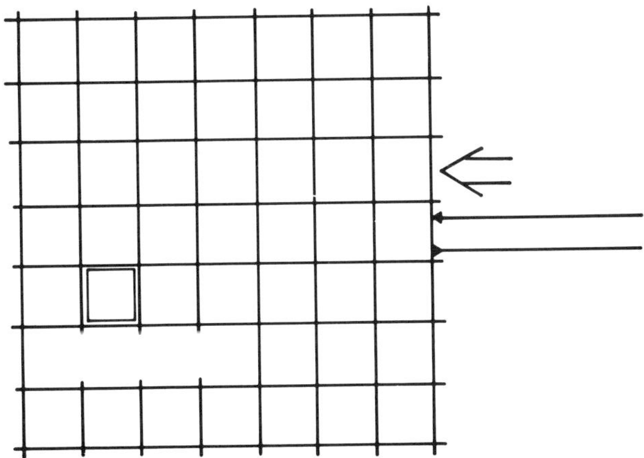

5. Match the words to the correct phrase.

a) CPU	An example of an output device
b) Supporting hardware	Is an I/O device
c) Memory	Executes the program in memory
d) System console	An example of an input device
e) Printer	Stores information
f) Keyboard	Controls signals to the CPU

6. Fill in the blanks:

   a) RAM stands for ________ ________ memory. The CPU can ________ and ________ to it.
   b) ROM stands for ________ ________ memory. The CPU can only ________ to/from it.

7. True or False?

   a) The CPU executes programs.
   b) A program is a series of instructions.
   c) Program instructions may be words, like PRINT and LET.
   d) The instructions the CPU executes are called machine code.
   e) Each instruction is placed in a random location in memory.
   f) BASIC is a short-cut to machine code.

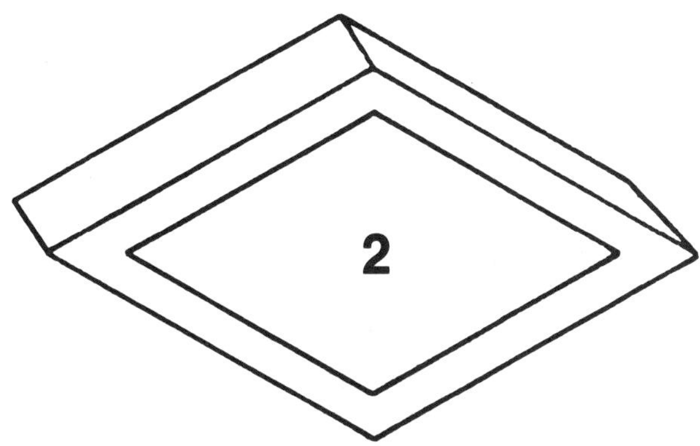

Beginning the Problem-Solving Process

In Chapter 1 we said that the function of a computer is to execute a program. If you have browsed through a computer magazine or looked around in a computer store, you know that there are programs to do almost anything. You might think there are very different programming methods to design program functions of such variety. However, this is generally untrue. In this chapter, we will begin a discussion of problem-solving techniques. The techniques can be used for *any* program you might write.

THE FUNCTIONS OF A PROGRAM

Although programs vary in complexity, they all have three things in common:

☐ Programs input information. Word processors input text; accounting programs input the description and amount of each transaction; a checkbook balancer inputs the amount of each check, the check number, the date of the check, and to whom the check was written; arcade games input commands that move the player and fire ammunition; and so on.

☐ Programs manipulate data. Word processors can replace text with an alternate piece of text. Accounting and checkbook programs add up figures. Arcade games constantly change the positions of the enemy, player, and missiles. Data manipulation includes changing the data the program reads in from the user, as well as creating new data from data it already has; the checkbook balancer would read the amount of a check, then compute the checking account's new balance.

☐ Programs output information. The data the program manipulates is made available to the user, when that data is useful for the user. The checkbook balancer would not print the subtotals it had computed, but will print the final balance.

When you write a program you must decide how the program will handle data, and how the operations performing the data-handling will relate to each other. A program rarely inputs all the information it needs, does all the manipulation, then does all the output. More often the processes overlap, performed many times throughout the program's run.

THE THREE STEPS OF PROGRAM CREATION

Knowing what a program *should* do is very different from knowing *how* to make the program do it. There are distinct steps taken to translate a problem into a program. We will examine three of these steps in this chapter, and the rest in Chapter 3.

Defining the Problem

A programmer must first ask, "What is the problem?" An important skill any programmer must develop is to properly identify a problem.

"I need a program to help manage my finances." This does not properly identify a specific goal. Should the program keep track of your checkbook? How about your budget? Do you have stock information you want to process? You must know in advance exactly what you wish your program to accomplish.

Often a program must solve more than one problem. For example, suppose a program is needed to keep track of phone numbers. What does this involve? First, the program must read people's names and numbers. Since our list may get large, it would be helpful if the list could be alphabetized. If a name needs to be removed from the list, we should be able to remove it, or change a number. We should be able to list the names, singly, by range (for example, names R-W), or the entire list. And, our program should save the list of names on a device such as a floppy disk, so they can be re-read and used later.

Let's look at our problem from the viewpoint of input, manipulation, and output:

☐ **Input**—The program inputs names and numbers. This means it may: do this in conjunction with adding a name to the list, or removing it; input what name or names are to be listed with their numbers; and input a list of names and numbers that have been previously saved.

☐ **Manipulation—**When a name is input, it will be stored in a specific area. When a name is deleted, it must be erased from this area. It must shuffle the order of the names when it alphabetizes them.

☐ **Output**—When a name or list of names is requested, it must output them. Also, it must output the names to a storage device to be used later.

Additionally, the program must also handle user commands—such as add new names. The program might first output a list of things the user may command it to do. Such a list is called a *menu*. A sample menu is shown in Fig. 2-1. After displaying the menu, the computer would wait for a response from the user telling the program what should be done next.

An important point to note here is that it is not always possible to know in advance exactly what the computer will input, or how it will manipulate the input, as we did in this problem. We had this foreknowledge because our problem was defined by what we wanted to input and what we wanted the computer to output. A different sort of problem would be one that computes the gas mileage of a car. We know that we want our program to output the car mileage, but what do we input? The next step will answer this question.

Determining an Algorithm

This step answers the question "What *method* will I use to solve the problem?" We analyze the different methods that could be used to see which is best for our problem. For example, we would decide how to alphabetize the list of names in the phone list problem. For the gas mileage problem, we would determine the formula to use to compute gas mileage. The formula we choose will tell us what inputs the program must handle.

The first two steps are interrelated. The goal of these procedures is to devise an *algorithm,* or series of steps, to solve a problem. The next procedure lets us put the algorithm we have mentally devised on paper.

Flowcharting

Flowcharting combines symbols and connecting lines, called *flow lines,* to show figuratively the operation of an algorithm. A flowchart can be thought of as a game board. The computer starts at the beginning of the flowchart and proceeds from symbol to symbol until it reaches the end. This analogy is a good one to keep in mind, since it reminds us that a computer can only be in one place at one time. If we can

```
Do you want to:

1)  Read in names that were saved

2)  Add a name to the list

3)  Alphabetize the names

4)  Print the names

5)  Save the list of names

6)  Stop the program
```

Fig. 2-1. A sample menu.

follow a flowchart so we know where we are and where we are supposed to go at any time, the computer will, as well.

The Start/Stop Symbol. Like any board game, we must know where to start. The symbol for this is shown in Fig. 2-2. The name of the symbol is the *start/stop symbol.* When used to show the beginning of a program, it contains the word START shown in Fig. 2-3. The symbol also uses a flow line, leaving from its bottom. The symbol is also used to show the ending of a flowchart; see Fig. 2-4. There is a flow line entering the top of the figure, with an arrow pointing toward the symbol. The arrow shows in which direction the flow line is flowing. There is no such thing as a "two-way" flow line. When an arrow is not present we know the flow line leads away from the symbol. If a flow line is very long, arrows may be added along the way to help the reader follow the flow line.

The start and stop symbols can be combined to form a simple flowchart, shown in Fig. 2-5. Start at the start symbol; the flow line leads to the stop symbol, which indicates the program is finished.

We can simplistically describe any flowchart we might write by the addition of an imaginary symbol. This universal chart is shown in Fig. 2-6. The "universal symbol" has only one flow line in and one flow line out. We will have to improve this flowchart, or refine it, by replacing this symbol with others better describing how the program operates. But no matter what symbols replace our universal symbol, and no matter how we connect them, only one flow line will lead into them, from the start symbol, and

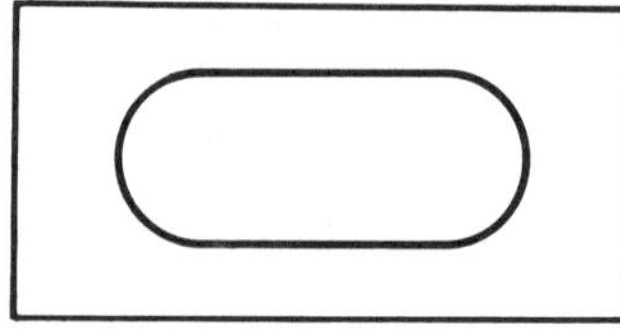

Fig. 2-2. The start/stop symbol.

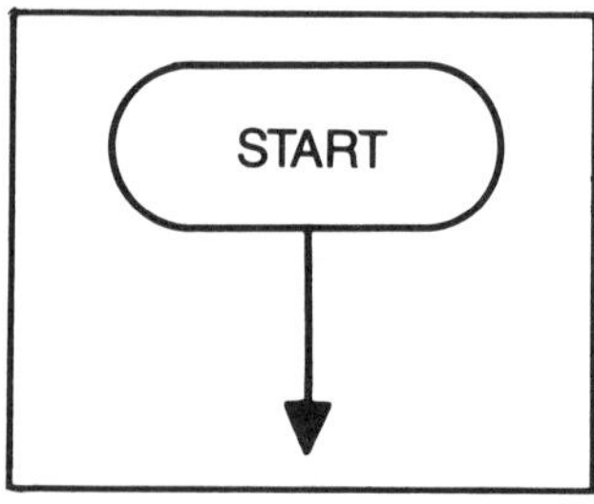

Fig. 2-3. The start symbol.

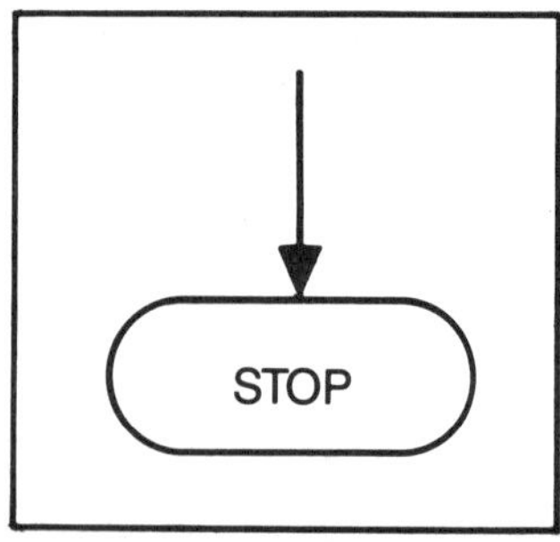

Fig. 2-4. The stop symbol.

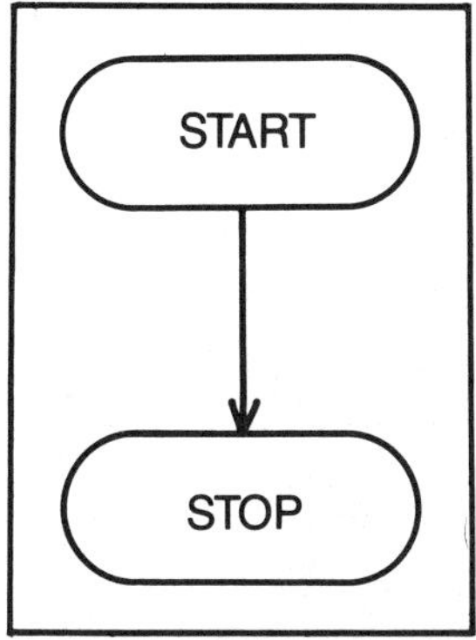

Fig. 2-5. Connecting the start and stop symbols.

only one flow line will lead out of them, to the stop symbol. When refining a symbol, the group of symbols we use must be connected to the rest of the flowchart in the same way the original symbol was connected.

The Read/Write Symbol. The next symbol to be looked at is the *read/write symbol,* shown in Fig. 2-7. This symbol shows the processes of input and output. A phrase that accurately describes the actions the read/write symbol stands for, such as "read in temperature" or "list the names," should be contained in it. The read/write symbol has two flow lines connected to it, one in and one out.

The Operation Symbol. Figure 2-8 represents a symbol used to direct the third goal of a program: manipulating data. The symbol is called the *operation symbol,* and like the read/write symbol, has a flow line leading into it and a flow line leading out. It shows any sort of data initialization, transfer, generation, or substitution.

To understand how these processes work, you must understand the concept of a variable. A *variable* can be thought of as a label that represents a part of memory used

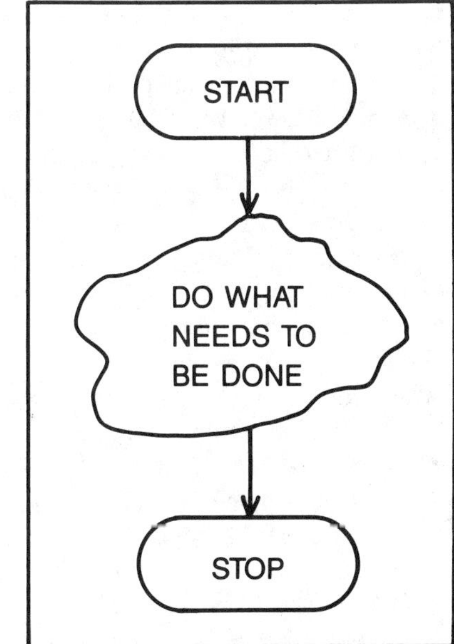

Fig. 2-6. The universal flowchart.

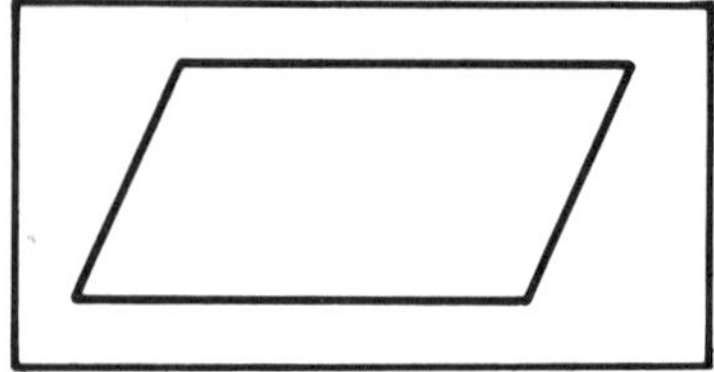

Fig. 2-7. The read/write symbol.

Fig. 2-8. The operation symbol.

to store information. For example, let's see how BASIC would handle the statement: **LET A = 10**. First, BASIC would look at this statement and recognize the letter **A** as a variable. If this were the first time BASIC saw this variable in the program, it would search in memory for free space. It would remember that from now on, the variable **A** will always refer to that part of memory. It would then store the value 10 there (in binary). If the variable **A** had previously been used, BASIC will have already set aside a place in memory for the variable. It therefore returns to that location to store the value 10. Any information already in that location will be destroyed. This is an example of storing information in a variable.

The statement: **LET B = C**, can illustrate how the function of reading from a variable is performed. If the variable **C** has already been used (assume it has the value 20 stored in it) BASIC returns to that location and reads the information stored there, but doesn't change anything. Had BASIC never seen **C** before, it would first set aside storage in memory. But there would be a problem: BASIC is asked to read from a variable that has never stored information. Rather than give us an error message, BASIC places a preset, or *default*, value in the location it sets aside from **C**. The default value BASIC uses is 0. Therefore, BASIC would designate a place for **C**, place a 0 there, read the 0, and then place the 0 in variable **B**. Study Figure 2-9, which shows the different possibilities for these two instructions.

The operation represented by the operation symbol that we have discussed is called *assignment* and it takes two forms: *initialization* and *transfer*. The **LET A = 10** instruction is an example of *initialization*, because it sets, or initializes, the variable to a preset value. The statement **LET B = C** is an example of *transfer*; it takes information stored in one place and transfers (copies) it to another place. A transfer does not disturb the information stored in the original location.

Generation involves computing a mathematical expression to generate a numeric value and placing it in a variable. For instance, the BASIC statement: **LET C = 2 * 4 / B** is an example of data generation. The BASIC processor's interpretation of the expression **2 * 4 / B** is placed in variable **C**. The value stored in **B** is used (or 0, if **B** has not been used before) in BASIC's interpretation. This does not affect **B**—its contents are not altered.

The last operation is the substitution operation. *Substitution* is a form of genera-

```
                    LET A = 10

Before                               After

A:  ---                              A: 10

A:   X                               A: 10

                    LET A = B

Before                               After

A: ---   B: ---                      A: 0    B: 0

A:  X    B: ---                      A: 0    B: 0

A: ---   B:  5                       A: 5    B: 5

A:  X    B:  5                       A: 5    B: 5
```

These tables show the results of each LET statement. --- means that the variable had never been used before. X means that the variable was storing a number, but its value is not important.

Fig. 2-9. Effects of storing values in variables.

tion, except that a value placed in a variable is related to the original contents of the variable. For example, consider the statement: **LET B = B + 1**. Its purpose is to replace the value of **B** with a number one greater than the value it originally contained.

The operation symbol will contain a description of the action the symbol represents, such as "shoe size = 10" or "miles per gallon = miles traveled / gallons consumed." The operation symbol has one flow line leading in, and one leading out.

EVALUATING MATHEMATICAL EXPRESSIONS

A *mathematical formula* or *expression* is a sequence of values and operations which results in one, and only one, value. This qualification leads us to create rules governing the evaluation of an expression. The easiest rule is: work from left to right. To evaluate: 2 + 4 + 6, first add 2 and 4, giving us 6, which we add to 6, giving us 12. Multiplication would be handled the same way as would subtraction and division. It is with these latter two operations that the rule we follow becomes important: If we evaluate the expression 6 − 4 − 2 left to right, we get 0. If, however, we subtracted 4 from 2 first, we would get −2.

We can extend this rule to expressions with combined operations; 2 + 4 × 6 would be 36. Without the rule, we could choose to multiply 4 and 6 together first and then add 2, a total of 26.

However, 26 is in fact, the correct answer to 2 + 4 × 6, because we give higher importance to multiplication than to addition. As well as the left-to-right rule, we establish what is called a *hierarchy of operations*, which tells us which operations are more important than others. Most programming languages, including BASIC, use a

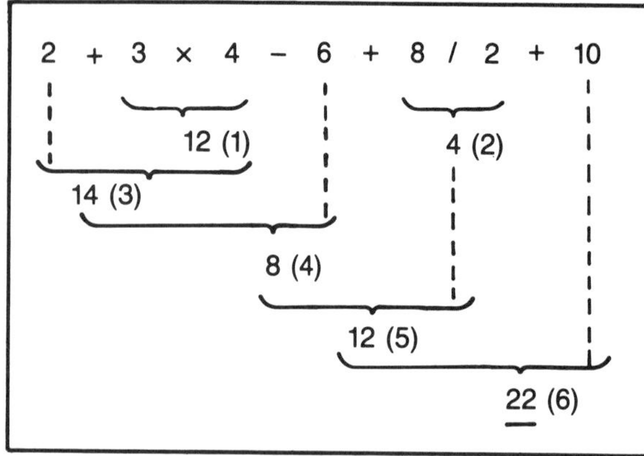

Fig. 2-10. Solving a mathematical expression.

hierarchy which places multiplication and division above addition and subtraction. Thus, to evaluate the expression 2 + 4 − 6 / 2, first divide 6 by 2. Then, as addition and subtraction are of equal importance, the order of operation takes place from left to right. The value of the expression is 3. If the hierarchy of operations hadn't been used, 0 would have been the answer.

It can be confusing to evaluate an expression containing many operations. Figure 2-10 shows a method using brackets to simplify computation. The key is to break down the expression, using the rules we have covered, into a series of operations between two numbers. Do all the multiplication and division first, working left to right, and then do all the addition and subtraction, again working left to right. Figure 2-11 is an example you can work for yourself.

You might be wondering how you can program BASIC so it ignores the rule of left-to-right and the rule of hierarchy, if it suits your purpose. The way to do this will be covered in the next chapter.

AN EXAMPLE

We now know enough to make a simple flowchart based on gas mileage problem. Let's

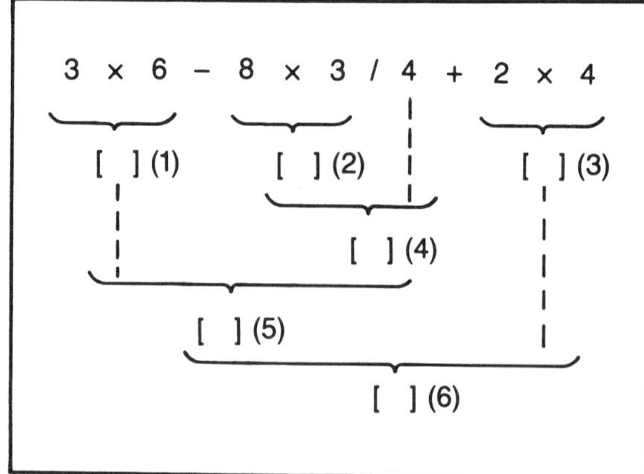

Fig. 2-11. An exercise in solving a mathematical expression.

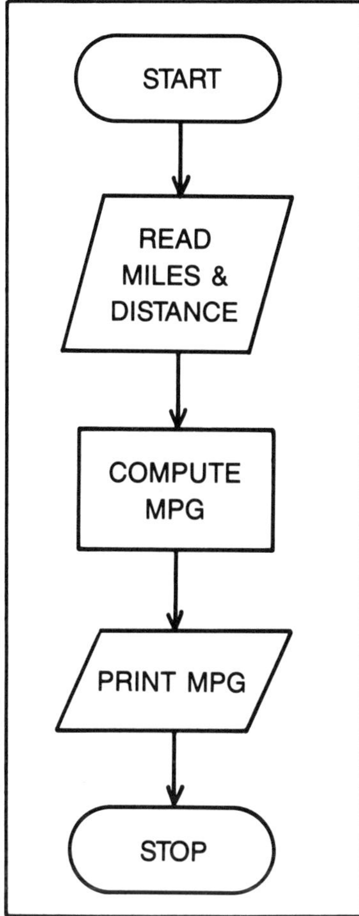

Fig. 2-12. Flowchart for MPG problem.

summarize what has been done: first, we identified the problem—we need a program to compute miles per gallon. We have established the way to do this—read in miles traveled and gallons consumed, figure MPG using the formula MPG = miles traveled /gallons consumed, and print the MPG. Without further ado, let's look at a flowchart accomplishing this task—Fig. 2-12.

Beginning at the start symbol, follow the flow line to a read/write symbol. It tells us to input how many miles traveled and gallons of gas used. Once we have done that, we travel to the operation box, where we generate data (the MPG). We leave the operation box and go to another read/write symbol, where we output the MPG. Finally we go to the stop box.

In the next chapter, we will discuss how we can take the flowchart just created and write a BASIC program—the goal of our efforts.

SUMMARY

The purpose of a program is to input information, manipulate it in some way, and output the results. All these functions may occur throughout the program.

The first three steps in writing a program are: problem definition, preparation of an algorithm, and flowcharting the process.

A flowchart diagrams a process by using symbols to represent different actions and flow lines to show the sequence of actions. The symbols covered so far are: the start/stop symbol, the read/write symbol, and the operation symbol.

A mathematical expression is a series of values and operators which yield one, and only one, result. The left-to-right rule and the mathematical hierarchy govern how expressions are evaluated.

EXERCISES

1. Name and describe the three functions of a program:

   1. ______________________________
   2. ______________________________
   3. ______________________________

2. Evaluate the following expressions:

   a) 2 × 3 + 4 = ________
   b) 1 − 2 + 10 = ________
   c) 5 + 1 × 4 = ________
   d) 4 − 12 / 3 = ________
   e) 5 / 10 + 4 × 9 = ________
   f) 6 + 4 × 2 − 8 / 2 × 3 = ________

3. Identify the contents of A, B, and C after each instruction. Assume the value of each variable isn't erased after each problem.

a) LET A = 10	A = ________	B = ________	C = ________
b) LET B = A × 2	A = ________	B = ________	C = ________
c) LET C = B + 1	A = ________	B = ________	C = ________
d) LET A = B × 2 + C × 3	A = ________	B = ________	C = ________
e) LET B = B × 2	A = ________	B = ________	C = ________

4. Identify the five operations in problem 3 as initialization, transfer, generation, or substitution.

   a) ____________ d) ____________
   b) ____________ e) ____________
   c) ____________

The next three questions deal with the following programming problem: Finding the average of two numbers.

5. Step 1: Describe the problem. What will be your input, computation, and output?

____

____

6. Step 2: How will you find the average? What formula will you use?

____

____

7. Describe your algorithm as a flowchart:

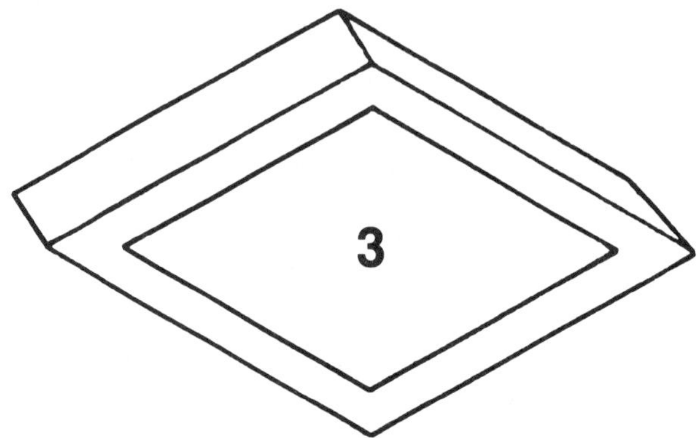

Finishing the Problem-Solving Process

In Chapter 2, we discussed identifying a problem, determining a solution to the problem, and representing the solution by a flowchart. This chapter will continue the process of using a flowchart as a tool for writing a BASIC program.

THE ROLE OF FLOWCHARTS

Look at Fig. 3-1. At the end of Chapter 2, we had reached step three in the process of flowcharting a program to compute MPG. We had produced a *macro-flowchart,* and were ready to proceed to step four. The macro-flowchart does not tell us exactly how our program will work; rather, it tells us how our program will function logically. For example, our first read/write symbol told us our program will read in the miles traveled and the gas used. It does not say *how* the program will do this.

A macro flowchart should tell you generally what your program should do; for example, the description T = H + 60 * M + 360 * S would not be as good as "compute time," even though we might anticipate that we will use the given formula in our program. We will adapt our algorithm for use on the computer in step four, creating a *micro-flowchart* that shows specifically how the program will work. At this point a formula might appear in place of the phrase "compute time."

The use of macro- and micro-flowcharts becomes most important when you begin to develop large, complex programs. A macro-flowchart will then serve as an important guide to your program design, as you work out many intricate details of a complex program. When writing large programs, you'll find it much easier to split the task into smaller subproblems, solve them separately, and then combine them. This means

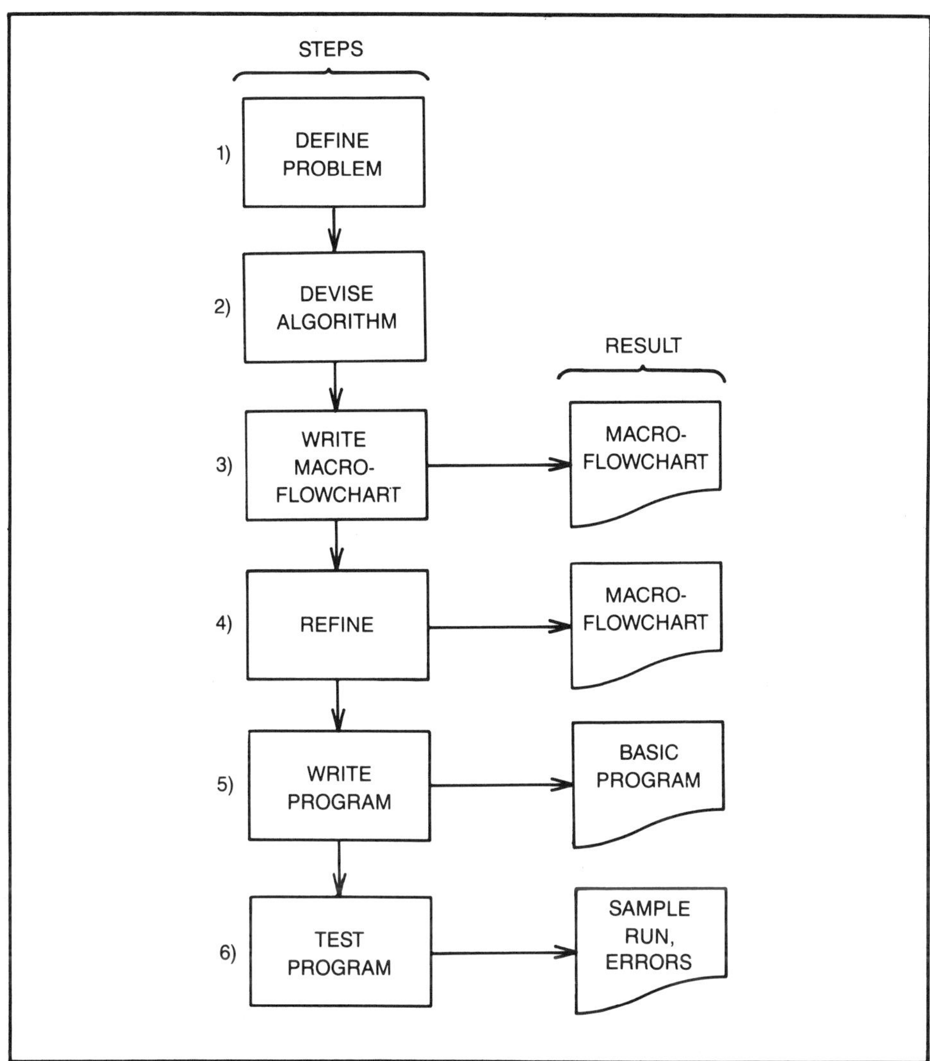

Fig. 3-1. The entire problem solving process.

that some steps will be repeated many times before the program is finished.

Think of the parts of a flowchart as building blocks which can be arranged in different ways. Flowcharting is not a procedure by which a program is written, but a tool a programmer uses to describe what he will develop. Flowcharts may also be used to document a program. Reading a flowchart is easier than scanning a program to understand how it works, or what it is supposed to do. Both macro-flowcharts and micro-flowcharts are useful for documentation purposes. By reading the macro-flowchart, a person learns what the program will do, and what logic is used to do it. By reading the micro-flowchart, you learn how the program actually works.

Flowcharts are also useful when a program needs to be modified. And micro-flowcharts are very useful for debugging a program. Using a flowchart, the programmer can "play computer" and step through the algorithm to ensure that it operates correctly.

CONCLUDING THE PROBLEM-SOLVING PROCESS

We will now examine the remaining steps in the problem-solving process in light of the gas mileage problem. The steps are designing a micro-flowchart; converting the micro-flowchart to a BASIC program: and testing the program.

Converting to a Micro-flowchart

In a macro-flowchart, each symbol represents a single logical process. One of these processes may take many BASIC instructions to perform. In a micro-flowchart each symbol represents a single BASIC instruction.

Figure 3-2 shows the macro-flowchart we constructed in Chapter 2. We must now decide how to implement our algorithm on the computer. We will take the ideas in our flowchart and make them acceptable to the computer. One refinement will be how we will handle the pieces of data, such as miles traveled, that our algorithm uses. Our programming language, BASIC, uses variables to store this kind of numeric data, so part of our task will be to make our micro-flowchart show how variables hold the various numeric values in our program.

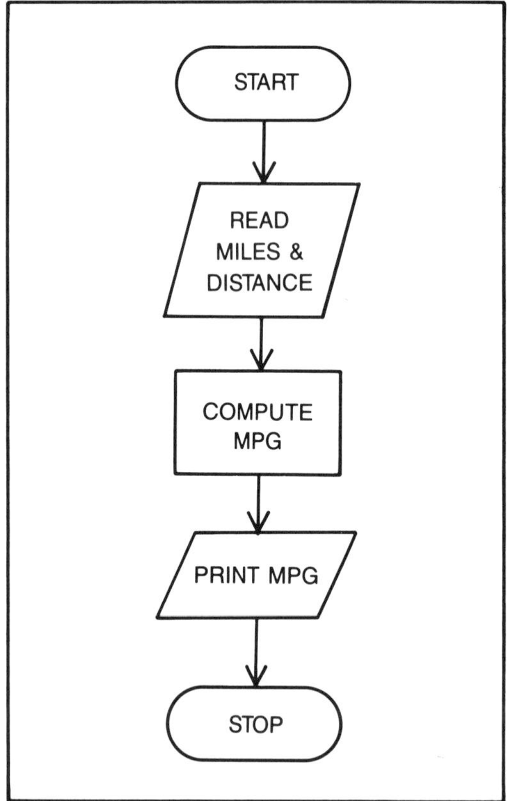

Fig. 3-2. Macro-flowchart for MPG problem.

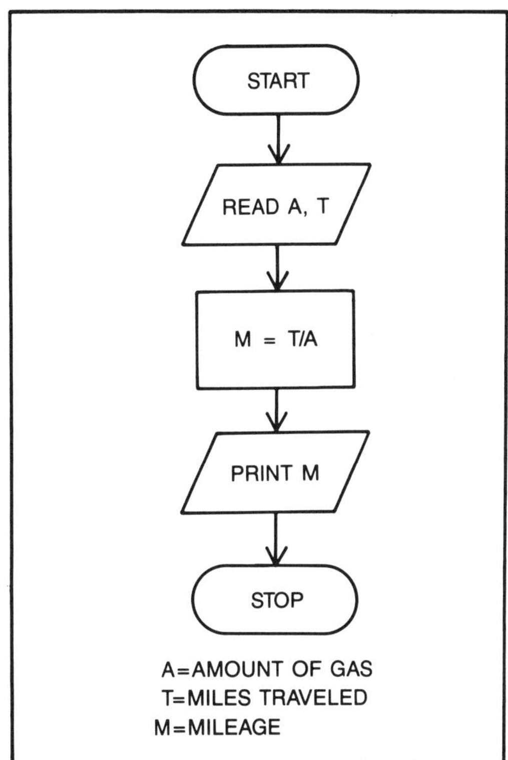

Fig. 3-3. Micro-flowchart for MPG problem.

Different versions of BASIC allow variables to take different forms. We will assume that a variable must start with a letter and be followed by an optional number. When you write programs on your own, be sure to read your BASIC manual to discover what forms of variables your computer will accept.

Our program handles three pieces of data: miles traveled, amount of gas used, and MPG. We will need three variables, and will use the following variables in this example: **T** will hold miles traveled, **A** will contain the amount of gas used, and **M** will store the MPG.

Our macro-flowchart is almost a micro-flowchart; besides the use of variables, little needs to be changed. The micro-flowchart that results is shown in Fig. 3-3. It included a variable chart so we will remember what each variable is supposed to contain. Also, the formula to compute MPG is shown in the operation symbol.

Converting to a BASIC Program

The test of how well we wrote our micro-flowchart is how easy it converts into a BASIC program. Refer to Fig. 3-4, which shows a BASIC program to compute gas mileage. The following explanation details the steps taken to convert the gas mileage micro-flowchart into this program.

The first symbol is the start symbol. It reminds us to write some comments. The comments, contained on lines 10-30, identify the program. They quickly tell a person looking at the program listing what the program does.

```
10 REM **********
20 REM GAS MILEAGE PROGRAM
30 REM **********
40 INPUT T
50 INPUT A
60 LET M = T / A
70 PRINT M
80 END
```

Fig. 3-4. BASIC program to compute MPG.

The next symbol tells us to read in variables **A** and **T**. The BASIC language uses the **INPUT** instruction for this, as shown in line 50. The operation symbol tells us to divide **A** by **T**, and place that value in **M**. Line 60 performs this calculation. Then we go on to the read/write symbol, that says to print **M**. The **PRINT** instruction is shown in line 70.

Finally, we come to the stop symbol. To end our program, we use the **END** statement.

Running and Testing the Program

A sample run is shown in Fig. 3-5. But it would be hard to use it if you didn't know what it is supposed to do. The program needs to be made *user-friendly*. The more user-friendly a program is, the easier it is to use.

We can begin to make our program user-friendly by changing line 20 from a **REM** statement to a **PRINT** statement. Then the purpose of the program will be printed on the screen. We can also insert **PRINT** statements before each of the **INPUT** statements, telling the user what to type. Finally, another **PRINT** statement inserted before the **PRINT** statement in line 60 will tell the user what the program is printing.

A listing of our improved program is shown in Fig. 3-6, and a sample run is shown in Fig. 3-7. A few **PRINT** statements make quite a difference.

There are many ways to make a program user-friendly, but we will concentrate on providing useful information to the user that will guide him to run the program. Because **PRINT** statements really have no bearing on the execution of the program, their presence is not noted in the flowchart. Were we to print a sizable piece of information, such as to describe what MPG is and how it is calculated, we might insert a write symbol, with the words "print theory of MPG" or some similar statement, in our flowchart.

What is put in a flowchart and what is left out is often a subjective choice. If you feel something would clutter your flowchart too much, leave it out, but exercise this

Fig. 3-5. Sample run of MPG program.

```
? 100
? 5
20
End in line 80
```

```
10 REM **********
20 PRINT "GAS MILEAGE PROGRAM"
30 REM **********
35 PRINT "ENTER MILES TRAVELED"
40 INPUT T
45 PRINT "ENTER AMOUNT OF GAS USED"
50 INPUT A
60 LET M = T / A
65 PRINT "YOUR MPG:"
70 PRINT M
80 END
```

Fig. 3-6. User-friendly MPG program.

option with great caution. What may seem insignificant now may have great importance later.

We were fortunate—our program ran correctly the first time. This is rare, and when errors occur, they must be fixed. An important skill a programmer needs to acquire is knowing where to look for an error. There are two main types of errors.

Syntax Errors. These are often the easiest to correct. A *syntax error* is simply a mistake in the form of command. Errors such as writing PINT instead of PRINT, or LET A B instead of LET A = B, are syntax errors.

Logic Errors. These are more difficult to find. They are errors in how the program is designed. These errors can occur most anywhere in the program development process, and include mistakes made when developing your algorithm. If your algorithm is wrong, chances are good the program is wrong.

To correct a logic error, it is often best to back up to step two and work your program out again. *Do not* try to insert instructions in your program to make it work correctly. Such changes, called *patches,* rarely work well.

A more subtle logic error is a *semantic error,* a misunderstanding about how the language you are using operates. For example, using the instruction: LET A = B to put the value of A into B is a semantic error; BASIC will allow you to do this, but the result will not be what you planned.

Depending on what errors have been made, one or more of the problem-solving steps will have to be redone. This process, called *debugging,* is what you will

```
GAS MILEAGE PROGRAM
ENTER MILES TRAVELED
? 100
ENTER AMOUNT OF GAS USED
? 5
YOUR MPG:
20
End in line 80
```

Fig. 3-7. Sample run of a user-friendly MPG program.

spend most of your time doing. Don't be discouraged if your program does not work; careful, methodic debugging will soon produce a running program.

REVIEWING THE PROBLEM-SOLVING PROCESS

Let's review the process of designing a flowchart and writing a program based on it:

1. We defined the problem—we needed a program that computed gas mileage.
2. We designed an algorithm—we discovered that gas mileage is miles traveled divided by the number of gallons of gas used. Our strategy was to find out how many miles were traveled and the gas used, perform the necessary computation, and print the MPG.
3. We designed our macro-flowchart, based on the algorithm just developed. This flowchart showed the logic of our algorithm.
4. We designed our micro-flowchart based on our macro-flowchart. This flowchart encorporated details that would enable us to write a program. For example, variables were used to hold data and changes were made in the operation symbol to reflect this use.
5. We converted our micro-flowchart to a BASIC program, by going through our flowchart and deciding what BASIC instructions were best suited for preforming the different tasks the flowchart described.
6. We tested our program to make sure it worked. Although it did run correctly, we decided **PRINT** statements should be inserted to make the program user-friendly. We felt it unnecessary to change the flowchart to reflect the addition of these statements.

EVALUATING EXPRESSIONS, PART 2

Let's digress to another topic we talked about in Chapter 2: evaluation of mathematical formulas. A mathematical expression yields one, and only one, solution. The operations most people are familiar with are addition (+), subtraction (−), multiplication (× or *) and division (/). These operations take two numbers and yield one number. Because they operate on two numbers, they are called *binary operators.*

We will evaluate an expression keeping in mind the fact that binary operators take two numbers and produce one as a result. The expression will be: $2 + 4 \times 5 - 3$. The first operation we perform is the multiplication between 4 and 5; multiplication is higher in the mathematical hierarchy than addition or subtraction. Replace 4×5 in the expression with 20, leaving us with: $2 + 20 - 3$. In our reduced expression, we next perform $2 + 20$. Addition and subtraction are equal in importance, but the addition operation is to the left of the subtraction operation. Our expression can now be written as $22 - 3$. We have only to subtract 3 from 22 to arrive at 19. The process of solving this expression is illustrated by the bracket method in Fig. 3-8.

You can alter the order by which a language evaluates an expression by using parentheses. If we enclose $2 + 3$ with parentheses to give us $(2 + 3) / 10$, BASIC will first evaluate the expression inside parentheses, regardless of any operations found outside them. In this case BASIC would add 2 and 3, then evaluate $5 / 10$, for a solution of 0.5. In the expression $2 \times (3 - 2 \times 4) + 3$, the expression $3 - 2 \times 4$ should be evaluated first: -5. Then the expression would continue as $2 \times -5 + 3$, or -7. More than one set of parentheses can be used in an expression.

Now let's show how to combine parentheses, or *nest* them. The expression is: (2

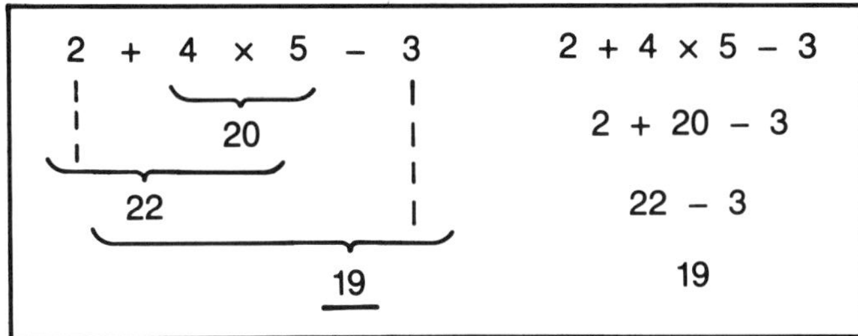

Fig. 3-8. Bracket method of solving expression vs. replacement method.

+ (15 − 7)) × 8. The rule to remember is: *start with the innermost pair.* Thus, we would subtract 7 from 15 to give (2 + 8) × 8. Evaluating this last expression should be easy by now; the answer is 80.

You may find an expression with more than two nested parentheses; just remember to start with the innermost pair and work outward. Here is an expression which will help cover all we have learned: (2 + ((3 − 2) + 4) × 5) − (3 × (5 − 2)). The correct value of the expression is 18.

We have so far used binary operators. There are also unary operators. A *unary operator* takes one number and produces another or *unary minus* operator, denoted by a minus sign, is a unary operator used to change the sign of a number; BASIC places the unary operator at the very top of the mthematical hierarchy. The negation operator can be placed in front of a number, in which case that number is negated, or it can be placed in front of an expression enclosed in parentheses, in which case the expression is negated once it is evaluated.

For example, in the expression 5 + − 3, BASIC recognizes − as a negation operator, so 5 is added to −3 to give 2. We could enclose the − 3 in parentheses, which doesn't affect the result of the expression, but does make its meaning more obvious to humans. In the expression: 5 × − (4 + 3), we evaluate 4 + 3 to give 7, then multiply 5 by − 7, to produce −35. The negation operator doesn't necessarily make something negative; − (6 − 10) × 4 becomes 4 × 4, or 16.

USING FORMULAS

While we must know how to evaluate expressions in BASIC, expressions like the ones we have shown almost never appear in a BASIC program! Instead, formulas are used. A *formula* is an expression containing one or more variables. For instance, **A + 3**, **12 * B / Z**, and **(− C + 4) * 12** are all formulas. A formula was used in the MPG program to compute the gas mileage.

The value of a formula cannot be determined until the value of each variable in the formula is found. Figure 3-9 shows the values of these three formulas for different values of the variables. If your understanding of expressions is good, you should have no problem with formulas.

USING THE ANNOTATION SYMBOL

Let us take a hypothetical situation and cover the entire problem-solving process. Imagine that you are a chef and have just purchased a computer hoping it can make your work easier. Our first step is to clearly define a problem that you can write a program to solve. We will keep it simple and say that a program is needed to help convert recipes designed for a certain number of people to the number of diners actually going to be

```
Formula:  A + 3

A = 10    Value = 13

A = -7    Value = -4

A = ---   Value = 3

Formula:  12 x B / Z

B = 2      Z = 4   Value = 6

B = 1.5    Z = 2   Value = 9

B = ---    Z = 5   Value = 0

B = 2      Z = 0   Value is undefined (you cannot
                        divide a number by 0)

Formula:  (-C + 4) x 12

C = 2     Value = 24

C = -1    Value = 60

C = ---   Value = 48
```

Fig. 3-9. Value of some formulas.

served. It will convert an amount of an ingredient in the recipe to the amount needed.

A key to the solution is to realize that if we wish to serve twice as many people as the recipe is designed for, we will need twice as much of an ingredient. Likewise, if we have one-third as many people, we will need one-third the amount of ingredient. The easiest way to determine what fraction of diners we have is to divide the number of people we have by the number of people the recipe is designed to feed.

If we have 10 people and the recipe is designed for 5, we have 10 / 5, or twice the people the recipe feeds. If we take this number and multiply it by the amount of ingredient called for, the result will be how much ingredient we need. This relationship is shown in Fig. 3-10. Looking at our formula, we see that in addition to finding out how many people are going to be served, our program must also find out how many people the recipe is for and how much of the ingredient the recipe calls for. The algorithm for our program is: read in the three pieces of data; compute the amount of ingredient needed; and print that amount. We can make our macro-flowchart based on this algorithm.

Begin with a start symbol, and connect a read symbol to indicate that the number

```
People to be served
------------------- x Amt. of Ingredient in Recipe = Amt. of Ingredient Needed
Servings in recipe
```

Fig. 3-10. Relationship between servings and amounts of ingredient.

of diners, the servings in the recipe, and the amount of each ingredient are to be read. We use an annotation symbol to "extend" the size of the symbol, allowing us to include all this information. The annotation symbol is connected by a slashed line, indicating that it is not a flow line, but is associated with the read symbol. When reading the flowchart, when we get to the read symbol we look to the annotation symbol to clarify the phrase in the read symbol.

After the read symbol, an operation symbol is attached, telling us to compute the amount of ingredient needed. To the operation symbol a write symbol is connected, instructing us to write the amount of ingredient we just computed. Finally, a stop symbol indicates we are finished.

All the arrows should show the flow from the start symbol to the stop symbol. A completed macro-flowchart is shown in Fig. 3-11.

Conversion to a micro-flowchart will be fairly easy. We will use variables to store the figures, and there is little else to modify. Try to create a micro-flowchart for this problem. How does it compare to that shown in Fig. 3-12? did you remember to include a variable table to indicate the uses for your variables? Did you show the formula that makes the conversion?

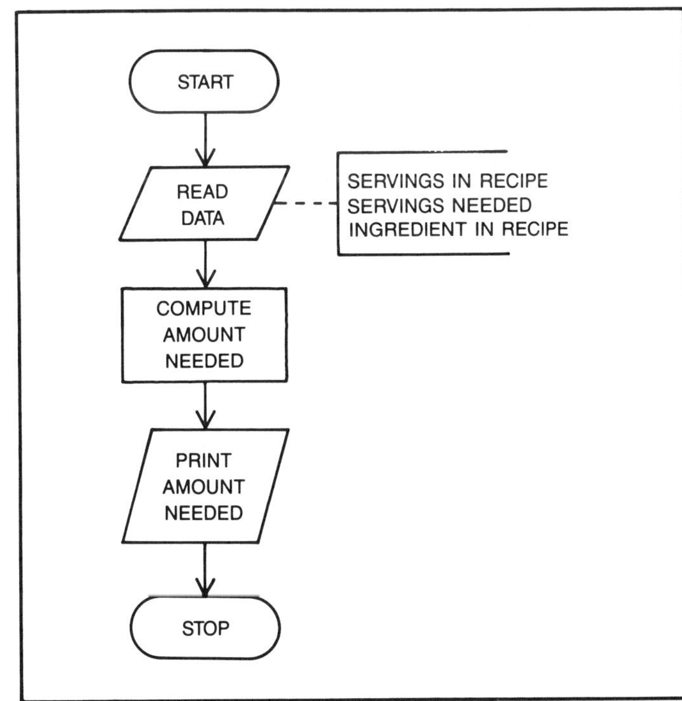

Fig. 3-11. Macro-flowchart for recipe problem.

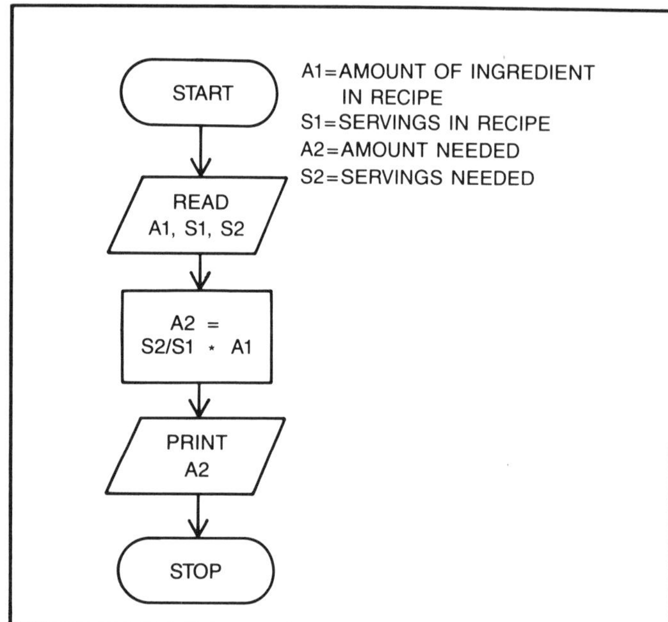

Fig. 3-12. Micro-flowchart for recipe problem.

Now that our micro-flowchart is complete, writing the program will be quite similar to the mileage program. Before you go on, write your own conversion program and run it on your computer. Remember to make it user-friendly. If you need help, refer to the program listing in Fig. 3-13. When you are done, compare your sample run to that in Fig. 3-14.

SUMMARY

The six steps of program development are: *problem definition, algorithm selection, macro-flowchart, micro-flowchart, program coding,* and *program testing.* These steps need not occur in a sequential order. In fact, when developing a large program, they may be done many times.

```
10 REM **********
20 PRINT "RECIPE CONVERSION PROGRAM"
30 REM **********
40 PRINT "AMOUNT OF INGREDIENT IN RECIPE"
50 INPUT A1
60 PRINT "SERVINGS IN RECIPE"
70 INPUT S1
80 PRINT "SERVINGS NEEDED"
90 INPUT S2
100 LET A2 = S2 / S1 * A1
110 PRINT "AMOUNT OF INGREDIENT NEEDED:"
120 PRINT A2
130 END
```

Fig. 3-13. BASIC recipe program.

```
RECIPE CONVERSION PROGRAM
AMOUNT OF INGREDIENTS IN RECIPE
? 2
SERVINGS IN RECIPE
? 4
SERVINGS NEEDED
? 10
AMOUNT OF INGREDIENT NEEDED:
5
```

Fig. 3-14. Sample run of recipe program.

A *macro-flowchart* attempts to show the logic behind a program. A *micro-flowchart* shows how the program executes that logic.

In addition to the left-to-right rule and the mathematical hierarchy, evaluation of mathematical expressions can be governed by the use of parentheses.

The *annotation symbol* can be used to add extra information to a symbol.

Formulas are mathematical expressions which contain one or more variables. The value of a formula can be found by replacing the variables with the data they store.

EXERCISES

The next three questions are a continuation from the exercises in Chapter 2.

1. Step 4: Create a program flowchart. Remember those variables!

2. Step 5: Write a BASIC program.

   10 ______________________________
   20 ______________________________
   30 ______________________________
   40 ______________________________
   50 ______________________________
   60 ______________________________
   70 ______________________________
   80 ______________________________

3. Step 6: Run your program.

4. Evaluate the following expressions:

   a) $3 \times (2 + 4) =$ __________
   b) $(2 + 3) \times (10 - 6) =$ __________
   c) $(4 - 2) / (5 + 3) =$ __________
   d) $(3 + (2 + 10)) \times 4 =$ __________
   e) $(3 \times -(2 - 6)) / 3 =$ __________
   f) $(3 + (4 + (6 - 9))) =$ __________

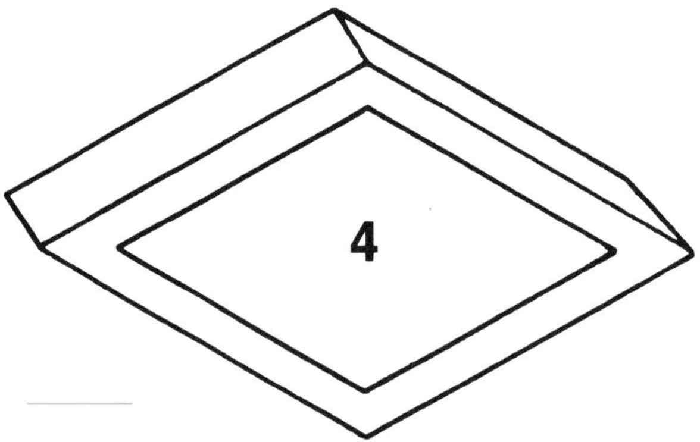

Making Decisions

The programs we have written so far execute a certain number of instructions in a top-to-bottom sequence. However, most problems must at some point make a decision between two or more possible paths. A *decision* is a test of information which has been input or created. The outcome of the test determines what instructions will next be executed. Decisions are also used to set up *loops*, a way to execute a set of instructions more than once. Looping is the topic of Chapter 5.

THE DECISION AND MERGE SYMBOLS

The decision symbol is shown in Fig. 4-1. The symbol has four points from which it is connected to other symbols. One flow line enters the symbol through the top point. The remaining three points are for outgoing lines. Inside the symbol a phrase describes the decision to be made, such as "What is the temperature?" or "Is the sky blue?" The outgoing lines are labeled to indicate what answer corresponds to it.

To label the outgoing lines we must know what answers are possible. The description of the outgoing lines can be classified as *absolute* or *relative.* For instance, if the question we must answer is, "Is the sky blue?", we could label one outgoing line "yes" and the other "no." This type of answer is an absolute answer. A relative answer makes a comparison.

If the question is "What is the temperature?", we might label one outgoing line "greater than 70" and the other "70 or less." When we desire this type of answer, the question inside the symbol should take the form *value 1: value 2.* We will label the outgoing lines to reflect a response that value 1 is greater than, equal to, or less than

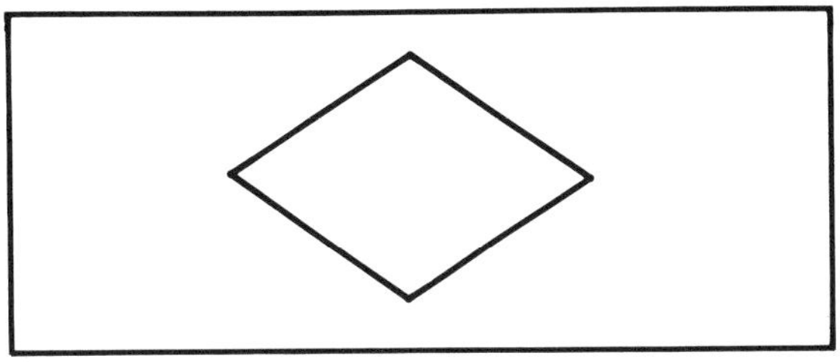

Fig. 4-1. The decision symbol.

value 2. In our temperature example, the phrase "Temperature: 70" would be placed in the symbol; one outgoing line would be labeled < (greater than), and the other = (less than or equal to). A decision symbol using three outgoing routes (greater than, less than, and equal to) would look like Fig. 4-2. We can sometimes make a decision relative or absolute depending on how we word it. Look at the symbols shown in Fig. 4-3. The left-most symbol uses the absolute form, while the right symbol uses the relative form. In either case, the same result is reached.

Decision symbols are flexible, but, we must follow some rules when deciding whether to use a relative or absolute question:

☐ No two branches should be equally valid choices. If our question is **A** : **B**, and one outgoing flow line is labeled **A** < = B, and the other **A** > = B, either flow line would be a valid choice if **A** equals **B**.

☐ Every possible condition between the branches should be taken into consideration. If our description is **A** : **B**, but one outgoing line is labeled **A** < **B** and the other **A** > **B**, there would be no line to follow if **A** equals **B**.

A symbol used with the decision symbol is the *merge symbol*, shown in Fig. 4-4. The merge symbol accepts two or more flow lines, but only one flow line leaves it. A decision symbol splits up flow lines which need to be rejoined at some later point. By rejoining flow lines with a symbol having no other function, we can be sure only one flow line will enter other symbols. Merge symbols also aid in converting a flowchart into a program, as we will see later.

Instead of using a merge symbol, flow lines can join at a *merge point*, shown in Fig. 4-5. This is often preferred, since the flowchart does not get as cluttered. Merge points will be used throughout the remainder of the book.

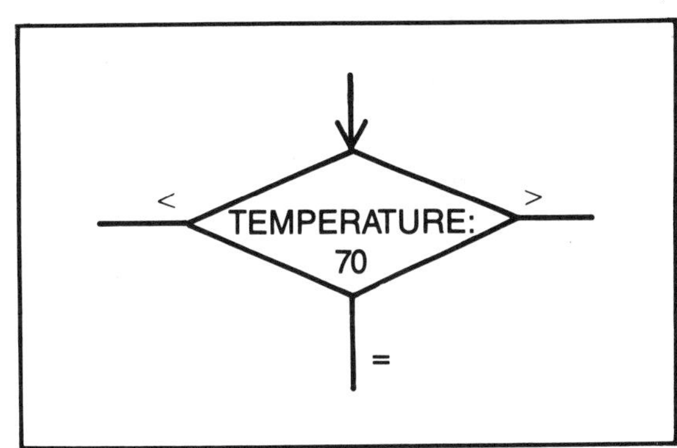

Fig. 4-2. Using decision symbol to go in three directions.

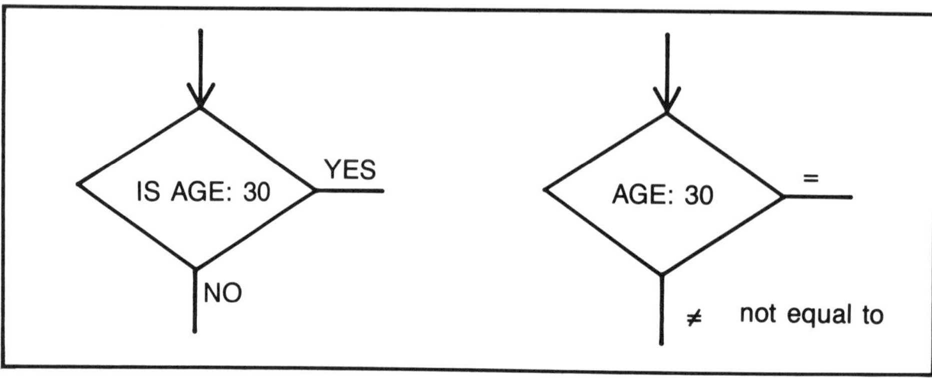

Fig. 4-3. Relative vs. absolute decision symbols.

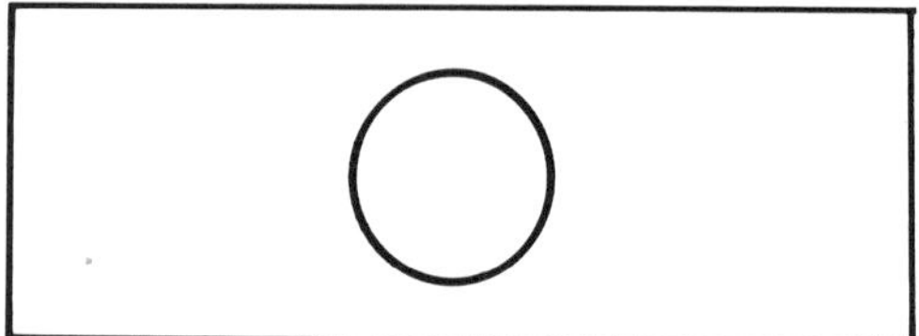
Fig. 4-4. The merge symbol.

USING THE DECISION SYMBOL

Let's look at an example using the decision symbol to flowchart a problem. We will analyze what a driver would do if a tire suddenly went flat. First we will consider the problem without making decisions, and create a preliminary flowchart using only operation symbols.

The first thing the driver would do is pull off the road at a safe location. Then he

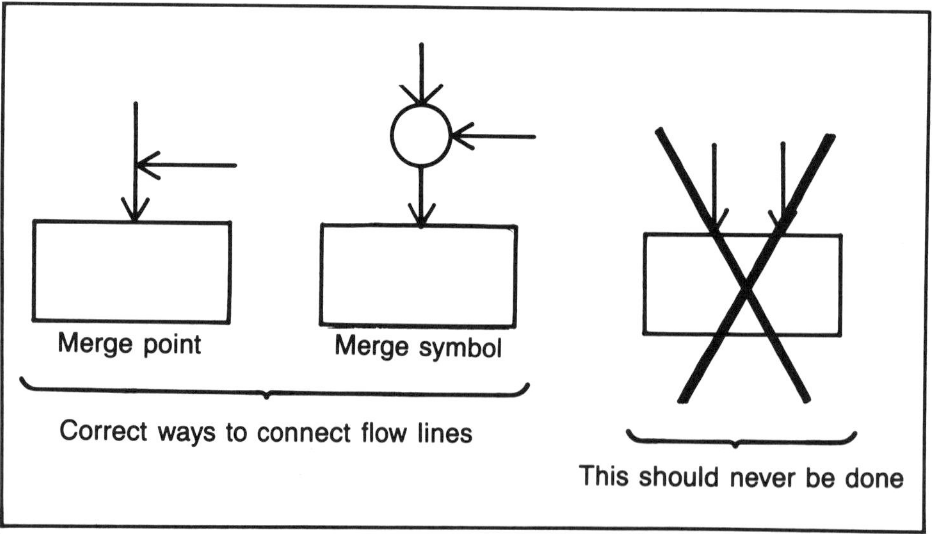

Fig. 4-5. Two correct ways of merging, and one incorrect way.

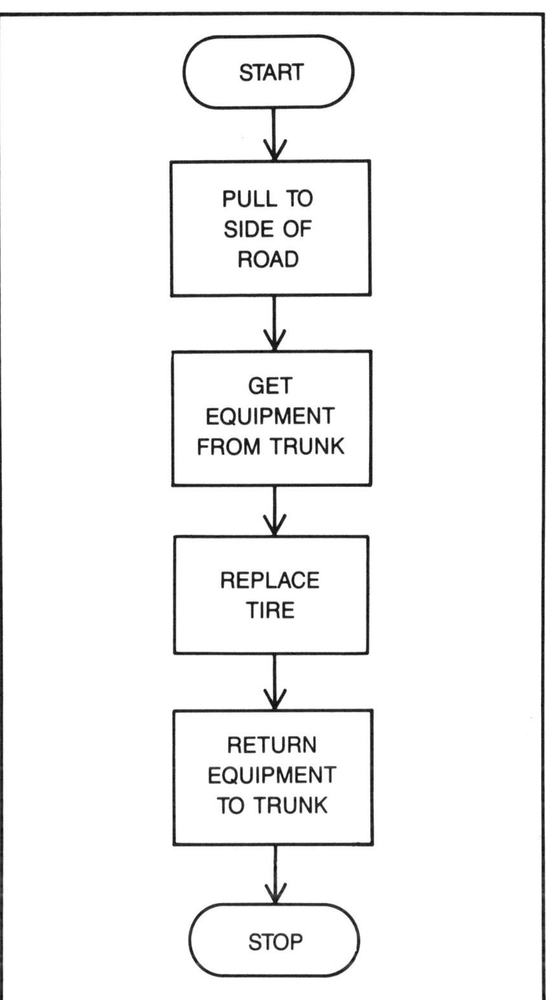

Fig. 4-6. Replacing a flat tire.

would get the spare tire from the trunk. While the trunk is open, he would remove the jack and tire iron. He would then jack up the car, replace the tire, and lower the car. Finally, the jack, tire iron, and flat tire would be placed in the trunk. Figure 4-6 shows a flowchart representing the steps just described.

You have probably thought of some exceptions to this procedure. For instance, the person may not be traveling when he realizes the car has a flat, or his spare also may be flat. The nuts may be stuck, and so on and on. When writing a program to deal with many alternatives like this, you must decide which circumstances to deal with, and which to ignore. Thousands of different things could happen when replacing a tire; we can't hope to cover them all in a short program.

For simplicity, we will only worry about what to do if the person is not driving when he discovers the flat, and what to do if the spare is flat. Let's decide what would be done differently if either of these circumstances occur. If the person is not driving, he would not have to pull over; if the spare is flat, he would have to flag down help.

Let's show these developments in a flowchart using decision symbols; look at Fig. 4-7.

We have arranged the flowchart so the order of what will most commonly occur is still top-to-bottom. The steps we believe will be less frequent are placed to the side. However, the side steps also travel in a top-to-bottom fashion; this careful arrangement helps us understand the flowchart better. Only absolute decisions have been used; notice the use of merge points.

This example helps to show the importance of the decision symbol. Could we know ahead of time whether the flat would be discovered while driving the car, and whether

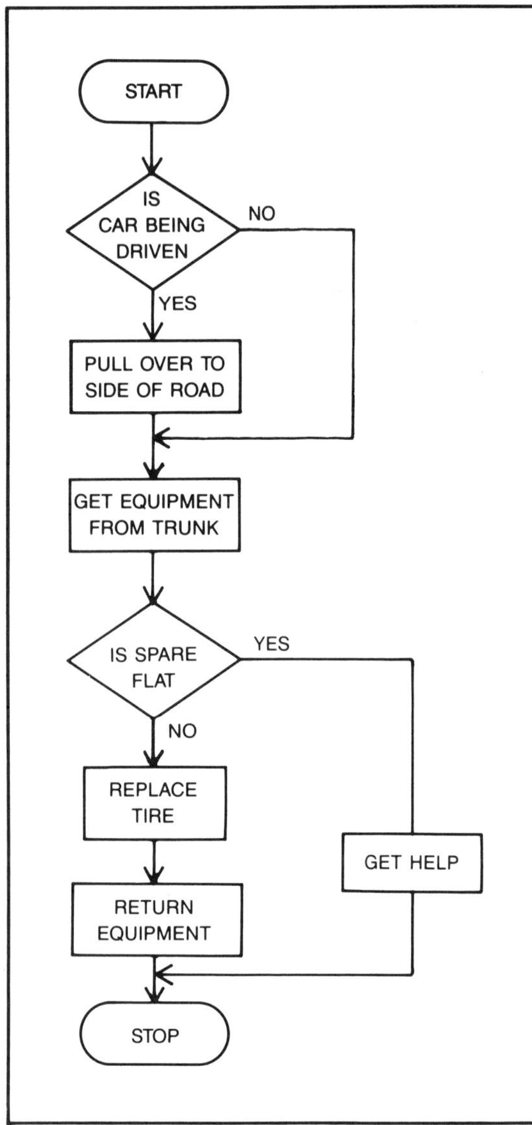

Fig. 4-7. Replacing a flat tire.

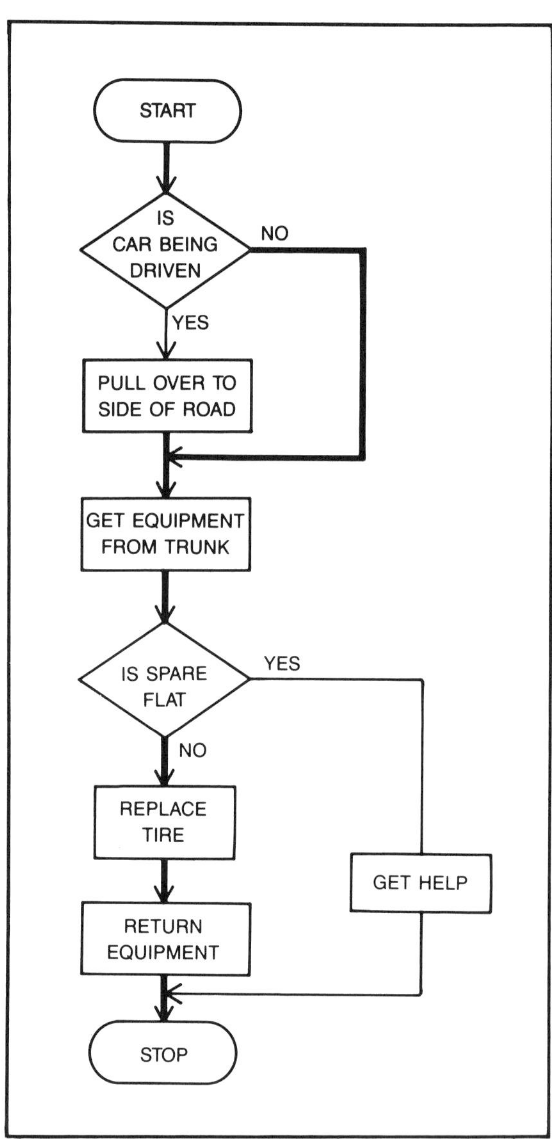

Fig. 4-8. Replacing a flat tire, with alternatives. Heavy lines showpath under alternate circumstances.

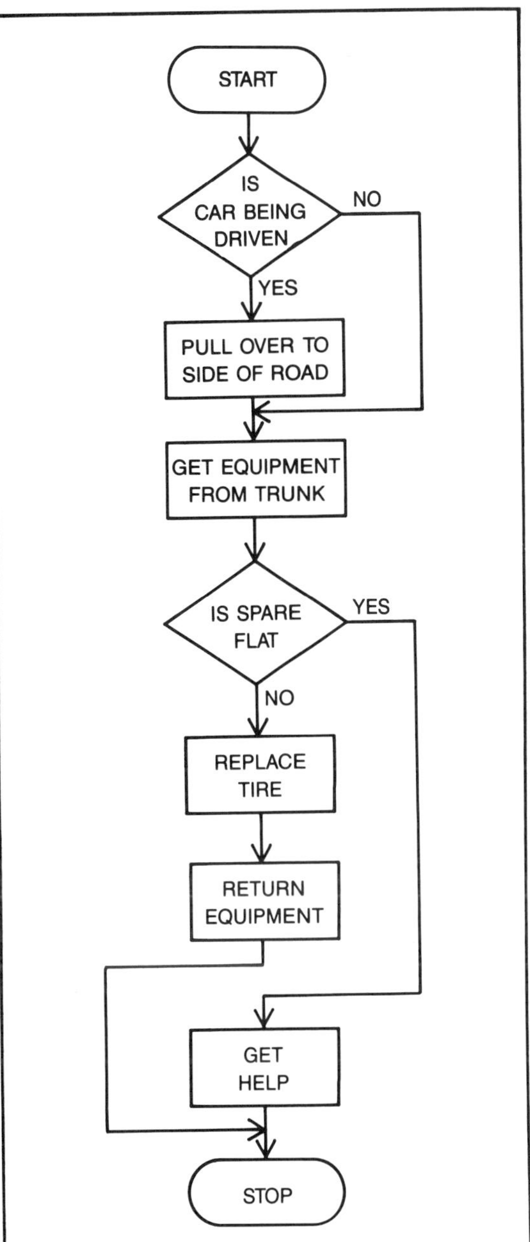

Fig. 4-9. Straightened flat-tire flowchart.

the spare was flat, we could write a flowchart using no decision symbols. However, this would have limited the flowchart to a solution that works only under those exact circumstanccs. Our currcnt flowchart is much more flexible.

It is still very easy to trace the flow, once we know the conditions under which we are traveling. If we assume that the care is *not* being driven and the spare is not flat, Fig. 4-8 shows we would follow the heavy flow lines.

IMPLEMENTING THE DECISION SYMBOL IN BASIC

In BASIC we have two statements that will help us turn our flowchart into a program. One statement is the **GOTO** statement. It lets us go from one part of a program to another, in an *unconditional transfer*. That is, the jump will occur every time the instruction is executed. The other instruction is the **IF-THEN** statement. This instruction lets us jump from one part of the program to another in a *conditional transfer*. That is, it will occur if and only if a certain condition exists.

The First Pass Through the Flowchart

Now we'll write a BASIC program based on the flat-tire flowchart. To represent a particular step in the process, we will simply use a **PRINT** statement to print the description. For instance, to represent jacking up the car, we will use the following **PRINT** statement: **PRINT "Jack up the car"**.

In our flat-tire flowchart, the order of instructions is slightly ambiguous. Also, none of the symbols indicate where **GOTO** statements are to be placed. In fact, depending on how we order the instructions, our need for **GOTO** instructions will change.

We will order the symbols first, as their order will affect our need for **GOTO** statements. A key to the solution is to realize that we have not affected the way the flowchart functions as long as the symbols remain connected in the same fashion. With that in mind, refer to Fig. 4-9 on the previous page.

This flowchart does not look exactly like the original one, but you can prove to yourself that it functions the same way by tracing some of the lines between symbols. Because they are all connected in the same order to the original flowchart, it *is* the same flowchart.

Let's implement this straight-line flowchart as a program, using **GOTO** and **IF-THEN** statements. Placing **IF-THEN** statements is easy; they replace the decision symbol. Placing **GOTO** statements is a little more tricky.

The way the symbols in the flat-tire flowchart are connected to each other are different than the connections we have used before. One type of connection connects a symbol to the symbol directly below it. Because BASIC executes instructions from top to the bottom, placing instructions right after each other, the second command is naturally executed after the first. But some of our connections indicate that after one instruction is executed, an instruction placed non-sequentially in the program and flowchart should be executed next. The GOTO instruction lets us make the transition from the one part to another.

When we are converting a flowchart into a program, and realize we must jump to a location further down the flowchart, that section will not have been converted into BASIC. We will not know what line number will correspond to the place we are jumping to. The solution is to write the program in two passes. In the first pass, we will write as much as we can, and leave room for the things for which we don't yet have an answer.

Figure 4-10 is the program that results from converting the flat-tire flowchart to BASIC in the first pass. Refer to it while we discuss how the program was written.

Lines 10-30 are introductory lines. Line 40 contains the **IF-THEN** statement that

```
10 REM **********
20 REM FLAT TIRE PROGRAM
30 REM **********
40 IF car is being driven THEN ***
50 PRINT "PULL OVER TO SIDE OF ROAD"
60 REM <MERGE POINT WITH 40>
70 PRINT "GET TIRE IRON, JACK, AND SPARE FROM TRUNK"
80 IF spare is flat THEN ***
90 PRINT "JACK UP CAR, REPLACE TIRE, LOWER CAR"
100 PRINT "PUT STUFF BACK INTO TRUNK"
110 GOTO ***
120 PRINT "GET HELP"
130 REM <MERGE POINT WITH 110>
140 END
```

Fig. 4-10. First pass through flat-tire flowchart.

replaces the first decision symbol. Notice the structure of the statement; the condition is placed between the words **IF** and **THEN**. The location to jump to follows **THEN**. At this point, we do not know where to jump, so we have placed some asterisks here to remind us we will have to add a line number before the program will work. Although we do not know where to jump, we do know what we want to accomplish; if the condition is true (the car is parked), we want to skip the part of the program that instructs us to pull over.

The next flowchart symbol tells us to pull over to a safe location. We agreed to use the **PRINT** instruction for actions; line 50 contains the instruction. Next we reach a merge point; line 60 contains the corresponding code. A **REM** statement is used to indicate that this point in the program stands for a merge point in the flowchart.

Now we know what line number should appear in the **IF-THEN** statement in line 40, but we will complete the rest of the flowchart first. Lines 70 and 80 take care of the open trunk and get equipment operation symbols. After these operation symbols we reach the second decision symbol, and the second jump, if the spare is flat. Again, use asterisks to remind us to later write in the correct line number to which to jump.

The next two operation symbols tell us what to do if our spare is not flat, and we use **PRINT** statements, lines 90-100. Following these symbols we reach a very interesting part of our flowchart. The flow line leading into the next symbol comes from the second decision symbol, and the one leading out goes to a point found later in the flowchart. Let us first look at the outgoing flow line.

As you remember, **GOTO** statements are used to indicate jumps to other parts of a program. The jump depicted by the flowchart occurs no matter what the conditions. Each time we execute the "return equipment" operation symbol, we go to another part of the program. However, we don't know where to go, so we again write **GOTO** ***.

Now we come to the operation symbol that says "flag down help." The flow line entering this symbol does not come from the symbol proceeding it. This is not a merge point; if you trace the flow line back to the symbol from which it originated, you will see that at no point do any other flow lines enter it. This symbol simply translates into another **PRINT** statement, shown in line 130.

After the third operation symbol is another merge point, and we add a **REM** statement as we did at the first merge point. Following the merge point is the stop symbol, and so we will add an **END** statement to finish off the program, in line 150.

Pass one of the conversion into a BASIC program is complete. Here is a quick summary:

☐ Start, stop, read/write, and operation symbols are converted to the appropriate BASIC code. In this program all operation symbols were translated as **PRINT** statements. This is not common practice.

☐ Decision symbols were replaced by **IF-THEN** statements. The condition placed between the **IF** and **THEN** is derived from the description inside the symbol. Where jump locations are unknown, asterisks (*) are put in place of line numbers.

☐ Merge points are indicated by **REM** statements to indicate from what part of the program the merging flow line originates.

☐ Where a flow line from a symbol runs to another symbol besides the one directly after it, **GOTO** statements are best. Again, we use asterisks to tell us we still need to determine the location to jump to.

☐ A line flowing into a symbol from another symbol besides the one directly before it has no special treatment.

The Second Pass

We now have only to go back through the program and fill in the details we left out in the first pass. Look again at Fig. 4-10; in the second pass, the line numbers not known in the first pass are entered. Go to the first place where asterisks were left as reminders; match it to the flowchart to see where the jump is made, find the location that the jump corresponds to, and replace the asterisks with that line number. In line 40, asterisks are replaced by reference to line 60; in line 80, the reference is to line 120; in line 110, the reference is to line 130. Only the line number (i.e., 60, 120, 130) is used.

BOOLEAN ALGEBRA

We have just prepared a fairly difficult program. Unfortunately, it is not a valid BASIC program, because the conditions in the **IF-THEN** statements are not in a suitable form. We will now study what expressions can be placed in **IF-THEN** statements.

True and False

When BASIC sees an **IF-THEN** statement it jumps to a given line number if the expression is true. If the expression is false BASIC goes to the instruction on the next sequential line. How BASIC determines truth and falsity depends on what version you are using. Most versions use the following rule: the number 0 is false and the number −1 is true. Thus, if BASIC encounters the instruction **IF 0 THEN 140**, it would not go to line 140, but to the next instruction line. If, on the other hand, BASIC encountered

Table 4-1. Boolean Operators.

Operator	Meaning
=	Equal to
<	Less than
<=	Less than or equal
>	Greater than
>=	Greater than or equal
<>	Not equal to

the instruction **IF −1 THEN 80**, it would jump to line 80.

These two instructions are never seen in a real program, though. Can you guess why? The first instruction, **IF 0 THEN** *line number*, never jumps to the specified line number. This instruction is a do-nothing instruction or *no-op* (no operation). It behaves like a **REM** statement; no operation is performed and execution always goes to the next instruction. Likewise, the **IF −1 THEN** *line number* instruction is never seen in a program, because it behaves just like a **GOTO** instruction; every time the instruction is encountered execution transfers to the specified line number.

Boolean Expressions

Now let's examine the expressions that give IF-THEN statements their power: Boolean expressions. Just like the mathematical expressions that produce a numerical result, Boolean expressions produce a result of −1 or 0. It is common practice to refer to the result of a Boolean expression as a Boolean value. A Boolean value has the value of true or false. To avoid confusion with numeric data, we will refer to true instead of −1, and false instead of 0.

Boolean expressions use operators, like mathematical expressions. However, while all mathematical operators take numbers and give numbers as a result, certain Boolean operators take numbers and give Boolean values, while others take Boolean values and produce Boolean values.

Relational Operators. The first type of Boolean operator is called a *relational operator*. These operators take two values and produce a true result if the relation is true, and false if the relation is false. Table 4-1 lists the relational operators and their meanings. As you may have already guessed, these are binary operators, because they need two numbers. Table 4-2 lists examples of Boolean expressions and their values. Either or both numerical arguments may themselves be numerical expressions. Because

Table 4-2. Results of Applying Boolean Operators.

True Expressions			False Expressions		
3	=	3	5	=	8
4	<	10	9	<	5
5	<=	7	2	<	2
6	<=	6	4	<=	3
8	>	2	3	>	7
8	>=	5	9	>	9
1	>=	1	2	>=	9
3	<>	5	4	<>	4

I will go to the beach if the weather is good AND I have the day off.

	The weather is not good	The weather is good
I don't have the day off		
I have the day off		X

Fig. 4-11. An example of the AND operator.

Boolean relational operators can be found in the same expression with mathematical operators, we must assign them a level of importance in our mathematical hierarchy. All relational operators are of lower importance than any mathematical operator. Thus, we compute the value of a Boolean expression *after* all mathematical expressions on either side of the operator have been evaluated.

Boolean Operators. Relational operators take numerical values and give Boolean values. Boolean operators take Boolean values and produces Boolean values. The operators are **AND**, **OR**, and **NOT**. Before we explore how they are used in BASIC expressions, let us see how they are used in everyday speech.

How might you describe the conditions under which you would go to the beach? Assume that there are two factors that decide whether you will be able to go or not: the weather and having the day off from work. You might say, "I will go to the beach if the weather is good **AND** I have the day off from work." The operator **AND** operates on the conditions "the weather is good" and "I have the day off from work." Both conditions must be true for the entire expression to be true. If either or both conditions false, the entire expression will be false.

Figure 4-10 shows this in a chart. This chart is called a *truth table.* The **X** indicates under what circumstances the expression will be true; in this case, if the weather is good and you have the day off.

The general function of the **AND** operator is shown in Fig. 4-11. It shows us that in order for **A AND B** to be true, both **A** and **B** have to be true. The truth table in Fig. 4-12 follows the accepted format; 0 is false and 1 is true. The table shows the value of **A AND B** for each possible combination of values **A** and **B** can have.

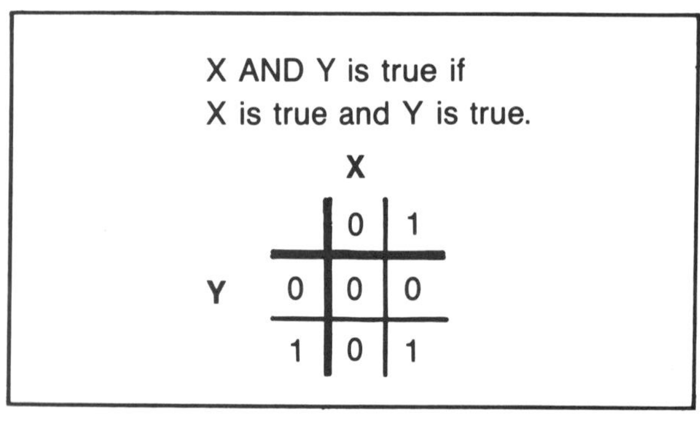

Fig. 4-12. Truth table for AND.

I will take an umbrella if it is raining OR rain was predicted.

	It is not raining	It is raining
Rain is not predicted		X
Rain is predicted	X	X

Fig. 4-13. An example of the OR operator.

The second Boolean operator is OR. Suppose you want to describe the conditions that would cause you to take an umbrella to work. You could say "I will take an umbrella to work if it is raining **OR** the weatherman predicts rain." Unlike the **AND** operator, the **OR** operator gives us a true response if either *or both* of the conditions are true. Figure 4-13 is the truth table that pictures this relationship; in Fig. 4-14 we have the general truth table for **OR**.

The final Boolean operator is the **NOT** operator. Unlike **AND** and **OR**, which are both binary operators, **NOT** is a unary operator. A use of the **NOT** operator in common speech might be, "I will go if he does **NOT** go." Thus, I will go only if the condition "he goes" is false (or, more correctly, if the Boolean **NOT** of "he goes" is true). **NOT** has the effect of reversing Boolean values; true becomes false and false becomes true. The general truth table for the NOT operator is shown in Fig. 4-15.

Combining Relational and Boolean Operators. To use Boolean operators we need Boolean operands, and the only way to obtain Boolean operands is to use Boolean expressions using relational operators. Because Boolean expressions are eventually intermixed with mathematical expressions, they are in the mathematical hierarchy. All of the operators are at the bottom of the hierarchy, below the relational operators. However, unlike relational expressions, which have the same priority among themselves, the Boolean operators have different priorities. **NOT** has the highest priority, then **AND**, and finally **OR**. Thus, when BASIC evaluates an expression, after the mathematical operators and relational operators have computed, all the **NOT**s are done, then the **AND**s and finally the **OR**s.

X OR Y is true
if X is true or Y is true.

		X	
		0	1
Y	0	0	1
	1	1	1

Fig. 4-14. Truth table for OR.

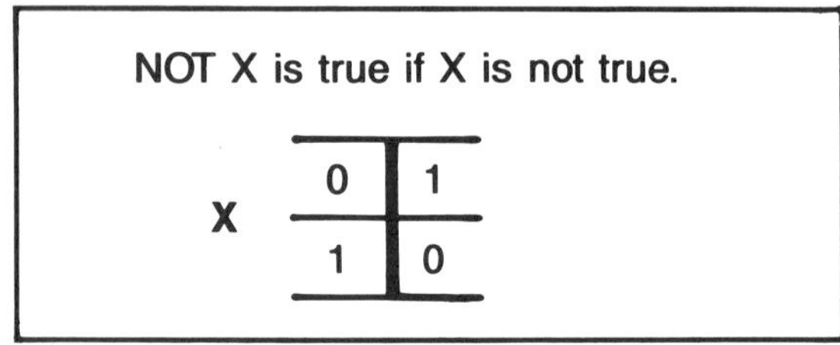
NOT X is true if X is not true.

X	
0	1
1	0

Fig. 4-15. Truth table for NOT.

Now let us see if we can evaluate some expressions containing Boolean operators. Our first expression will be B > A AND B < C. To evaluate this expression, BASIC would first determine whether B > A was true or false and then B < C. Then it would compute the value of the AND operation. Suppose A is 5, B is 7, and C is 11. B > A would be 7 > 5, which is true. B < C is also true. Finally, **true AND true** is true: the final answer. If, on the other hand, C is 4, B > A is true, but B < C is false. **True AND false** is false, so the result of the expression is false.

THE FLAT TIRE PROBLEM REVISITED

Let's see if we can adapt the flat tire problem to use the proper expressions. Before we do, we must rethink a few points.

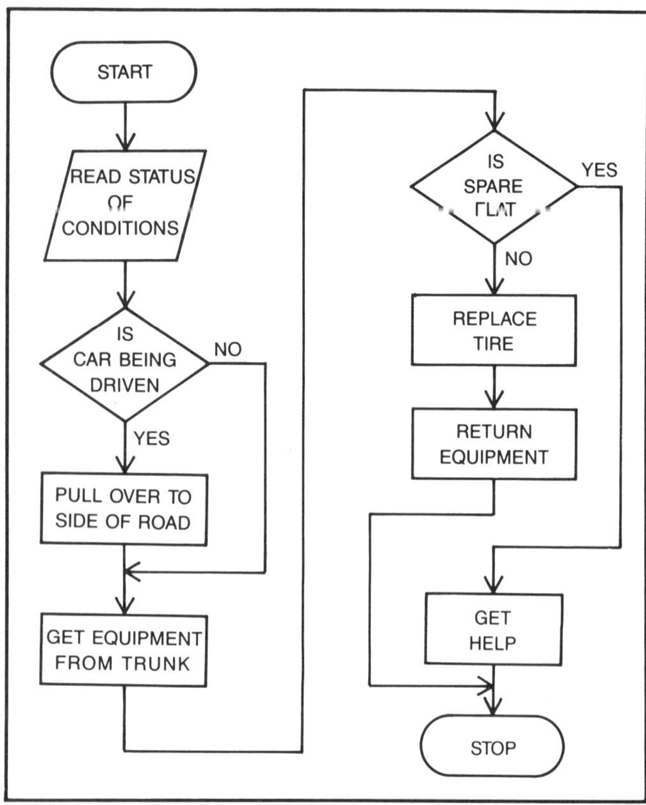

Fig. 4-16. New macro-flowchart for flat tire program.

Our first step is to define the problem. We said we want a flowchart that explains the procedure of replacing a flat tire. Let us modify that to say we want a flowchart to print out what would happen if we attempt to replace a flat tire. We want the explanation to show exactly what will be done depending on whether we are driving the car or not, and whether our spare is good or not. A macro-flowchart to represent this is shown in Fig. 4-16. This flowchart shows us that we must first read in the status of these two conditions before the instructions are printed out.

Convert the macro-flowchart into a micro-flowchart. We are first told to read in two conditions. How do we do this? All the data we have been using has been numerical data: data that represents a quantity of something. However, now we must store a different type of data, data that does not represent a quantity, but a fact or condition.

Storing information like this is easy. The type of variable we can use is called a *switch*. A switch can be either on or off. For our flat tire problem, we will need two switches. We will use one switch to store the status of the motion of the car when the flat tire is detected. If the switch is on, we will say we are driving at the time, and if it is off, we will say we are parked. The second switch will be used to store the status of the spare tire. If it is on, the spare is good, and if it is off, the spare is flat. Fig. 4-17 shows this information in a chart.

Now the solution to our problem is easy. We simply read in the values of the two switches, and then print out the directions, referring to the value of the switches when necessary. How are switches implemented in BASIC? There are different ways. The one we will use is probably the easiest; we will use a variable, and agree on a value that represents on and another value that represents off. A 0 will represent off, and a 1 will represent on, and we will be consistent with the notation used in truth tables.

It is not possible to store other values (e.g., 5, −3, 9482.57). To cover this possibility, we will say that if the switch does not contain either of the agreed-upon values, it is "undefined". If a switch is undefined we will treat it as an off value. In programs where such an assumption might cause unwanted errors, it would be best to have the program print an error message and then halt or perform some sort of correction when an undefined value is detected.

We can now begin to prepare the micro-flowchart. Two variables are needed to contain the two switches; D will be used for the switch that tells us whether we are driving, and S will note whether the spare is flat. To implement the read symbol, we simply read in the values of these two variables. The rest proceeds as before.

Switch	On (1)	Off (0)
D	Person is driving	Person is not driving
S	Spare is good	Spare is flat

Fig. 4-17. Switches for flat tire program.

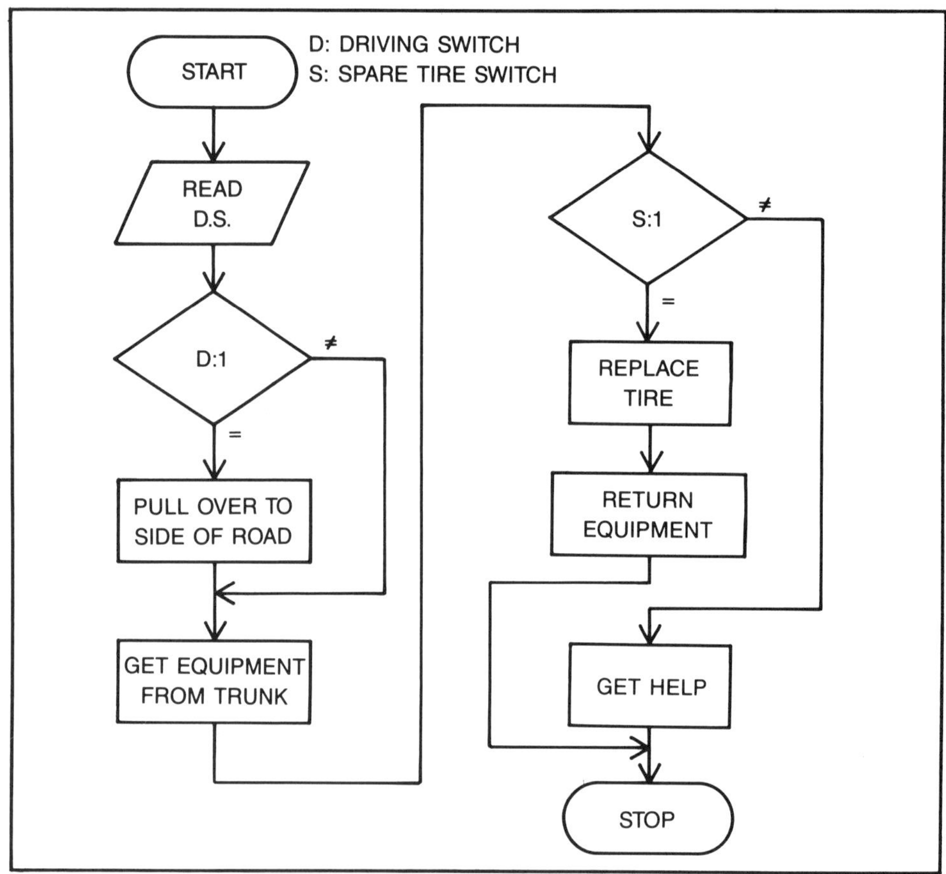

Fig. 4-18. New micro-flowchart for flat tire program.

The completed micro-flowchart is shown in Fig. 4-18. We have replaced the expressions in the decision symbols with expressions that incorporate the switches and proper Boolean expressions. From the micro-flowchart, conversion to a BASIC program is straightforward.

Figure 4-19 is the BASIC listing after two passes through the flowchart. Look at the expressions used in the **IF-THEN** statements; the first corresponds to the decision symbol that asks whether we are driving. If we are not, we want to branch past the next instruction. Therefore, the expression must be true when the condition (we are driving) is *not* present. We might have used **D = 0**, but we agreed that undefined values would be the same as a zero. This expression does not take that into account.

The correct expression is **D < > 1**. Thus, if **D** is 0, or any undefined value, **D < > 1** will be true and the jump will take place. The second **IF-THEN** tests whether the spare is good. If the spare is bad, we want to jump to a later part of the program. We encounter the same problem; we must jump if **S** is 0 or any undefined value. **S < > 1** is the correct expression.

Conversion during the second pass merely involved replacing asterisks with line numbers for jumps in lines 80, 120, and 140. Sample runs are shown in Fig. 4-20.

```
10 REM *********
20 PRINT "FLAT TIRE PROGRAM"
30 REM *********
40 PRINT "ENTER 1 IF YOU ARE DRIVING OR 0 IF YOU ARE NOT"
50 INPUT D
60 PRINT "ENTER 1 IF SPARE IS GOOD OR 0 IF IT IS NOT"
70 INPUT S
80 IF D <> 1 THEN 100
90 PRINT "PULL OVER TO SIDE OF ROAD"
100 REM <MERGE POINT WITH 80>
110 PRINT "GET TIRE IRON, JACK, AND SPARE FROM TRUNK"
120 IF S <> 1 THEN 160
130 PRINT "JACK UP CAR, REPLACE TIRE, THEN LOWER CAR"
140 PRINT "PUT STUFF BACK INTO TRUNK"
150 GOTO 170
160 PRINT "GET HELP"
170 REM <MERGE POINT WITH 150>
180 END
```

Fig. 4-19. Second pass through new flat tire flowchart.

SUMMARY

A *decision* is a test on data made during a program. Depending on the outcome of the test, different instructions are executed. A decision can be either absolute or relative.

The *decision symbol, merge symbol,* and *merge point* are used to show decisions in flowcharts. It is important that flow lines converge at a merge symbol or merge point and not at any other symbol.

The **IF-THEN** and **GOTO** instructions are used to implement decisions in the

```
FLAT TIRE PROGRAM
ENTER 1 IF YOU ARE DRIVING OR 0 IF YOU ARE NOT
? 1
ENTER 1 IF SPARE IS GOOD OR 0 IF IT IS NOT
? 0
PULL OVER TO SIDE OF ROAD
GET TIRE IRON, JACK, AND SPARE FROM TRUNK
GET HELP
End in line 180

------

FLAT TIRE PROGRAM
ENTER 1 IF YOU ARE DRIVING OR 0 IF YOU ARE NOT
? 0
ENTER 1 IF SPARE IS GOOD OR 0 IF IT IS NOT
? 1
GET TIRE IRON, JACK, AND SPARE FROM TRUNK
JACK UP CAR, REPLACE TIRE, THEN LOWER CAR
PUT STUFF BACK INTO TRUNK
End in line 180
```

Fig. 4-20. Sample runs of flat tire program.

language BASIC. When coding a micro-flowchart in BASIC, it is not possible to finish instructions which jump to a location which hasn't yet been coded. These unresolved references are filled in during a second pass through the micro-flowchart.

A *Boolean expression* has a value of true or false. Boolean expressions are formed using *relational operators* and (optionally) *Boolean operators*. Relation operators are below mathematical operators in the mathematical hierarchy. Boolean operators are lower still: **NOT** is computed first, **AND** second, and **OR** last.

EXERCISES

1. Describe the two types of conditions that can be placed in a decision symbol:

   a) ______________________________

   b) ______________________________

2. What are two rules to remember about decision symbols?

   a) ______________________________

   b) ______________________________

3. List the relational operators:

   a) ______________________________

   b) ______________________________

   c) ______________________________

   d) ______________________________

   e) ______________________________

   f) ______________________________

4. List the Boolean operators from highest to lowest priority:

   a) ______________________________

   b) ______________________________

   c) ______________________________

5. Evaluate the following expressions:

   a) 4< = 2 = __________

   b) 3< > 2 = __________

   c) 4 < 19 OR 5 > 3 = __________

   d) 2 > 9 AND 4 < 2 OR 4 < 6 = __________

   e) NOT (2 < 3 AND 3 < = 3) = __________

   f) 2 * 5 - 2 < (4 - 2) * 9 = __________

6. Problem: To determine whether number 1 is equal to number 2 × number 2. Have the program print our YES if this is true, and NO if it is not. Go through all six steps of the problem solving process. How user-friendly can you make the finished program?

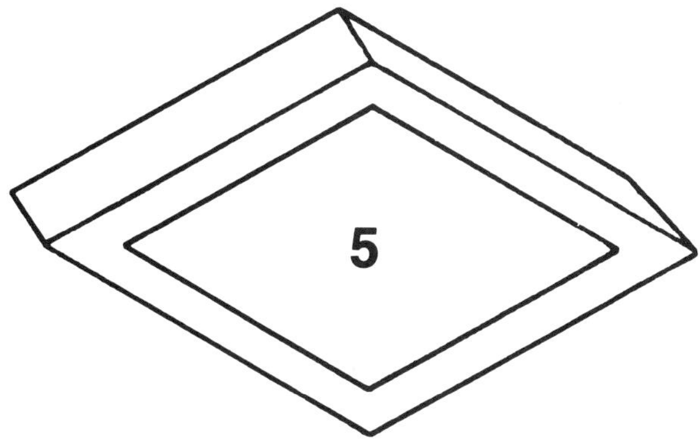

Looping

The programs we have developed have executed each instruction only once. There are many times when we will want to execute an instruction or group of instructions several times.

Repeated execution is directed by jumping to a location just preceding the jump. Figure 5-1 is a flowchart using such a jump. Each time the operation symbol is processed, the flow line leads back to a merge point above the operation symbol, causing the operation symbol to be executed over and over. A stop symbol is not used because the program never stops executing the operation symbol. We say the flowchart contains an *infinite loop.* We will look at looping after we have briefly discussed another important topic.

FORMULAS AND FUNCTIONS

We have used formulas in several of our programs. Because formulas are so prevalent, it is often convenient to represent them by a symbolic name which includes the variables in the formula. For example, if you use the formula 3 * Y − Y * Y quite often, you could choose a short name to call the formula, for instance, HAHA. Designing the name so it has some relevance to the formula it represents makes it easier to identify.

To complete the name we must define values to replace the variables in the formula. We make a *declaration* like the following: HAHA(Y) = 3 * Y − Y * Y. This declaration creates the *function* HAHA. It tells us that HAHA uses one variable, and shows us how it is used in the formula. HAHA(3) would be $3 \times 3 - 3 \times 3$ or 0, and HAHA(7)

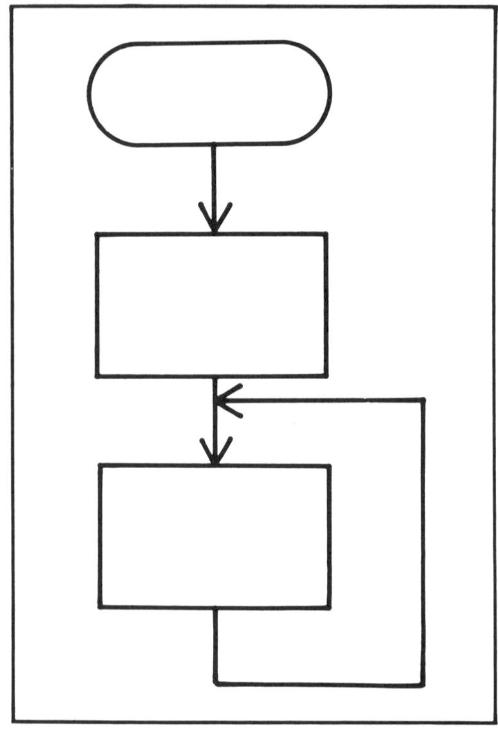

Fig. 5-1. A flowchart with an endless loop.

would be −28: 3 × 7 − 7 × 7. Variables can also be used in the function; **HAHA(A) = 3 * A − A * A**, etc. A function using more than one variable can also be defined: **HOHO(M,N) = M − 2 * N**. In this kind of function, the ordering of the variables is very important. **HOHO(6,5)** is −4, while **HOHO(5,6)** is −7.

Most languages, including BASIC, supply many built-in functions that perform many useful jobs which would be difficult to do otherwise. **SIN(X)** computes the sine of angle **X** (where **X** is in radians). The **RND(X)** function returns a random number between 0 and 1 (e.g., .83871209). The value we pass to it has no bearing on the number produced, so it is common practice to use 1. A value passed to a function that ignores the value is called a *dummy variable* because it is there simply to preserve the form of the function. The exceptions to this rule in the RND function are: **RND(0)**, which returns the last random number generated, and negative numbers, which cause a new series of random numbers to be generated.

THE CONDITIONAL LOOP

Let's study looping by writing a simple game. The object of the game will be to guess a number the computer has selected. The user keeps guessing until he gets the right answer. Every time a guess is made, the computer will state whether the guess is too high or too low.

Figure 5-2 is the macro-flowchart describing this game. The decision symbol is the vehicle by which the loop is created. It tests whether the guess was right, and loops back on an incorrect guess.

To convert the macro-flowchart into a micro-flowchart two pieces of data are used: the number the computer has selected, and the guess the player has made. Two variables can be used: **N** for the computer's number and **G** for the player's guess.

The first operation symbol tells us to pick a random number **N**. We want **N** to be between 0 and 1000. The **RND** function is used for this. **RND(1)** produces a number between 0 and 1; **RND(1) * 1000** will produce a number in the correct range. This alone will produce numbers like 492.38573 and 91.283741. To chop off the unwanted decimal part of the number BASIC provides another intrinsic function. **INT(X)** is the *integer function;* it returns the integer part of the number given to it (the part to the left of the decimal point). **INT(7.34)** is 7, and **INT(602.834)** is 602. The compute command we will use is **INT(RND(1) * 1000).**

To evaluate this expression, **RND(1)** is first computed. Let's say the function returns .63966293. **INT(.63966293 * 1000),** or **INT(639.66293),** is 639.

Figure 5-3 is the micro-flowchart. The first operation symbol shows how the expression we just created is used. The write symbol in the macro-flowchart has been expanded to several symbols better describing how to print the hint if a player gives a wrong answer.

To make sure the flowchart works, pick a value for **N** and then see how you would trace the flow through the remaining symbols. This technique is shown in Fig. 5-4 through Fig. 5-6 for different values of **G**. Note that we are testing for a guess that was less than, greater than, and equal to the value picked by the computer, to test every possibility that could occur. Look at the flowchart in Fig. 5-7; it is almost identical to

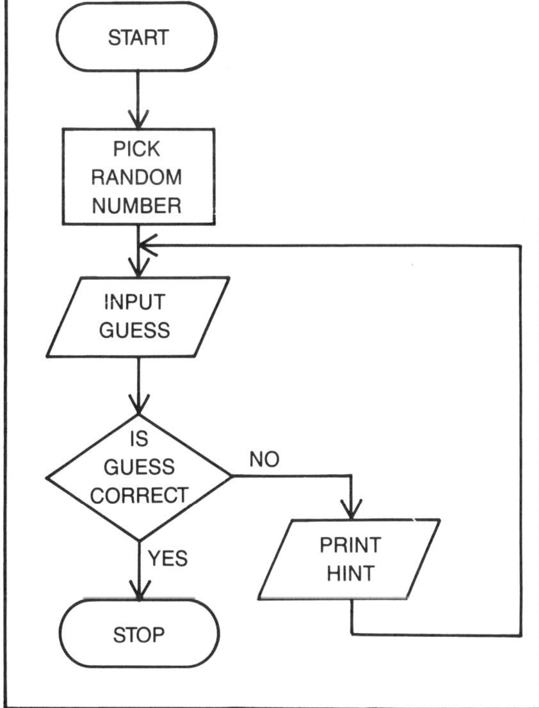

Fig. 5-2. Macro-flowchart for guessing game.

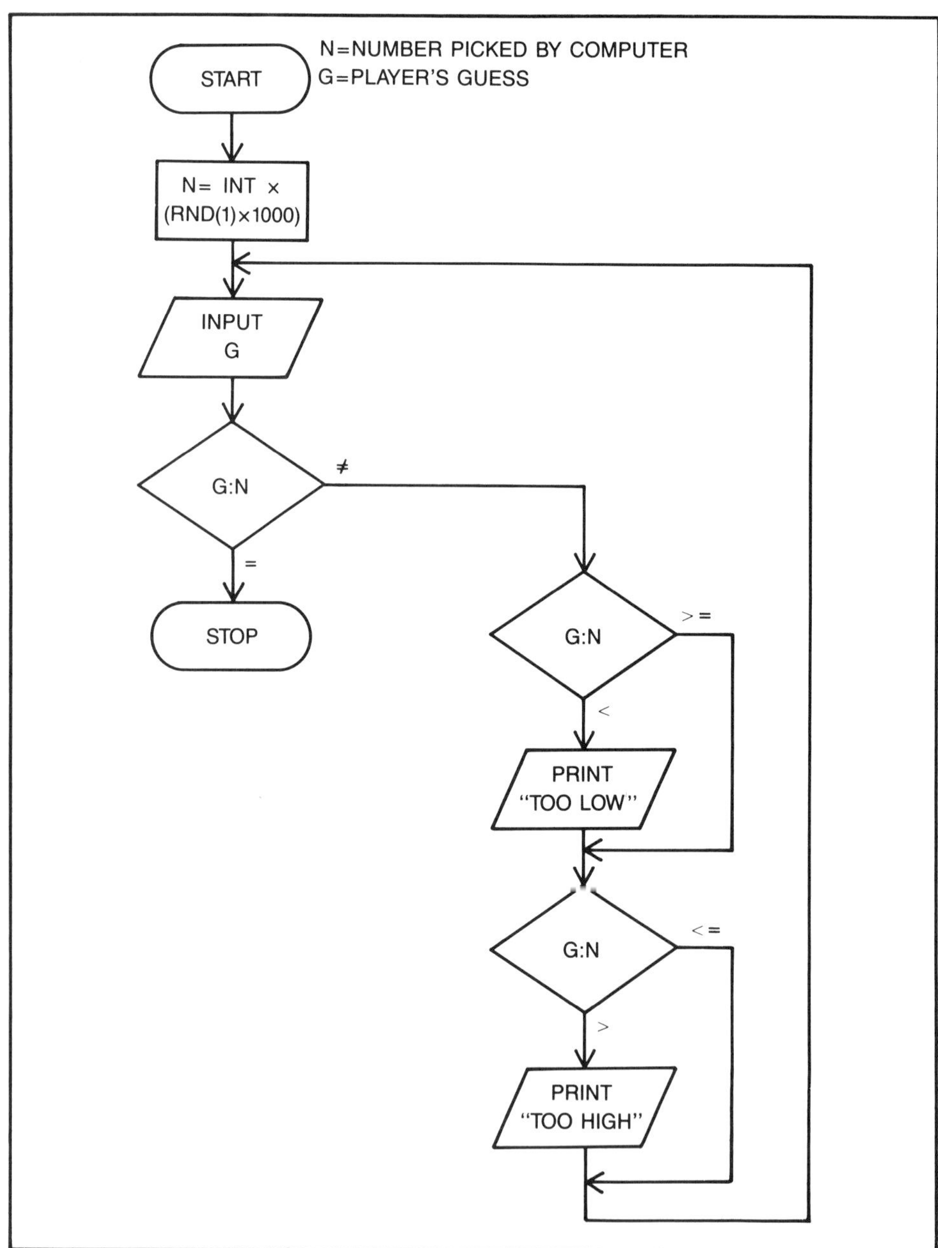

Fig. 5-3. Micro-flowchart for guessing game.

Fig. 5-3, with one small change. This error is highlighted when we apply the same test as that for Fig. 5-4. Figure 5-8 shows a trace through the flowchart in Fig. 5-5. Notice that the computer prints both hints if a user guesses too low.

Conversion into a program is more complicated than the flat tire program, but is still straightforward. Figure 5-9 shows the flowchart crunched into a straight line. The same rules presented in the previous chapter still apply when you do this, but be careful of flow lines traveling up as well as down. Both passes of the program are shown in Fig. 5-10 and a sample run is shown in Fig. 5-11. Not all merge points have had a **REM** statement associated with them; only jumps made over long distances have been noted.

The looping we used here is known as *conditional looping:* the program continues to loop until a particular condition exists. Another frequently-used method of looping

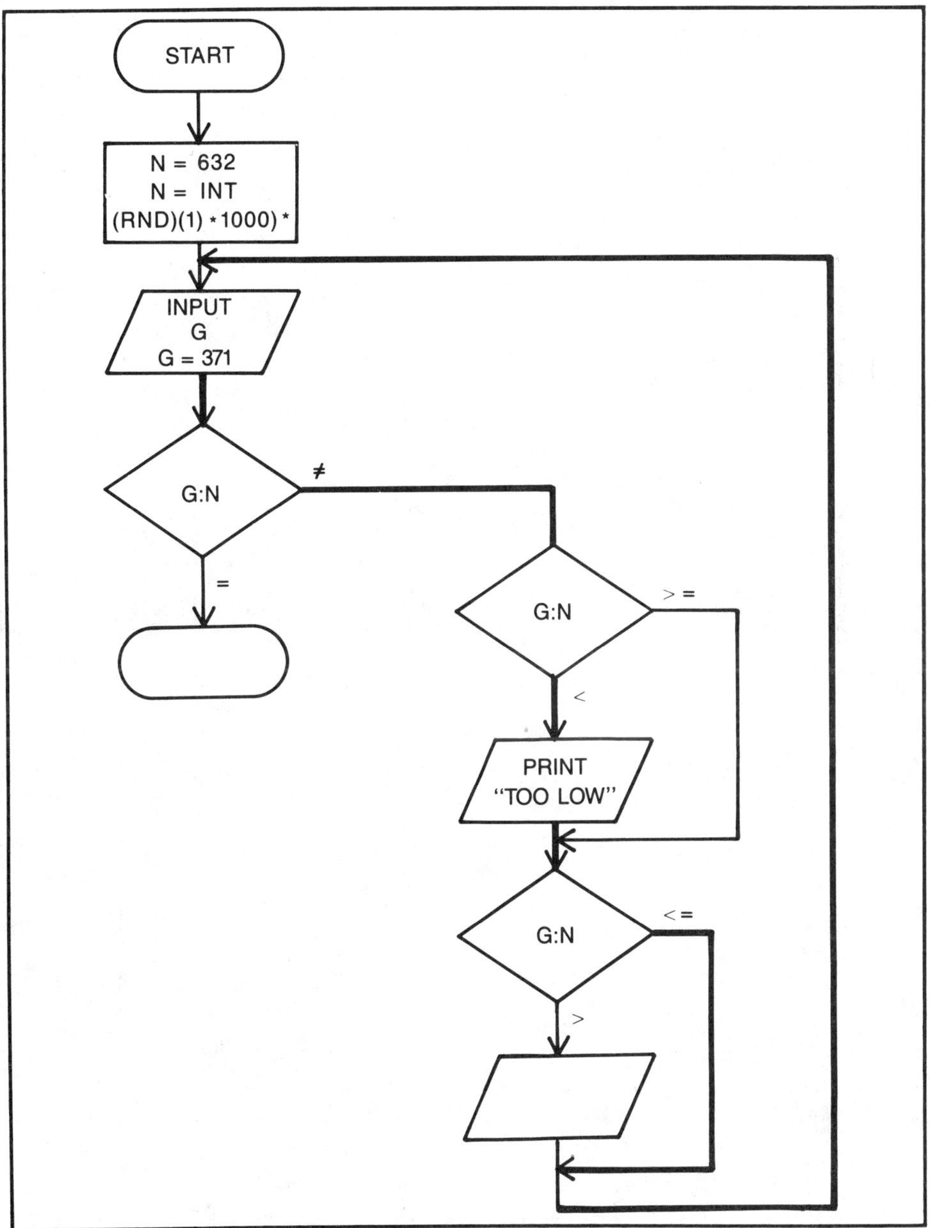

Fig. 5-4. Trace through the guessing game flowchart for a too-low guess.

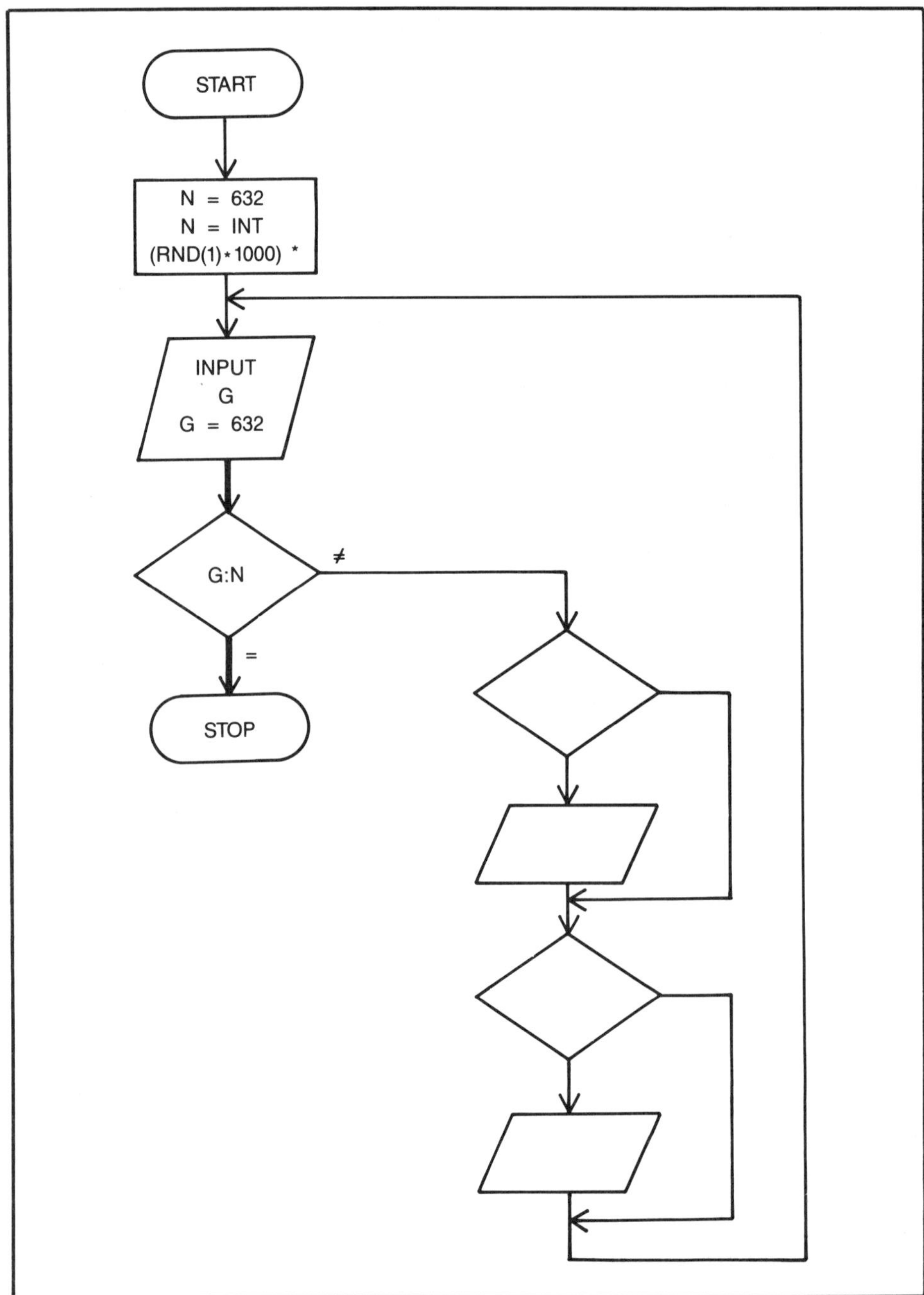

Fig. 5-5. Trace through the flowchart for a correct (i.e., equal) guess.

is known as *iterative looping*. This loop is repeated a certain number of times, determined before the looping takes place. The power of this type of looping can be seen in conjunction with the use of an array.

ARRAYS

An *array* is a collection of variables. Each variable in the array is referenced by the name of the array, in the same way ordinary variables are referenced, and by a subscript. A *subscript* is a numerical value that identifies each element of an array. Each element

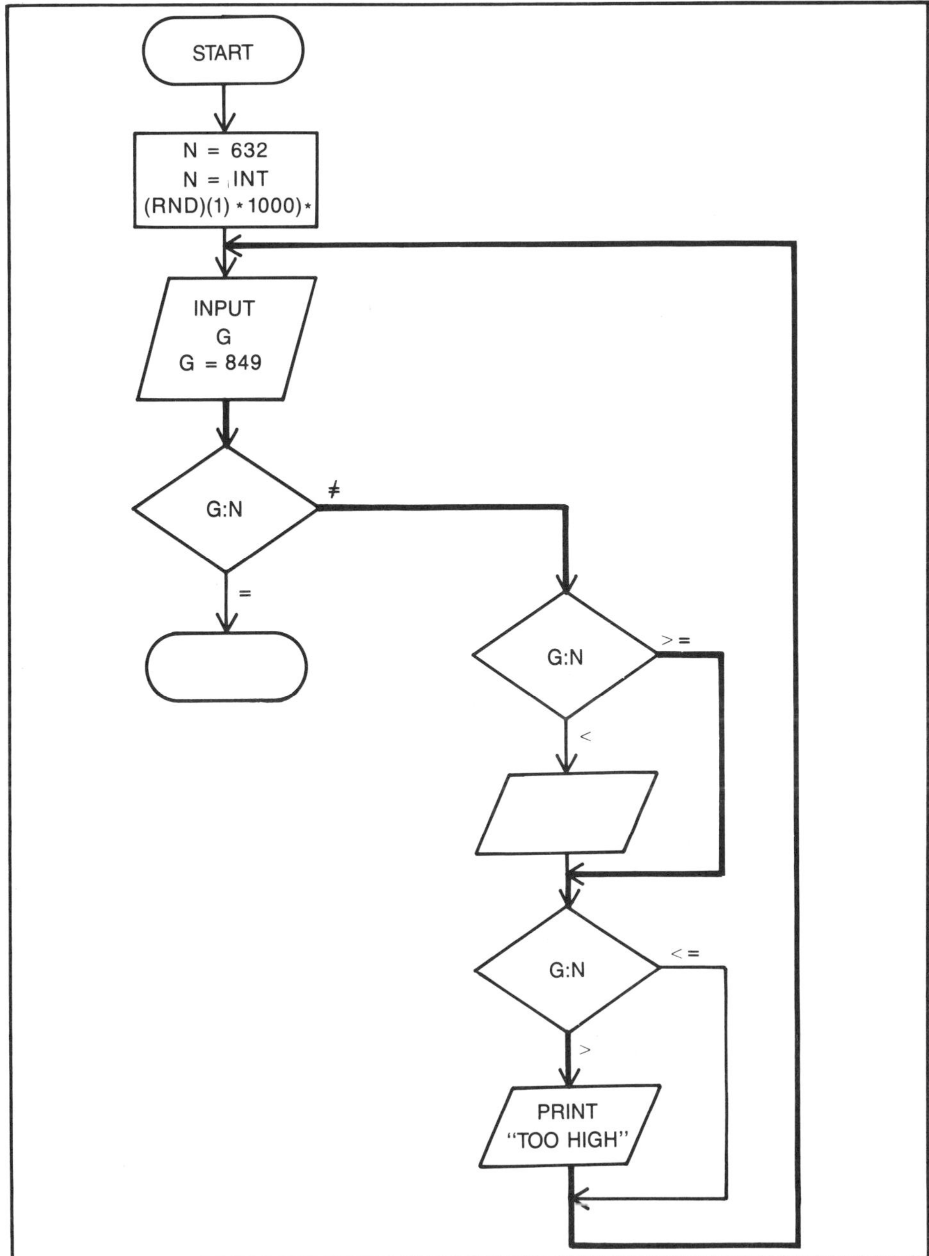

Fig. 5-6. Execution path for a too-high guess.

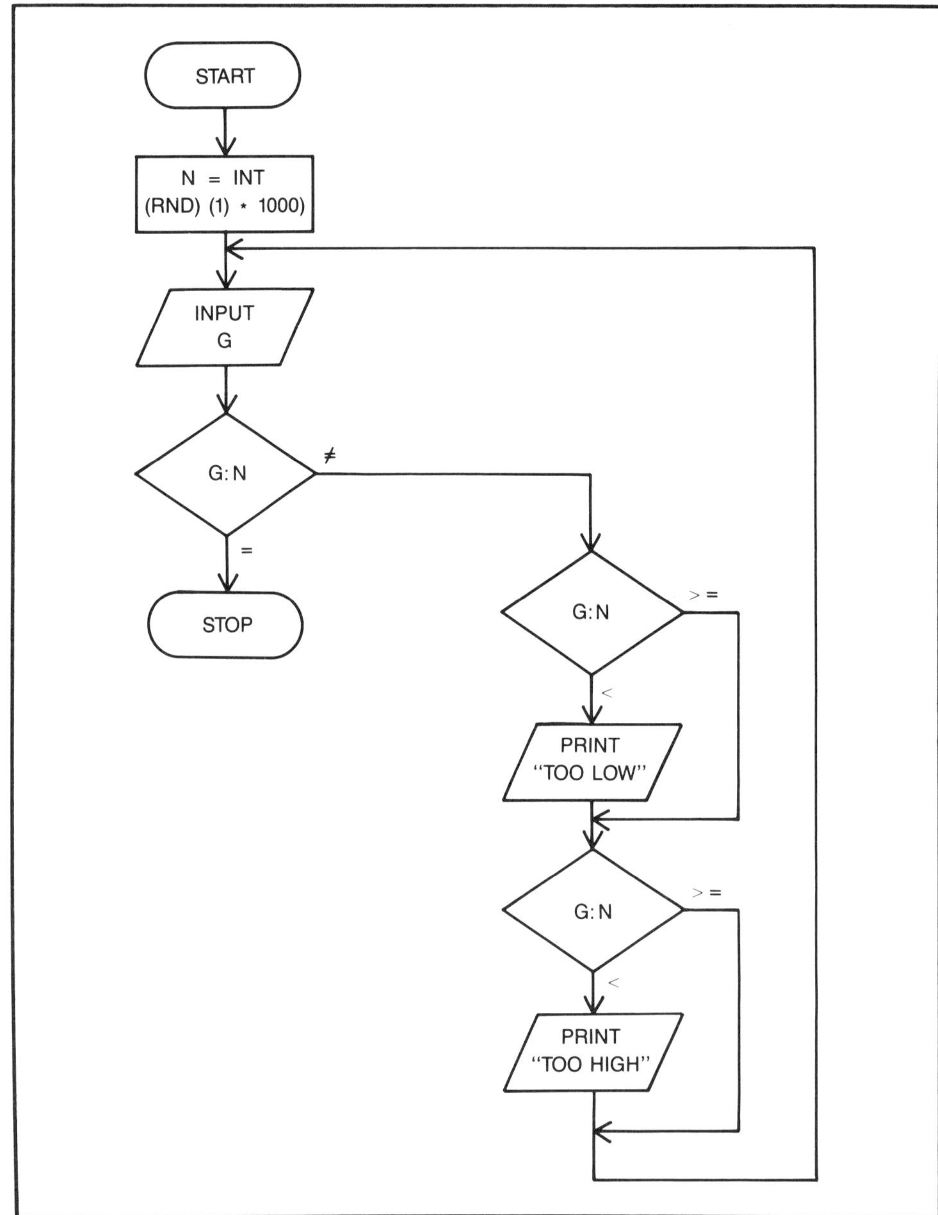

Fig. 5-7. Micro-flowchart for guessing game containing an error.

is independent of the others; modification of one element has no effect on any of the other members.

Before we can use an array, we must *dimension* it; this lets your programming language know how large the array is. As you remember, BASIC sets aside memory for every variable used in a program. With ordinary variables, the amount of memory set aside is constant, usually one or two bytes. However, since arrays can have different numbers of elements, BASIC must be told how many will be used before reserving memory.

To use an array (let's call it A) with ten elements, we would use the following instruction in our program:

10 DIM A(10)

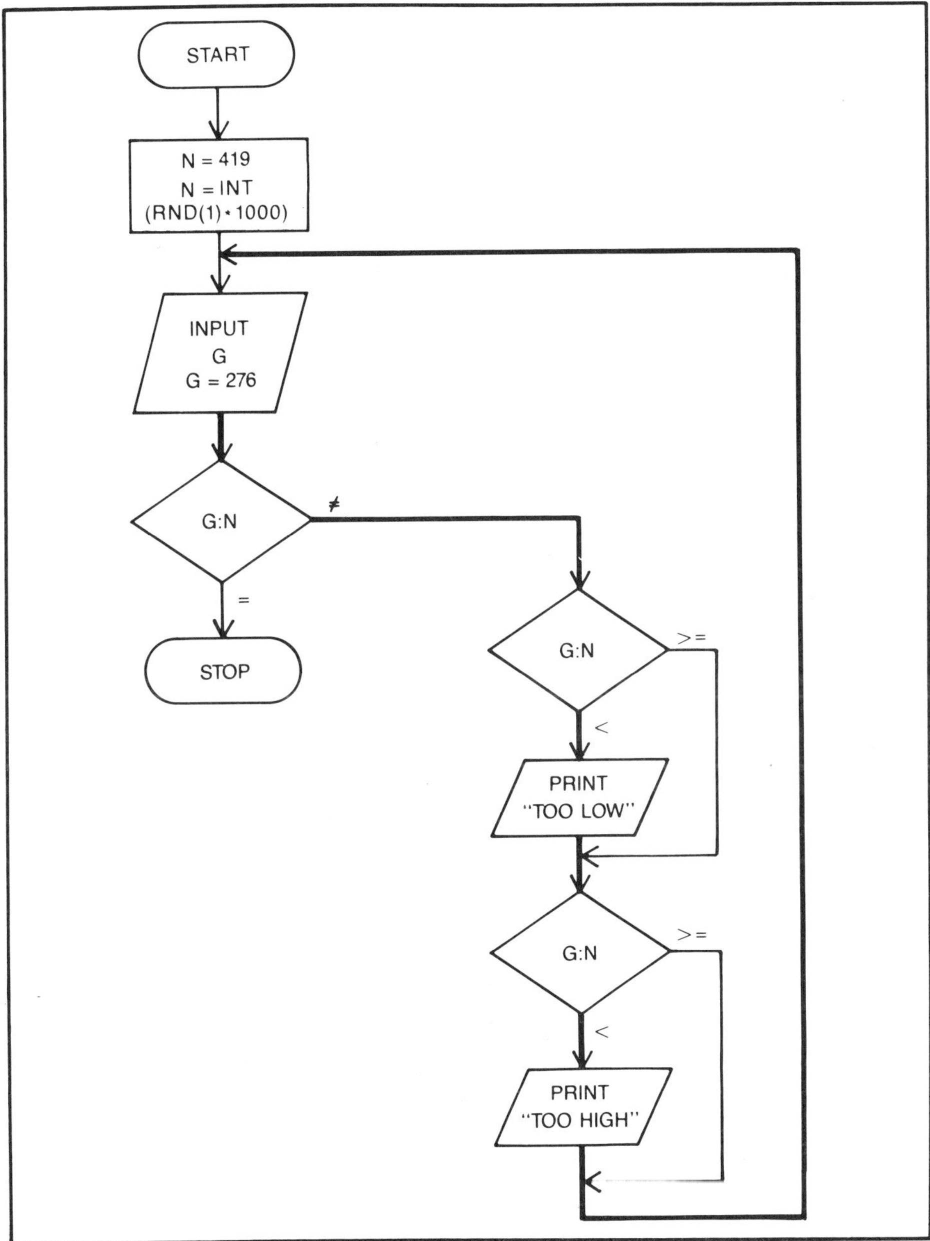

Fig. 5-8. Trace through erroneous guessing game flowchart.

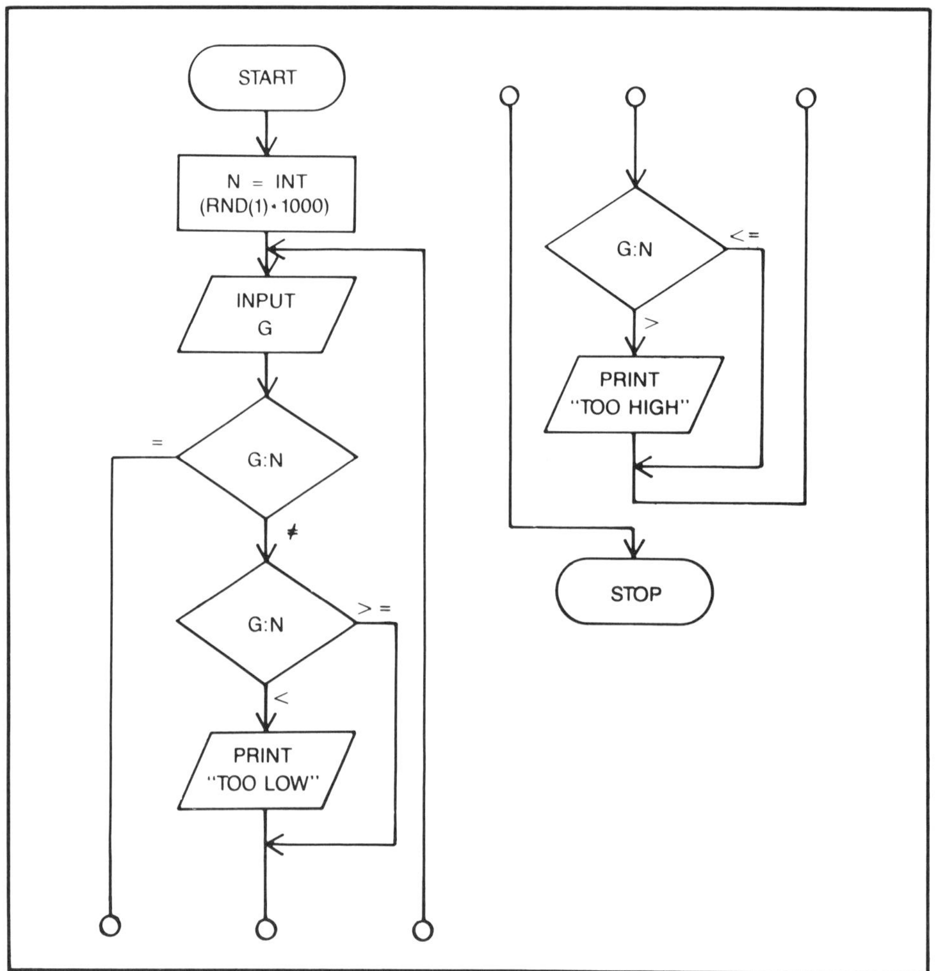

Fig. 5-9. Straight line micro-flowchart for guessing game.

Your BASIC language processor will set up enough memory to store the ten elements. Each element can be referenced by the name **A** and its index. The first element of the array would be **A(1)**, and so on. (Some versions of BASIC call the first element in **A A(0)**, and the last **A(9)**. Check with your manual first.)

The index numbers of the array are true numbers, unlike the 1 in the ordinary variable **A1**. This means instead of writing **A(1)**, we could write **A(5 – 4)** or **A(3*4 – 11)**. As long as the value inside the parentheses equals an integer number between 1 and the limit we set on the array in the dimension statement, the denotation is correct.

THE ITERATIVE LOOP

Consider the following problem: Since the purpose of many programs is to perform calculations on a large quantity of data, we must often enter many related data items, such as a series of banking transactions. We will forget about looping and arrays for

```
10 REM *********
20 PRINT "GUESSING GAME"
30 REM *********
40 LET N = INT(RND(1) * 1000)
50 REM <LOOP FROM LINE ***>
60 PRINT "GUESS THE NUMBER"
70 INPUT G
80 IF G = N THEN ***
90 IF G > N THEN ***
100 PRINT "TOO LOW"
110 IF G < N THEN ***
120 PRINT "TOO HIGH"
130 GOTO 50
140 REM <BRANCH FROM LINE 80>
150 PRINT "CORRECT!"
160 END
-----------
```

```
10 REM *********
20 PRINT "GUESSING GAME"
30 REM *********
40 LET N = INT(RND(1) * 1000)
50 REM <LOOP FROM LINE 130>
60 PRINT "GUESS THE NUMBER"
70 INPUT G
80 IF G = N THEN 140
90 IF G > N THEN 110
100 PRINT "TOO LOW"
110 IF G < N THEN 130
120 PRINT "TOO HIGH"
130 GOTO 50
140 REM <BRANCH FROM LINE 80>
150 PRINT "CORRECT!"
160 END
```

Fig. 5-10. Passes one and two of guessing game program.

```
GUESSING GAME
GUESS THE NUMBER
? 500
TOO HIGH
GUESS THE NUMBER
? 200
TOO LOW
GUESS THE NUMBER
? 300
TOO LOW
GUESS THE NUMBER
? 350
TOO HIGH
GUESS THE NUMBER
? 330
TOO LOW
GUESS THE NUMBER
? 335
CORRECT!
End in line 160
```

Fig. 5-11. Sample run of guessing game.

```
10 INPUT A1
20 INPUT A2
30 INPUT A3
40 INPUT A4
50 INPUT A5
60 INPUT A6
70 INPUT A7
80 INPUT A8
90 INPUT A9
100 INPUT A0
110 END
```

Fig. 5-12. Reading ten values into ten variables.

```
10 DIM A(10)        70 INPUT A(6)
20 INPUT A(1)       80 INPUT A(7)
30 INPUT A(2)       90 INPUT A(8)
40 INPUT A(3)       100 INPUT A(9)
50 INPUT A(4)       110 INPUT A(10)
60 INPUT A(5)       120 END
```

Fig. 5-13. Reading ten values into an array.

a moment and see how to read ten numbers into ten variables. Figure 5-12 is a BASIC program that does this; it places the ten data items in variables **A1-A10**.

This is an awkward solution to our problem. We can duplicate the program, using an array of dimension 10, as shown in Fig. 5-13. Your first impression is probably that using an array is worse, since both programs require 10 lines to read the data, but the array method needs still another instruction for the dimension statement. However, using a loop can cut this number and greatly simplify the array program.

First let's look at a program that will give us a hint as to how we should write a loop. Figure 5-14 shows a program in which we use a variable to index the array in each **INPUT** statement. This change makes every **INPUT** statement exactly alike; what makes the difference is that the value of I is different each time, so the **INPUT** statements will cause the data to be placed into different elements of the array.

Figure 5-15 shows how a loop can be set up to read 10 values into an array called **A**. The flowchart also uses a new symbol: the preparation symbol. The *preparation symbol* shows actions which could be placed in an operation symbol but are not directly related to the creation or manipulation of data. The DIM statement is a good example of what should be placed in a preparation symbol. It is an operation, but does not create or change data in any way. We will see the preparation symbol again shortly.

Figure 5-16 is the program that reads in data with a loop. Variable **I** is modified so the **INPUT** statement is incremented by 1 every time it is executed. After this is repeated 10 times, the program ends.

Fig. 5-14. Reading ten values into an array using an index variable.

```
10 DIM A(10)        120 LET I = 6
20 LET I = 1        130 INPUT A(I)
30 INPUT A(I)       140 LET I = 7
40 LET I = 2        150 INPUT A(I)
50 INPUT A(I)       160 LET I = 8
60 LET I = 3        170 INPUT A(I)
70 INPUT A(I)       180 LET I = 9
80 LET I = 4        190 INPUT A(I)
90 INPUT A(I)       200 LET I = 10
100 LET I = 5       210 INPUT A(I)
110 INPUT A(I)      220 END
```

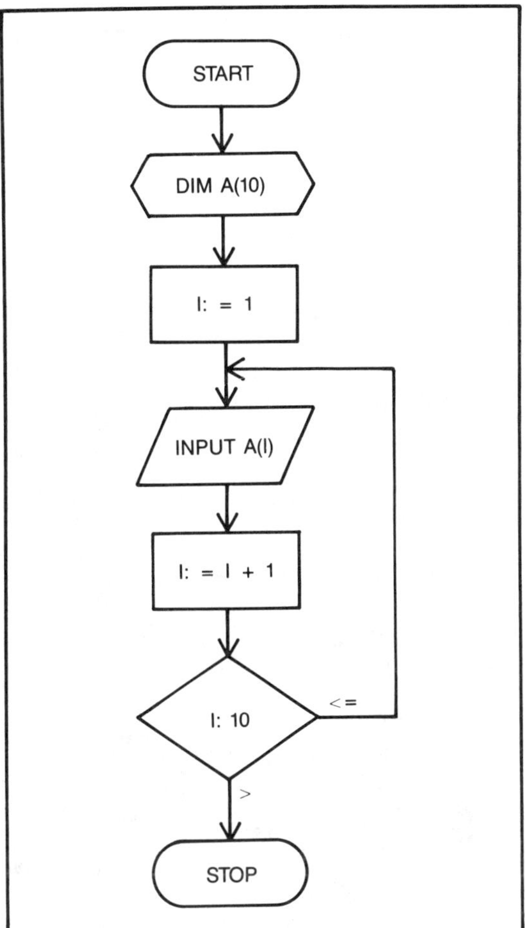

Fig. 5-15. Using a loop to read ten values into an array.

Although this program is shorter than the original, you might think it not worth the trouble. First look at these two important facts:

☐ The size of the first program would grow were we to read more numbers, while the loop method always stays the same size.

☐ The loop program can vary the quantity of numbers it reads during execution. The program could first read a number that tells it how many data items to read; Fig. 5-17 shows how this would be done.

```
10 DIM A(10)
20 LET I = 1
30 INPUT A(I)
40 LET I = I + 1
50 IF I <= 10 THEN 3
60 END
```

Fig. 5-16. BASIC program to read data into an array.

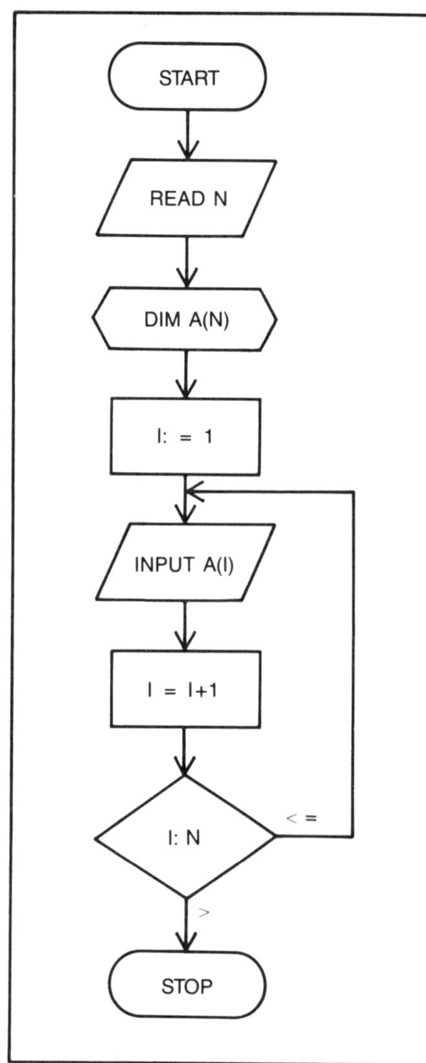

Fig. 5-17. Varying the amount of data to be read in.

THE FOR-NEXT STATEMENT

Although the loop in Fig. 5-15 can be viewed as a conditional loop, it is really a more specialized type of loop, known as an *iterative* loop. All iterative loops have a similar format, shown in Fig. 5-18. The index is a variable. Once it is set to the initial value, it is not changed—but it can be referenced—by the body of the loop, except when it has the increment value added to it. The process of executing the instructions inside the loop and adding the increment value to the index is repeated until the index becomes greater than the final value. We can also specify a final value *less* than the initial value; a negative value should be given for the step. BASIC adds the increment value to the index until it is *less* than the final value.

Because iterative looping is done so often, we have a special way to represent it in a flowchart, using the *preparation symbol.* Figure 5-19 shows how an iterative loop

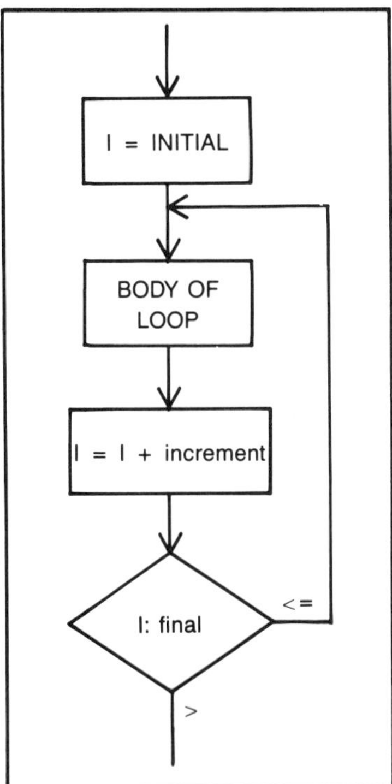

Fig. 5-18. Flowchart of an iterative loop.

is represented. The preparation symbol marks the beginning of the loop, and the decision symbol containing the index variable marks the end. The preparation symbol is used because setting the index variable to the initial value at the beginning of the loop is an action the preparation symbol is better suited for than the operation symbol. This

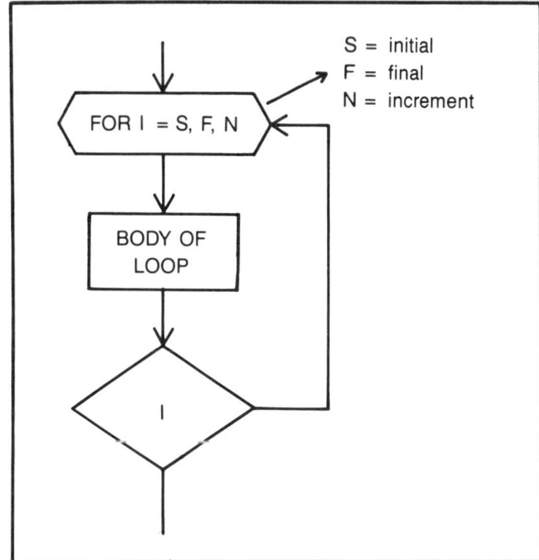

Fig. 5-19. Representing an iterative loop.

convention has not been followed; the preparation symbol is used in this book only for iterative loops and operations such as dimensioning arrays. The phrase: **FOR I = S, F, N** inside the preparation symbol gives us all the necessary information about the loop: I is the index variable, S is the starting value of the index variable, F is the final value of the index variable, and N is the increment value of the index variable. If a value is not present, we assume N to have a value of 1.

FOR I = S, F, N is often read as **FOR** *index* **EQUALS** *initial* **BY** *increment* **TO** *final.* To see how these two symbols are used together, refer to Fig. 5-20, a modified version of the flowchart that reads in values to an array.

Flowcharts using this type of notation are particularly appropriate for programs in BASIC. The **FOR** and **NEXT** statements are used for iterative loop control. The **FOR** statement is written as **FOR** *index* = *start* **TO** *final* **STEP** *increment.* **STEP** *increment* can be left out if we wish to use an increment of one (usually). The **NEXT** statement is written as **NEXT** *index.* The **FOR** statement is placed at the beginning of the loop, at the same location as the preparation symbol in the flowchart. The **NEXT** statement is placed at the end of the loop, at the same location as the decision symbol.

Even though we specify what the increment and final values are in the **FOR** statement, the increment is added to the index and checked against the final value when BASIC executes the **NEXT** statement. Figure 5-21 shows the program derived from Fig. 5-20, using **FOR-NEXT** statements.

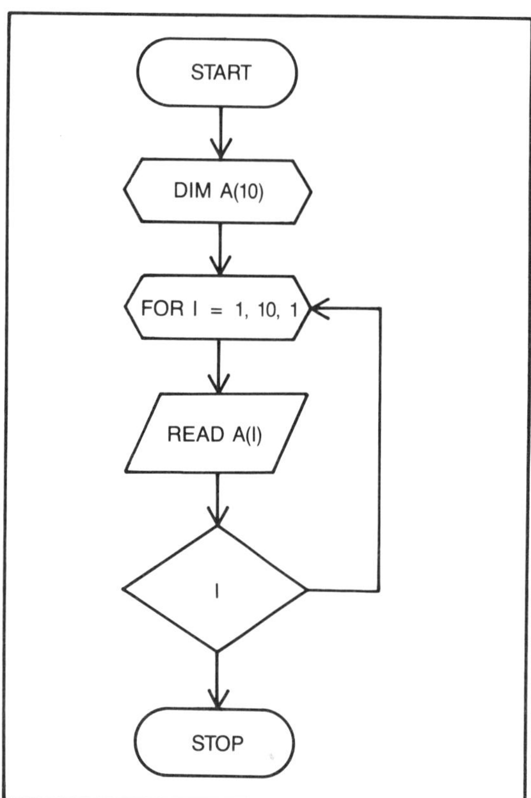

Fig. 5-20. Using an iterative loop to read data into an array.

```
10 DIM A(10)
20 FOR I = 1 TO 10
30 INPUT A(I)
40 NEXT I
50 END
```

Fig. 5-21. BASIC program to read data using FOR-NEXT statements.

SUMMARY

Looping is created by a jump which causes one or more instructions to be executed one or more times. There are two types of loops: conditional and iterative.

A *conditional loop* loops while a particular condition is true. Iterative loops execute a certain number of times. Each iterative loop has an associated *index variable.* The index is set to an initial value before the loop begins. Each time through the loop an *increment* (usually one) is added to the index. When the index becomes greater than the final value, the loop terminates.

Functions represent formulas by a symbolic name. If the formula uses variables, the variables must be declared along with the name. When the function is used, either constant values or variables can be substituted for the variables used to declare the function.

An *array* is a collection of variables. Each element in an array can be accessed by referring to the array name and the element's index. If the array's name is A, A(1) is the first element, etc.

EXERCISES

1. Consider the following two functions:

ALPHA(X) = X + 2 and BETA(X) = X * 3

Compute the following values:

a) ALPHA(3) = _________
b) BETA(12) = _________
c) A = 5, ALPHA(A) = _________
d) C = 9, BETA(C) = _________
e) A = 12, ALPHA(A / 3) = _________
f) C = 2, BETA(C - 3) = _________
g) Q = 3, ALPHA(BETA(Q)) = _________
h) Q = 4, BETA(ALPHA(Q) + 3) = _________

2. How many times will the following iterative loops repeat?

a) FOR X = 1 TO 10 — _________
b) FOR Y = 3 TO 21 STEP 3 — _________
c) FOR Z = 15 to 1 STEP -2 — _________

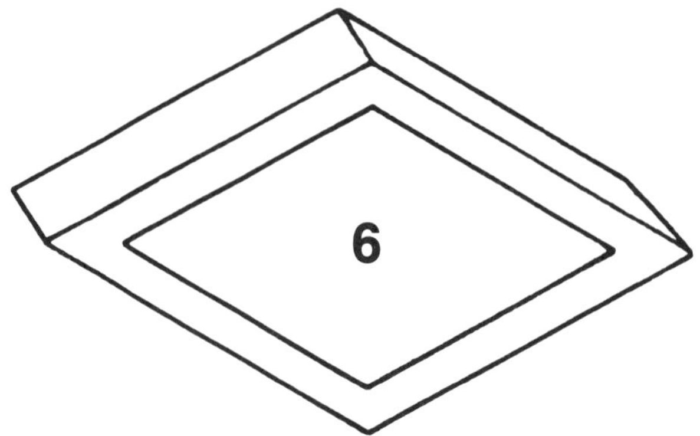

Program Design Language

Now let's take a look at some theory of structured programming. *Structured programming* is a programming technique that follows rules which govern the way a program is structured. For all practical purposes, BASIC is an unstructured language. PDL, on the other hand, is a language in which structured programs can be written. Out strategy will be to learn PDL and then see how it can be used to develop BASIC programs.

AN OVERVIEW OF PDL

Many structured languages share similar *control constructs*—statements that control the execution of other statements. Program Design Language (PDL) or Informal Language (IL) is often used to design programs. A PDL program is easily modified to become any specific structured programming language.

PDL can vary slightly in the manner in which it is written, but it always can be divided into two general syntax categories:

□ An inner syntax describes specific information processes. It allows instructions such as "compute the average" or "process next input." These are phrases found inside a flowchart's operation or read/write symbols.

The programmer can make the inner syntax as general or specific as he wants. A common strategy is to use general commands early in program development and then gradually replace them with more specific commands.

Inner syntax is generally written in lowercase. Another rule that should be observed is the use of the := symbol (read as "is made equal to") to denote assignment. **A := B** has the same meaning as the BASIC statement **LET A = B**. This operator is used to prevent confusion with the statement **A = B**, which is an assertion of the fact that **A** equals **B**.

☐ PDL uses an outer syntax which governs the manner in which the inner syntax is executed. The rules governing the outer syntax are well defined. The instructions allowed by the outer syntax are called *control constructs*. A control construct is a collection of key words, one or more inner syntax commands, and sometimes a qualifier. The inner syntax contained by a control construct is executed zero, one, or many times depending on the control construct and the value of any qualifier present.

Control constructs affect the inner syntax of the program only through the relative positions of the inner and outer syntaxes. For example, an instruction placed between two **FOR** and **NEXT** instructions in a BASIC program will be executed repeatedly in the loop while instructions not located between a **FOR** and **NEXT** will not. This is not the same as a **GOTO** statement which causes a loop: The instructions in the loop created by the **GOTO** statement are controlled by the value of the line number in the **GOTO**, not by their positions relative to the **GOTO** statement.

WHAT IS A PDL PROGRAM?

Before we go on to describe PDL in detail, we will take a look at a PDL program. A program written in PDL is shown in Fig. 6-1. The underlined words are the control constructs. The other phrases comprise the inner syntax of the program. You can now see why I emphasized relative control of outer syntax over inner syntax: there are no line numbers! A statement can only be controlled by a control construct by being in-

```
do
  input X
  while
    X < 10
  do
    print "X isn't ten yet."
    X:= X + 1
  od
  if
    X = 10
  then
    print "X is ten."
  else
    print "X must be greater than ten now."
  fi
od
```

Fig. 6-1. An example of a PDL program.

```
do
   input A
   input B
   C:= A + B
od
```

Fig. 6-2. Using DO.

side it. The indentation of lines helps show what statements are inside a particular control construct.

PDL programs are usually easier to write and modify than flowcharts, and their popularity has grown. Even though BASIC supports few PDL statements, making conversion from PDL to BASIC not an easy task, program development in PDL is often beneficial because a PDL program can easily be converted into a flowchart, which in turn can be converted into a BASIC program. Languages such as Pascal, Modula-2, Ada, and C are designed to encourage—even force—structured programming, making the conversion from PDL to flowchart to code far easier.

THE CONTROL CONSTRUCTS

All control constructs have single entry points and single exit points. The entry point in a PDL program is the first key word of the construct (e.g., DO or IF) and the exit point is the last key word (e.g., OD or FI, respectively). After the exit point of a control construct is reached, control passes to the entry point of the control construct immediately following it.

The DO Statement

The first control construct to be looked at is DO. DO consists of two keywords, DO and OD (DO spelled backwards). It groups together one or more inner syntax commands. The entire group is then considered to be one inner syntax command, which can be used by other control constructs. An example is shown in Fig. 6-2. It shows how three statements—INPUT A, INPUT B, and C:= A + B—are grouped together.

When control is passed to DO, it executes its statements in the order they appear.

```
do
   input A
   input B
   do
      C:= A + B
      D:= A - B
   od
   print D / C
od
```

Fig. 6-3. Nesting DO's.

```
do
   input A
   input B
   C:= A + B
   D:= A - B
   print D / C
od
```

Fig. 6-4. Program without nested DO's.

After the last statement is processed control exits through **OD** and goes to the next statement. Because **DO** is considered to be a single inner syntax statement, it can be combined inside other **DO**s. Figure 6-3 shows an example of this combination.

After the **INPUT** statements are executed, control passes to the inner **DO**. The values of **C** and **D** are computed and control leaves the inner **DO**. Finally, the values of **C** and **D** are written and control leaves the outer **DO**. This program is identical to Fig. 6-4, which does not contain an inner **DO**; the same statements in each are executed in the same order. The purpose of **DO** is not to modify statement execution, buy to group statements together. Figure 6-5 is a version of the gas mileage program using PDL and illustrating **DO** statements.

The IF Statement

The **IF** construct consists of four key words, a qualifier, and two inner syntax statements. The key words are **IF** (the entry point), **THEN**, **ELSE**, and **FI** (the exit point). The qualifier is a Boolean expression. The organization of **IF** is shown in Fig. 6-6. When control enters **IF** the Boolean expression is evaluated. If it is true, the statement between **THEN** and **ELSE** is executed. If it is false, the statement between **ELSE** and **FI** is executed.

An alternate form of **IF** is shown in Fig. 6-7. Here **ELSE** and the second statement are not used. If the qualifier is true, the statement is executed; if it is false, control exits through **FI** with no action taken.

You might think this somewhat limited; however, the **DO** statement lets us replace one or both of the statements in **IF** with a group of statements we want to be executed

```
do
   print "Enter miles traveled"
   input T
   print "Enter gas used"
   input A
   M:= T / A
   print "Your mileage"
   print M
od
```

Fig. 6-5. Gas mileage program in PDL.

```
if
  (boolean expression)
then
  (statement to be executed if true)
else
  (statement to be executed if false)
fi
```

Fig. 6-6. Format of IF construct.

```
if
  (boolean expression)
then
  (statement to be executed if true)
fi
```

Fig. 6-7. Alternative form of IF.

```
if
  X > Y
then
  do
    statement A
    statement B
    statement C
  od
else
  do
    statement D
    statement E
  od
fi
```

Fig. 6-8. Using IF.

if the qualifier is true or false. An example of such an application of the IF and DO constructs is shown in Fig. 6-8. When IF is executed, the statements A, B, and C will be executed if the condition is true, and statements D and E will be executed if the condition is false.

As with DO, IF can be used as an inner syntax statement, making it possible to write the program shown in Fig. 6-9, which reads two numbers and prints the larger. As a final example of the IF construct, refer to Fig. 6-10, which shows the flat tire program from Chapter 3.

```
do
  input A
  input B
  if
    A > B
  then
    print A
  else
    print B
  fi
od
```

Fig. 6-9. Nesting IF under DO.

The WHILE Construct

The **WHILE** construct is probably the most differently structured construct found during the various dialects of BASIC. **WHILE** sets up a loop that is executed while a particular condition remains true. It uses the keyword **WHILE**, a qualifier which is a Boolean expression, and a **DO** construct. The syntax of **WHILE** is shown in Fig. 6-11.

When control is passed to **WHILE**, the Boolean expression is evaluated. If the result is true, the statements inside **DO** are executed. If the result is false, control is passed to the statement after **OD**. On the surface, this might seem like the IF construct. However, if the qualifier is true, it is re-evaluated after **DO** is executed. If the result is again true, **DO** is executed again, and the whole process is repeated. Only when the qualifier becomes false does control pass to the next statement.

Figure 6-12 shows a PDL program for the guessing game we designed in the previous chapter. The computer picks a number and asks the player for a guess. Then,

```
do
  if
    car is being driven
  then
    pull over to side of road
  fi
  remove tire iron, jack, and spare from trunk
  if
    spare is good
  then
    jack up car, replace tire, then lower car
    return equipment to trunk
  else
    flag down help
  fi
do
```

Fig. 6-10. Flat tire program in PDL.

```
while
  (boolean expression)
do
  (statements to be executed)
  •
  •
  •
od
```

Fig. 6-11. Format of WHILE construct.

"while" the player's guess is incorrect, the computer prints a hint and asks for another guess. When the player guesses correctly, the computer prints "RIGHT!" and stops.

If the player's first guess is right, the expression GUESS < > NUMBER becomes false immediately. In this case the statements in WHILE will not be executed at all. On the other hand, if the first guess is incorrect, GUESS< > NUMBER will be true. This causes the program to keep printing hints and asking for guesses until GUESS < >NUMBER is false. Then the WHILE loop will finish. Notice that the WHILE loop is used as an inner syntax statement inside a large DO.

The REPEAT Statement

The REPEAT construct is very similar to WHILE. In fact, I suggest that WHILE be used unless it is really necessary to use REPEAT.

Similarly to WHILE, REPEAT uses the keyword UNTIL, a Boolean expression for a qualifier, and DO. The general format of REPEAT is shown in Fig. 6-13. REPEAT sets up a loop which is executed while a condition is false. That is, the loop is executed *until* the condition becomes true. Also, and this is a very important characteristic, the condition is tested *after* DO is executed. If the condition is false, DO is repeated again until the condition is true.

An example is probably the best way to illustrate the way REPEAT operates; refer

```
do
  N:= random number between 0 and 999
  input G
  while
    G <> N
  do
    print out hint
    input G
  od
  print "You win!"
od
```

Fig. 6-12. Guessing game in PDL using WHILE.

```
do
   (statements to be executed)
   •
   •
   •
until
   (boolean expression)
od
```

Fig. 6-13. Format of REPEAT construct.

to Fig. 6-14, another version of the guessing game. The computer picks a number, then control passes to **REPEAT**, which asks the player for a guess. After it prints a hint, it tests the expression **NUMBER = GUESS**. If this is false, **DO** is re-executed. This process is repeated until the number is equal to the guess. Control then leaves **REPEAT** and the program prints "RIGHT!" and stops.

If this method is used the "give hint" statement is executed even when the player guesses correctly. Knowing this, the programmer should design the program so that when the player guesses correctly, nothing is printed for a hint.

The FOR Loop

FOR is formed like **WHILE** and **REPEAT** loops: the keyword **FOR**, a qualifier (in this case the phrase *index* := *initial* to *final* by *increment*"), and **DO**, as shown in Fig. 6-15. It operates exactly like the **FOR** loop we studied in Chapter 5. The index is set to an initial value, then **DO** is executed and the increment added to the index. This process is repeated until the final value is exceeded.

The testing takes place after **DO** is executed; thus, as with **REPEAT**, **DO** is executed at least once. Figure 6-16 is an example of **FOR** which reads the values of an array.

PDL CONCEPTS

Now we have seen the PDL constructs, we will look at two concepts that are useful when combining them.

```
do
   N:= random number between 0 and 999
   do
      input G
      print hint
   until
      G = N
   od
   print "You win!"
od
```

Fig. 6-14. Guessing game in PDL using REPEAT.

```
for
  (index):= (initial) to (final) by (increment)
do
  (statements to be executed)
  .
  .
  .
od
```

Fig. 6-15. Format of FOR construct.

The first concept is *scope*. Scope is an attribute associated with every control construct. It is the range of instructions controlled by the construct. For example, the scope of DO is the statements placed between DO and OD. Any statements not between DO and OD are said to be outside the scope of the construct. The scope of IF is the instructions between IF and FI; the scope of WHILE is the instructions between WHILE and its associated OD.

The next concept is *nesting*. When a statement is placed within the scope of a construct, it is said to be nested under that construct. The nesting level of a statement is equal to the total number of constructs whose scope it falls into.

An example illustrating scope and nesting is shown in Fig. 6-17. It shows the scope of the different control constructs, as well as the nesting level of each statement. Knowing what scope and nesting are is necessary to determine what outer syntax statement(s) control a particular inner syntax statement.

A PDL PROGRAMMING EXAMPLE

We will examine the various PDL constructs as we solve a programming problem introduced in Chapter 1: how to maintain a telephone directory system. As you may recall, the program had to read telephone numbers, print the telephone number of a particular person or persons, delete names, alphabetize the list of names, and save the

```
do
  dimension A(10)
  for
    I:= 1 to 10
  do
    input A(I)
  od
od
```

Fig. 6-16. Reading data into an array in PDL.

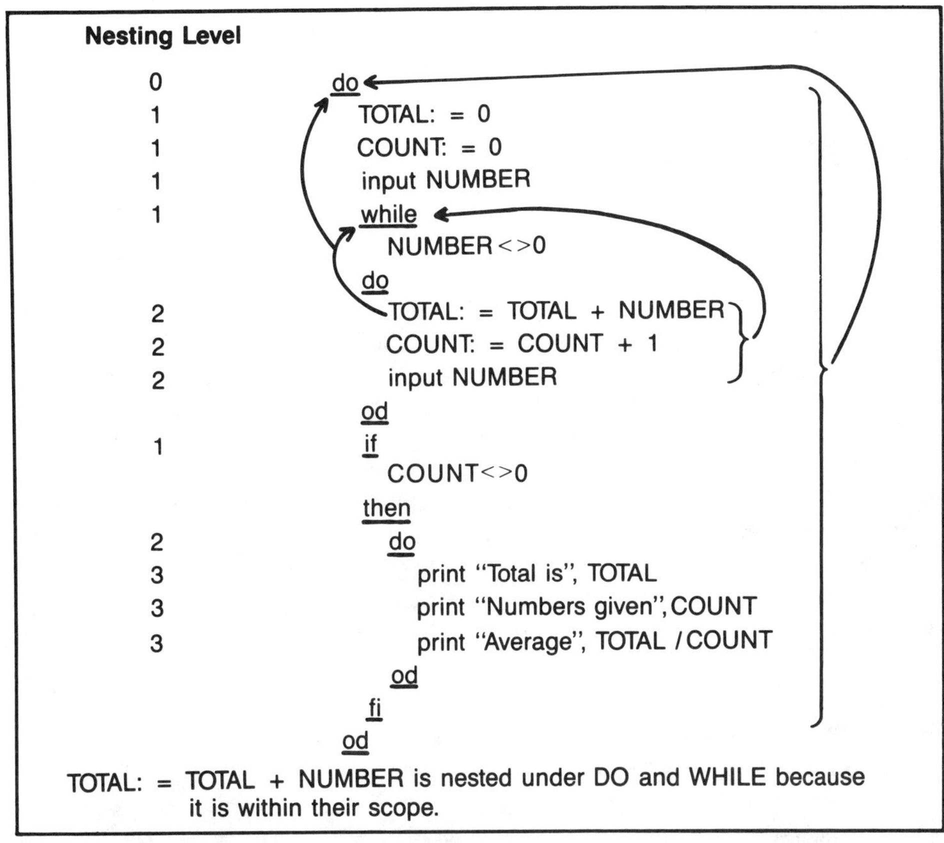

Fig. 6-17. Nesting and scope in a PDL program.

list on disk for later use. Because we are not yet introduced to all the concepts needed to write a program confirming to all these specifications, the requirements will be modified as follows:

- ☐ The program must be able to read a name and the telephone number associated with that name. If the name already exists on the list, the number associated with the name will be changed to a new number and the user will be informed.
- ☐ Removal of a name—a name is read and if it exists on the list, it is deleted. A message stating that the name was deleted or was not on the list shall be printed.
- ☐ A name or names can be looked up; a string of letters is read and all the names that begin with that string and their telephone numbers are printed. The entire list may also be printed.

We won't concern ourselves with solving the different features, but will try to see how the program will choose which function is to be performed, by referring to a command input by the user.

We said in Chapter one that a menu is an appropriate way to let the user know what options are available and how to invoke them. The menu is Fig. 6-18. It indicates

```
1) Add a name
2) Delete a name
3) Print out a name or names
4) Quit
```

Fig. 6-18. Menu for phone directory program.

what functions are available and what command corresponds to each. For example, to add a name to the list, command 1 is entered. Once the program knows what function to perform, it can execute the appropriate instructions. Since a user will usually want to execute more than one function, a loop will be created in which the menu is presented, the user's command read, the command carried out, and the process repeated. To let the user leave this loop an **END** command causes the program to terminate.

You know enough to write your first PDL program; it is shown in Fig. 6-19. It prints a menu, asks for a command, executes the command, and repeats. The process uses the **REPEAT** control construct. Now our task will be to more clearly define what each inner syntax statement does, until we have enough detail to write a BASIC program.

First look at Fig. 6-19 again. By embedding the **REPEAT** loop inside a **DO** construct, we have added an "initialize data" statement. Although it is not apparent now, certain pieces of data (the list of names) will have to be set up at the beginning of the program. This will become clear later on.

Successive Refinement

We will now employ *successive refinement* to develop our PDL program gradually to one which makes conversion to a BASIC program relatively easy. In this process we select an inner syntax statement and write another PDL program which does the same thing. The new PDL program can be reinserted into the original PDL program where the inner syntax line used to be. This process is considered a *single refinement* of the PDL program. Technically, a single step of refinement is when most or all inner syntax statements are changed so their levels of abstractness remain the same. This prevents a program from becoming very detailed in some areas and very abstract in

```
do
  initialize data
  do
    print out menu
    input command
    execute command
  until
    quit command is given
  od
od
```

Fig. 6-19. PDL version of the phone directory program.

others. When this process is repeated, each successive refinement of the program will naturally contain more detail.

When we developed a program from flowcharts, we made a transition between a conceptual piece of data to data which was structured by the way it is stored by the computer. For example, when developing the gas mileage program, an algorithm was developed using "miles traveled" that was later changed to use a numerical variable T. Since PDL programs are refined gradually, this change becomes difficult to implement. A programmer often determines what data will be needed and how the programmer often determines what data will be needed and how the program will manipulate it at the very start of the PDL design process. In the telephone directory program, a numerical variable C will be used to store the user's command. C will contain the appropriate menu number of the process the user wishes to perform.

Sometimes, to save space, the DO constructs immediately inside an IF statement are dropped. An example is shown in Fig. 6-20. Because the statements are clearly indented, it is easy to know where each statement "belongs." If indentation is not done carefully, a situation like that shown in Fig. 6-21 can occur, in which it is difficult to decide under what control constructs an inner syntax statement is nested.

Strings

The only form of data we have been able to manipulate is numbers. Most versions of BASIC can handle another type of data as well, these are called *strings.* A string is a sequence of letters, digits, and other characters. We can represent a string constant by enclosing the constant in quotation marks, such as "cow", "flight 109", and "This is an example of a string containing quite a few letters". The quotation marks are necessary because blanks are perfectly valid in a string.

The quotation marks are called *delimiters*; delimiters show the ends of a string. Because they are used as delimiters, quotation marks cannot be used inside a string, as in "Mary said, "Look at this.""

(A)
```
if
  X < Y
then
  do
     T:= X
     X:= Y
     Y:= T
  od
else
  do
     X:= Y
     Y:= Y - 1
  od
fi
```

(B)
```
if
  X < Y
then
  T:= X
  X:= Y
  Y:= T
else
  X:= Y
  Y:= Y - 1
fi
```

Fig. 6-20. Removing DOs inside an IF construct: (A) With DOs (B) Without DOs.

```
Ⓐ  if
      X < Y
   then
   if
      Y < Z
   then
      Z:= X
   fi
   else
      Z:= Y    --->  Is statement executed if Y < Z is false or X < Y is false?
   fi

----------

Ⓑ  if
      X < Y
   then
      if
         Y < Z
      then
         Z:= X
      fi
   else
      Z:= Y
   fi
```

Fig. 6-21. (A and B) Ambiguity caused by poor indentation.

Just as numerical values can be stored in variables, so can strings. A string variable is denoted by a dollar sign following the variable name (**C$ or Z1$**). A statement such as:

LET A$ = "orange"

would assign the string "**orange**" to the variable **A$**. If we printed **A$**, the word *orange* (without quotation marks) would appear on the screen.

We can also use the **INPUT** statement to request a string from a program user. A variety of functions are supported by BASIC to manipulate strings. One, that we will use shortly, is **LEFT$**. Unlike the other functions we have seen so far, **LEFT$** requires two arguments; a string or string variable, and a number. The function returns the left most characters of the string specified by the number. For example, the statement:

B$ = LEFT$ ("HOTDOG", 3)

would store the string "HOT" in variable B.

Be careful; the number specified cannot be greater than the number of digits in the string. If we use a constant, as above, this is not a problem. However, if we have a variable **M$**, and did not know how many characters it contains, we could check its length first. A function that accomplishes this is **LEN**. **LEN** uses a single parameter, a string, and returns the number of characters (including spaces) in that string. Thus:

L = LEN ("HOTDOG")

stores the number 6 in L. We could have written:

```
H$ = "HOTDOG"
L = LEN(H$)
```

to accomplish the same thing.

An Abstract View of Lists

It is important to ascertain how data will be stored and retrieved before program development takes place, but sometimes it is impractical to do so. Consider the list of names and phone numbers our program is going to manipulate; it would be silly to waste time determining how the list will be implemented. Instead, an *abstract data type* (ADT) is used. In this case, the ADT would be a list. Operations which can be performed on the ADT should be defined. These are operations that let data be stored in and retrieved from the ADT. It doesn't yet matter how the ADT is stored or how the ADT functions operate. We can develop the program without this information.

The best way to understand this is to look at an example. First we will develop a list ADT. A list can be thought of as a sequence of similar items. An analogy to the real world one might make is that of a box of index cards; although each card contains different information, the type of information is the same: it would not make sense to file recipes with financial records. The following terms will be used to define a list:

□ Field—this is an entry in a record, containing a single piece of information. A field might be used to contain a numeric value, such as the balance of a bank account, or a string value, such as a name or address.

Every field has a meaning or type associated with it. Although a type restricts the type of data that can be stored in the field, its purpose is to restrict how that information is interpreted. For example, if we had a field of type "age," we could not store the letter "a" in the field because we would use a numeric variable, which doesn't allow letters to be stored in it. But the real purpose would be to restrict how we interpret the stored numeric value; it is not a weight, I.Q., etc.; it is an age.

Fields usually contain data which can be stored in a single variable. You must decide prior to program development how to store a field. Sometimes fields are themselves an ADT. In this case, the ADT must be defined containing simple fields, or be defined as yet another ADT containing simple fields, and so on.

□ Record—This is analogous to the index card in the shoebox file. Each record in the list must contain the same kind of fields, in the same order. The information is accessed by finding the correct record, and reading the information contained in the correct field or fields. If records were formatted differently it would be extremely difficult to find information quickly, if at all. Fortunately, the need for a list containing records of different types is very rare and should not be considered here.

□ List—a list is a series of records strung together. The order of the records is important. Each records has one record following it (except the last) and a record preceding it (except the first). We can represent a list as R1, R2, R3, R4. This is a list containing four records; R1 is the first record; R4 is the last record. Note that R1, R2, R3, R4 is not the same as R1, R3, R2, R4.

To create a list of names and numbers, we will make the following definitions:

☐ **Fields:** We will define three field types: FIRST_NAME, LAST_NAME, and PHONE_NUMBER. Since FIRST_NAME and LAST_NAME will store text information, they are defined as strings. PHONE_NUMBER can be defined as a numeric variable.

☐ **Record:** A single record in the list will contain the field FIRST_NAME, the field LAST_NAME, and the third field, PHONE_NUMBER. We will call such a record NAME_NUMBER_ENTRY.

☐ **List:** The list of names and phone numbers will be defined as a list of NAME_NUMBER_ENTRYs. We will call a list of this type NAME_NUMBER_LIST.

List Manipulation

To use an ADT, ADT functions must be defined to operate on the ADT. To facilitate in processing the list ADT, the idea of *currency* is used. Currency refers to the last or most current piece of data refered to in the list. It is a marker in the shoebox of index cards which reminds us which card was looked at last. Currency can be modified in one of two ways:

☐ It can be reset to the beginning of the list. When this is done, the proverbial slate is wiped clean. The current record is the first record in the list.

☐ It can be incremented to the next record in the list. This enables the list to be scanned, record by record. Once the end of the list is reached, the current record remains on the last record until a reset operation is performed.

By restricting ourselves to the two operations above, a *sequential mode of operation* is established. The list is read through until the end is reached, at which time access must start back at the beginning. To access a record located before the current record, the current record must be reset to the beginning of the list and the list scanned to the desired record. Though this might seem restrictive, all necessary list functions can be performed using this type of access. The four functions required are:

☐ Lookup—This is an attempt to find a piece of data in the list. A particular field or fields are selected, and the list is scanned until a record with fields meeting some requirement is found.

Two types of look up can be done. We can specify that we want to look for the first record, in which case the current record is reset to the first record and the list is scanned until an acceptable record is found or the end of the list is reached. If there is more than one occurrence of an acceptable record in the list, the search can be made without first resetting the current record. For example, if our list contained more than one record with the last name "Smith," and we want to find all those records, we would find the first by resetting the current record and searching. The remaining records will be found in succession by searching without resetting the current record.

☐ Insertion—An additional record is added to the list. Although it is possible that some fields will be identical to others, no record should be identical to any other record in the list. The record to be inserted is set up in a temporary memory area. When it is time to insert the record, the current record is moved to a record either immediately before or after the place the new record will be inserted. Two insertion methods are needed so that records can be inserted before the first record (where it is impossible to move the current record ahead of the place of insertion) and after the last record (where it is impossible to move the current record past the place of insertion).

☐ Deletion—A record is removed from the list. A look up operation sets the current record to the record targeted for deletion. The record is then deleted.

☐ Modification—The data in one or more fields is changed in an existing record. A look-up operation sets the current record to the record containing the fields we wish to modify. The new information is then placed into the record. This operation can be thought of as two operations (deletion and insertion) combined into one.

Figures 6-22 through 6-26 show how a list (represented by the shoebox analogy) is affected when various operations are performed.

Global Data

Global data is an important concept in program design. The word *global* implies that a particular piece of data remains valid from the time it is initialized throughout the program. At no point after initialization will it contain an invalid piece of data. For example, a text editing program might use a variable to store the name of the file con-

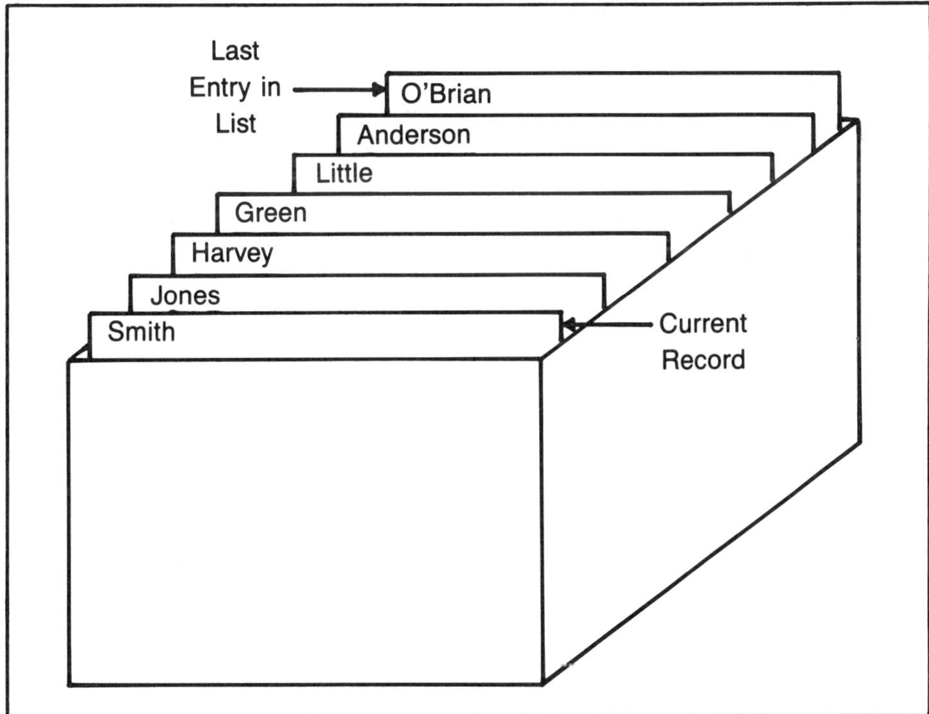

Fig. 6-22. Representation of an initialized list structure, with the first entry as the current record.

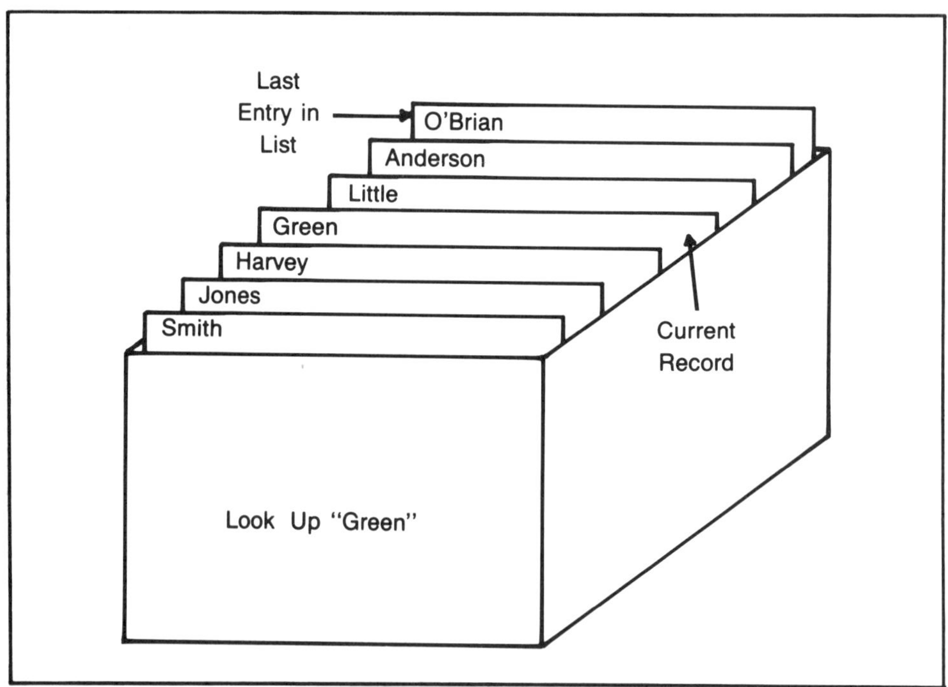

Fig. 6-23. The list after a lookup operation.

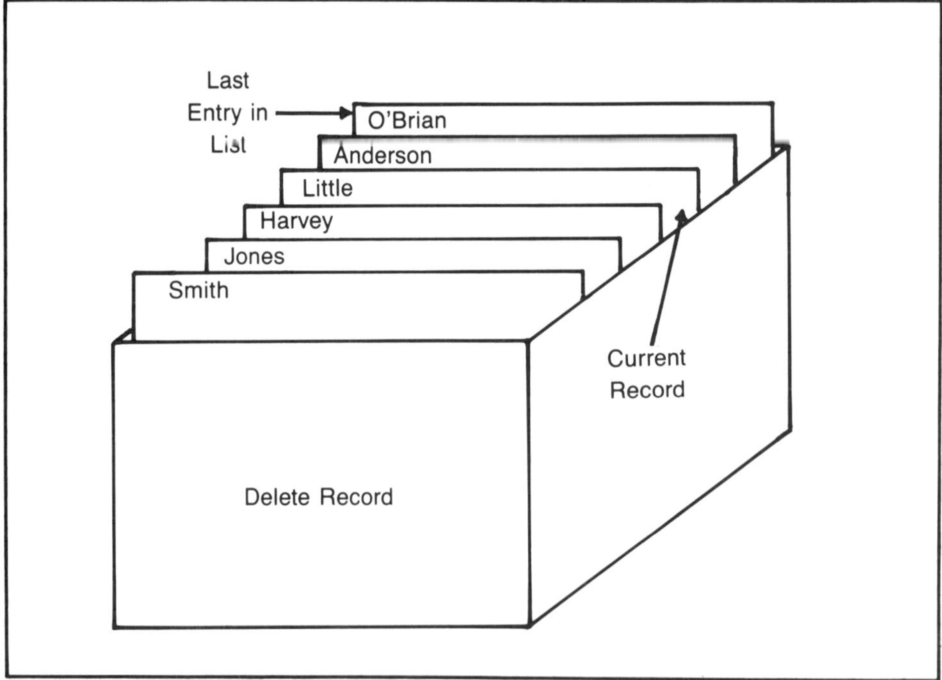

Fig. 6-24. Effect of a deletion on the list structure.

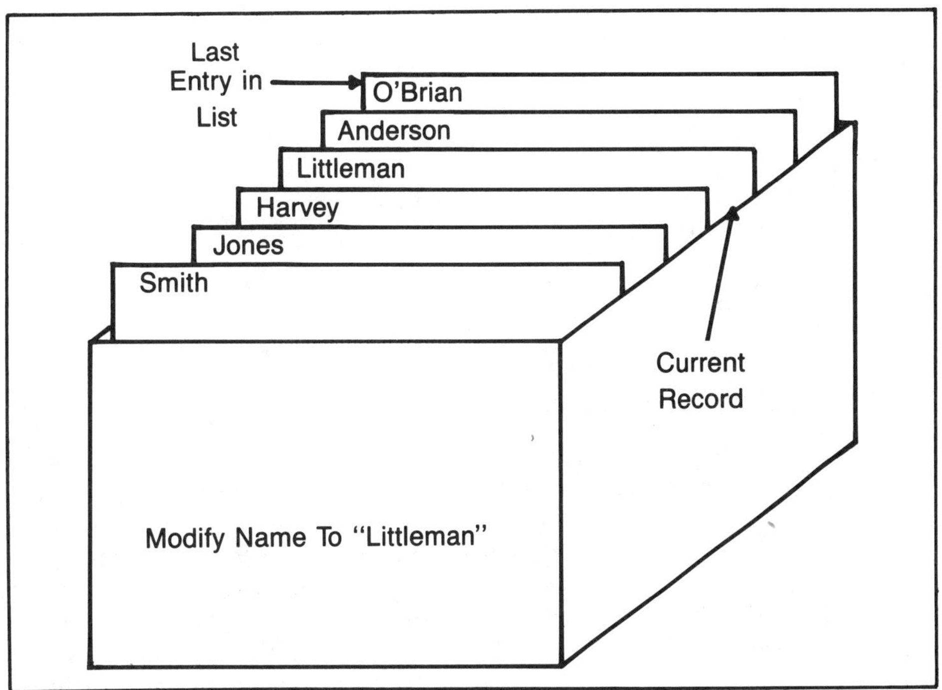

Fig. 6-25. A modification operation on the list.

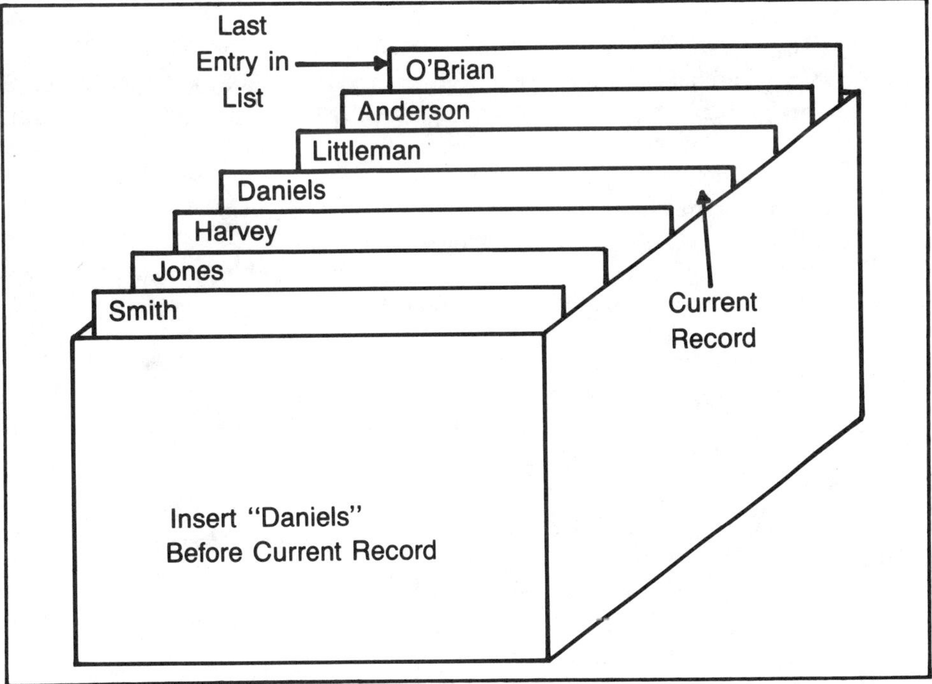

Fig. 6-26. Insertion of an item into the list.

```
10 PRINT "Enter Age"
20 INPUT N
30 PRINT "Age is ", N
40 PRINT "Enter Height"
50 INPUT N
60 PRINT "Height is ", N
70 PRINT "Enter Weight"
80 INPUT N
90 PRINT "Weight is ", N
100 END
```

Fig. 6-27. Using non-global data.

taining the text being edited. This variable is initialized when the program asks the user for it; afterwards, the variable will always contain the filename. Later, if the program replaces the text in the file, the appropriate filename still exists in the variable. The program can store the text without having to ask the user for the filename again.

In our telephone directory program, we need to store names so they can easily be accessed by many different parts of the program (since different parts of the program all modify or read the list in some way). We must define a *data structure,* data that conforms to a particular ADT, which will contain the list from the time it is initialized until the program ends. Then any part of the program can use the list by referencing the data structure. Another piece of global data our program will use is the user's command.

Not all data in a program is global. A typical example of non-global data is using one variable to do similar functions. One might use the variable N every time a number is read in. Figure 6-27 is a program containing several INPUT statements; the first time something is read, N contains a person's age; the second time, N contains their height; the third time, it contains their weight. N does not contain the same piece of data everywhere in the program—its contents depend on what part of the program is executing at the time. N is therefore non-global.

If we modify the program, as shown in Fig. 6-28, we would then make use of global data. After the first read statement, A contains an age—from that time on we can

```
10 PRINT "Enter Age"
20 INPUT A
30 PRINT "Enter Height"
40 INPUT H
50 PRINT "Enter Weight"
60 INPUT W
70 PRINT "Age is ", A
80 PRINT "Height is ", H
90 PRINT "Weight is ", W
100 END
```

Fig. 6-28. Using global data.

```
clear L
clear C
initialize any other data
```

Fig. 6-29. Refining Initialize Data statement.

use variable **A** knowing that **A** contains the age; and likewise with variables **H** and **W**.

Just because we say a particular variable will contain a global piece of data does not mean we cannot change its value. Nothing prevents us from switching the contents of **A** in the program above to the time of day, for example. We must be careful to abide by the self-imposed rules we create.

The First Level of Refinement

Before refining our program, we must define two pieces of global data. **L** will be the list of names and phone numbers and have the ADT type **NAME__NUMBER__LIST**. **C** will contain the last command issued by the user and be a numerical variable.

We can now go through our PDL program and expand the inner syntax statements. The first statement, "initialize data," will be replaced with statements which clear out **L** and **C**. The code appears in Fig. 6-29. Although we can do it "by the book" by enclosing the instructions with **DO**, common sense tells us this is not necessary. Check this by inserting the new code into the original PDL program and seeing that removing the **DO** does not affect how the inner syntax is executed.

The second statement to be replaced is the "read in command" instruction. The original statement can be replaced with "read in C."

```
if
  C = 1
then
  add a name
fi
if
  C = 2
then
  delete a name
fi
if
  C = 3
then
  print out a name or names
fi
if
  C = 4
then
  print "Bye."
fi
```

Fig. 6-30. Refining Execute Command statement.

Finally, "execute the command" could be replaced by "execute **C**," but this is a cheap solution. A better code is shown in Fig. 6-30. It shows how the value of the command is tested and the appropriate code is executed to carry out the command. Again we see why it is important to assume that **C** is not changed to something other than the last command entered by the user. If we modify **C** in the "insert name" portion of code, we might inadvertently cause one of the other sections to be executed as well.

The complete PDL program after this first pass of refinement is shown in Fig. 6-31. We have replaced all the original inner syntax statements with expansions. Another important change, to the outer syntax of the program, was made as well: the expression in the **REPEAT** loop was changed to make use of variable **C**. We have included the global variables next to the PDL program to remind us of their presence.

```
do
  clear L
  clear C
  initialize any other data
  do
    print out menu
    input C
    if
      C = 1
    then
      add a name
    fi
    if
      C = 2
    then
      delete a name
    fi
    if
      C = 3
    then
      print out a name or names
    fi
    if
      C = 4
    then
      print "Bye."
    fi
  until
    C = 4
  od
od
```

Fig. 6-31. First refinement of phone directory program.

```
do
  input name and phone number
  reset current of record
  lookup name in L
  if
    name is found
  then
    modify phone number
    print "Name already on list, number changed"
  else
    go to end of L
    insert new information
    print "New name entered"
  fi
od
```

Fig. 6-32. Refining Add Another Name statement.

The Second Refinement

As we refine our program again, we still will not concern ourselves with how the list of names will be implemented, but we will begin to incorporate different operations to manipulate the list.

First we will expand "read in C." As you may recall from Chapter 1, the idea is to print a menu containing all the options available to the user so the user may type in a number corresponding to the desired command. We therefore replace the statement with two statements: "display menu" and "read in **C**."

The first IF statement is responsible for adding another name and number. We must expand the statement "add another name to **L**." To add another name, we must first read in the new information (the name and the telephone number) and then insert it into the list. However, our program is supposed to check to see if the name is already in the list. Therefore, a look up procedure must first be performed. If the name is present, the phone number will be modified and a message given to the user. Otherwise, the name and number will be inserted. The code to do this is shown in Fig. 6-32.

Next we refine the statements to delete a name, to print a name or names, and to quit, much in the same way we refined the procedure to add a name. The conditions in the IF's are modified appropriately, and we expand the statements as shown in Fig. 6-33.

The complete program after the second pass of refinement is shown in Fig. 6-34.

Implementing a List

There are many different ways the list of names and numbers ADT can be stored. The following method is probably the most understandable.

The strategy is to use an array to store the contents of a particular field. To store the list of names and numbers, three arrays are needed: one for **LAST_NAME**, and

```
   do
(A)  input name
     reset current of record
     lookup name in L
     if
       name is found
     then
       delete entry
       print "Name deleted"
     else
       print "Name not found"
     fi
   od
(B)do
     input string
     reset current of record
     do
       lookup entry whose last name begins with
       string
       if
         entry is found
       then
         print name and number
       else
         print "End of list reached."
       fi
     until
       end of list reached
     od
   od
```

Fig. 6-33. Refining other statements: (A) Delete name (B) Print name(s).

one for FIRST_NAME, and one for PHONE_NUMBER. We can choose N1$, N2$, and P to store them, respectively. A record is stored by setting the same element in each array to the appropriate field. For example, one record each would be stored in N1$ (1), N2$(1), and P(1). The names will be arranged so that if there are N number of names, they will be stored in elements 1-N of the arrays.

We also have to define a *null entry*—an entry that contains nothing. A null entry is stored by setting the first and last names to "" and the phone number to 0. Finally, the maximum number of names in the list must be determined; once the arrays are dimensioned it is impossible to store more names in the list once it is filled. For our program, we will pick 100. We will often want to refer to this number; it is a good idea to store the value in a global variable and to refer to that variable throughout the course of the program. Should it become necessary to store more names, the only change

```
do
  clear L
  clear C
  initialize any other data
  do
    print out menu
    input C
    if
      C = 1
    then
      input name and phone number
      reset current of record
      lookup name in L
      if
        name is found
      then
        modify phone number
        print "Name already on list, number changed"
      else
        go to end of L
        insert new information
        print "New name entered"
      fi
    fi
    if
      C = 2
    then
      input name
      reset current of record
      lookup name in L
      if
        name is found
      then
        delete entry
        print "Name deleted"
      else
        print "Name not found"
      fi
    fi
    if
      C = 3
    then
      input string
      reset current of record
      do
        lookup entry whose last name begins with string
        if
          entry is found
        then
          print name and number
        else
          print "End of list reached."
        fi
      until
        end of list reached
      od
    fi
    if
      C = 4
    then
      print "Bye."
    fi
  until
    C = 4
  od
od
```

Fig. 6-34. Second refinement of phone directory program.

```
do
  input N1$, N2$, P
  R:= 1
  while
    N1$(R) <> N1$ and N2$(R) <> N2$ and R < N
  do
    R:= R + 1
  od
  if
    N1$(R) = N1$ and N2$(R) = N2$
  then
    P(R):= P
    print "Name already on list, number changed"
  else
    N:= N + 1
    R:= N
    N1$(R):= N1$
    N2$(R):= N2$
    P(R):= P
    print "New name entered"
  fi
od
```

Fig. 6-35. Third refinement of the add-name function.

```
do
  input N1$, N2$
  R:= 1
  while
    N1$(R) <> N1$ and N2$(R) <> N2$ and R < N
  do
    R:= R + 1
  od
  if
    N1$(R) = N1$ and N2$(R) = N2$
  then
    N1$(R):= N1$(N)
    N2$(R):= N1$(N)
    P(R):= P(N)
    N:= N - 1
    print "Name deleted"
  else
    print "Name not found"
  fi
od
```

Fig. 6-36. Third refinement of the delete-name function.

```
do
  input S$
  R:= 1
  do
    while
       LEFT$( N1$(R),LEN(S$) ) <> S$ and R < N
    do
       R:= R + 1
    od
    if
       LEFT$( N1$(R),LEN(S$) ) = S$
    then
       print N1$(R), N2$(R), P(R)
    else
       print "End of list reached."
    fi
  until
    R = N
  od
od
```

Fig. 6-37. Third refinement of the print-name function.

needed to the program is to initialize the global variable to a higher value.

Finally, we must define a numerical variable **R** as our current record, where **R** contains a particular element number. If the first element in the list is the current record, **R** = **1**, etc. If the list is empty **R** will contain 0.

Creating the two elementary functions which operate on the current record becomes trivial, now. To reset the current record to the beginning, **R** is reset to 1 or 0 if the list is empty. To go to the next element, **R** is incremented by 1 if doing so doesn't pass the last element in the list.

The Third Refinement

In the final refinement, all references to the list L and the list operations must be modified to reflect how the list is implemented. Figures 6-35 through 6-38 shows refinement of the procedures to add, delete, and print information in the list to make use of the list's implementation. The following describes how the list operations were performed:

☐ Lookup name in list—Each entry in the list was scanned until a match was found or the last entry reached. When the loop finishes, the current record will point to either a record with the name in it or the last record in the list.

☐ The condition "name is found"—To test whether the name was found, the program simply looks at the record pointed to by the current record.

☐ Insert new information—To add another record, the pointer to the end of the

```
do
  dim N1$(100), N2$(100), P(100)
  N:= 0
  R:= 0
  for
    I:= 1 to 100
  do
    N1$(I):= ''
    N2$(I):= ''
    P(I):= 0
  od
od
```

Fig. 6-38. Third refinement of the clear-L function.

```
do
  dim N1$(100), N2$(100), P(100)
  N:= 0
  R:= 0
  for
    I:= 1 to 100
  do
    N1$(I):= ''
    N2$(I):= ''
    P(I):= 0
  od
  C:= 0
  do
    print out menu
    input C
    if
      C = 1
    then
      input N1$, N2$, P
      R:= 1
      while
        N1$(R) <> N1$ and N2$(R) <> N2$ and R < N
      do
        R:= R + 1
      od
      if
        N1$(R) = N1$ and N2$(R) = N2$
      then
        P(R):= P
        print "Name already on list, number changed"
      else
        N:= N + 1
        R:= N
        N1$(R):= N1$
        N2$(R):= N2$
        P(R):= P
        print "New name entered"
      fi
    fi
    if
      C = 2
    then
      input N1$, N2$
      R:= 1
      while
        N1$(R) <> N1$ and N2$(R) <> N2$ and R < N
      do
        R:= R + 1
      od
      if
        N1$(R) = N1$ and N2$(R) = N2$
      then
        N1$(R):= N1$(N)
        N2$(R):= N1$(N)
        P(R):= P(N)
        N:= N - 1
        print "Name deleted"
      else
        print "Name not found"
      fi
    fi
    if
      C = 3
    then
      input S$
      R:= 1
      do
        while
          LEFT$( N1$(R),LEN(S$) ) <> S$ and R < N
        do
          R:= R + 1
        od
        if
          LEFT$( N1$(R),LEN(S$) ) = S$
        then
          print N1$(R), N2$(R), P(R)
        else
          print "End of list reached."
        fi
      until
        R = N
      od
    fi
    if
      C = 4
    then
      print "Bye."
    fi
  until
    C = 4
  od
od
```

Fig. 6-39. Third refinement of phone directory program.

list is incremented. The data for the new record is then inserted at this new location. For simplicity, no check was performed to make sure N does not exceed the size of the array.

☐ Deletion of a record—A record might be deleted by simply setting all the fields to null values. However, this would leave a hole in the middle of the list, a waste of space. To compact the data, the last record in the list can be copied into this empty location. Then the pointer to the end of the list is decremented back over the old location of the record.

This last refinement produces a PDL program shown in Fig. 6-39, in which the inner syntax statements all represent operations which can be performed in BASIC. It can be likened to the micro-flowcharts developed in the previous chapter. Now we need to convert the outer syntax into operations which can also be performed in BASIC. That is the topic of the next chapter.

SUMMARY

PDL was introduced and used as a way to develop a program. PDL is divided into an inner syntax which describes opertions such as input, output, data manipulation; and an outer syntax which controls how the inner syntax is executed.

There are five main *control constructs* used in PDL: **DO**, **IF**, **WHILE**, **REPEAT**, and **FOR**. These control constructs can in turn be used as an inner syntax statement of another control construct. Control constructs all have *scope*—the range of inner syntax statements that it controls. All inner syntax statements are considered *nested* under a control construct when it is within the scope of the control construct.

Successive refinement is the development of a PDL program. Inner syntax statements are replaced by larger pieces of PDL code which better describe the function of the original statement. Usually, the type of data that will be used is decided upon early in the development process.

A *list* is a sequence of similar items called records. A set of list operations can be used on a list to access and change the data it contains. Each list has an associated *current record* which points to the last record referenced.

Global data is data maintained throughout the program.

EXERCISES

1. The **LEFT$** function does not work with a string length of 0. That is, the expression **LEFT$(" ",0)** will usually cause an error. Therefore, modify the PDL programs so that by entering " " as a name, the entire list will be printed out. Start with the first refinement and then the second and third refinements.

2. Change the program so there can be more than one record with the same name, but different numbers. Modify the delete routine so that when a name is removed, all entries are deleted, Or, allow the user to select which entries will be deleted.

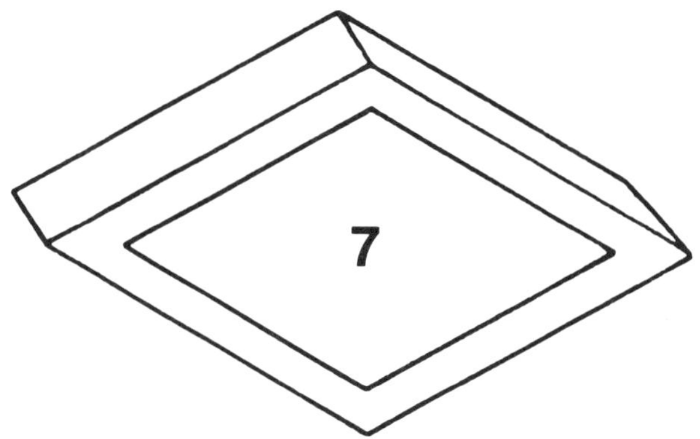

Flowcharts and PDL

While PDL permits program development in a fairly straightforward manner, it is still useful to have a flowchart as a guide for coding BASIC programs. The program we will use as an example in the following discussion is shown in Fig. 7-1. It uses some control constructs and has several levels of nesting.

SYMBOLIC REPRESENTATION OF PDL PROGRAMS

Our first attempt to convert from PDL to a flowchart will be to represent a PDL program symbolically. We will represent control constructs by rectangles with a description of the control construct at the top. Smaller interior rectangles represent the inner syntax nested inside the construct. Figure 7-2 shows an example of the symbol that represents the **WHILE**, **REPEAT**, and **FOR** constructs. The **IF** construct is represented in Fig. 7-3. The **DO** construct can be represented as shown in Fig. 7-4. In no symbol have provisions been made for flow lines, because none are needed.

Control enters through the top of each rectangle and passes through the bottom to the next rectangle. In the **DO** symbol, each sub-rectangle is executed in the order in which it appears. By nesting the symbols the way the constructs they represent are nested, you can represent a PDL program. Figure 7-1 would be arranged as shown in Fig. 7-5.

A Closer Look at Symbolic Representation

Flowcharts are composed of discrete or separate symbols connected by flow lines;

```
do
  TOTAL:= 0
  COUNT:= 0
  input NUMBER
  while
    NUMBER <> 0
  do
    TOTAL:= TOTAL + NUMBER
    COUNT:= COUNT + 1
    input NUMBER
  od
  if
    COUNT <> 0
  then
    do
      print "Total is", TOTAL
      print "Numbers given", COUNT
      print "Average", TOTAL / COUNT
    od
  fi
od
```

Fig. 7-1. PDL program to convert.

our task now is to create a symbolic representation of PDL which allows the outer and inner syntaxes to be placed in different symbols. Perhaps the easiest construct to modify is DO. An example is shown in Fig. 7-6. The outer, claw-like symbol, represents the outer syntax. The inner operation symbols denote inner syntax statements.

The DO symbol operates by passing control to each operation symbol in order of appearance. When control leaves the last operation symbol, control is passed to the

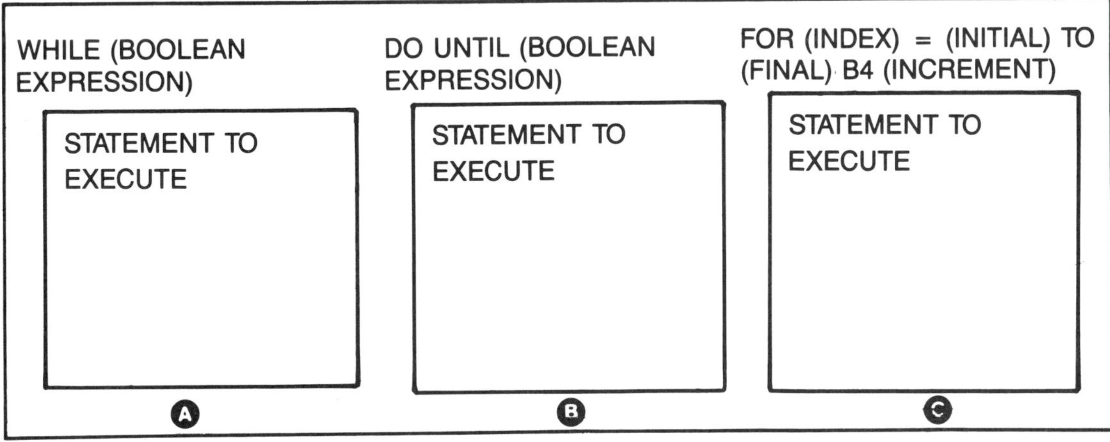

Fig. 7-2. Symbolic representations of: (A) WHILE (B) REPEAT (C) FOR.

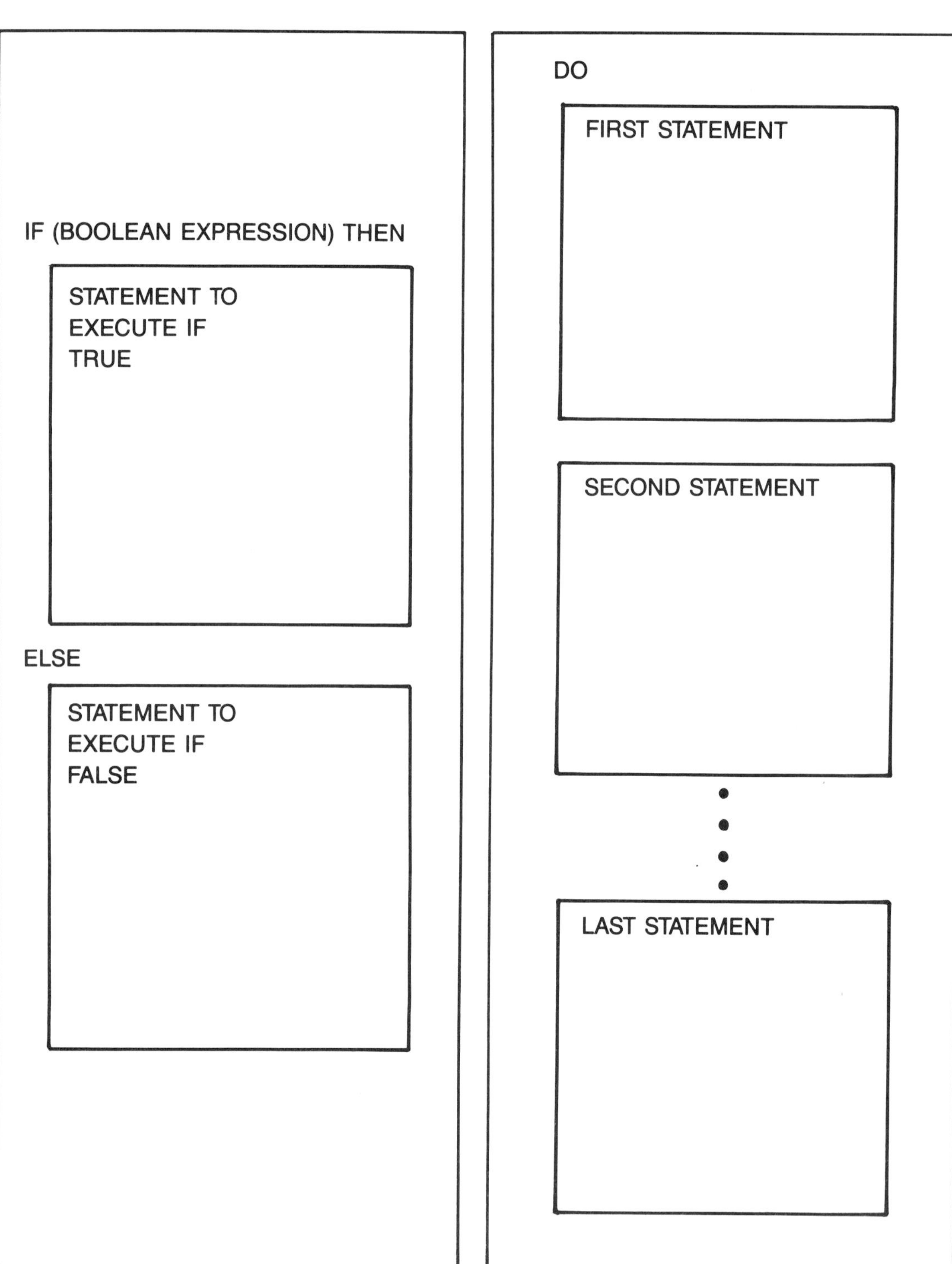

Fig. 7-3. Symbolic representation of IF.

Fig. 7-4. Symbolic representation of DO.

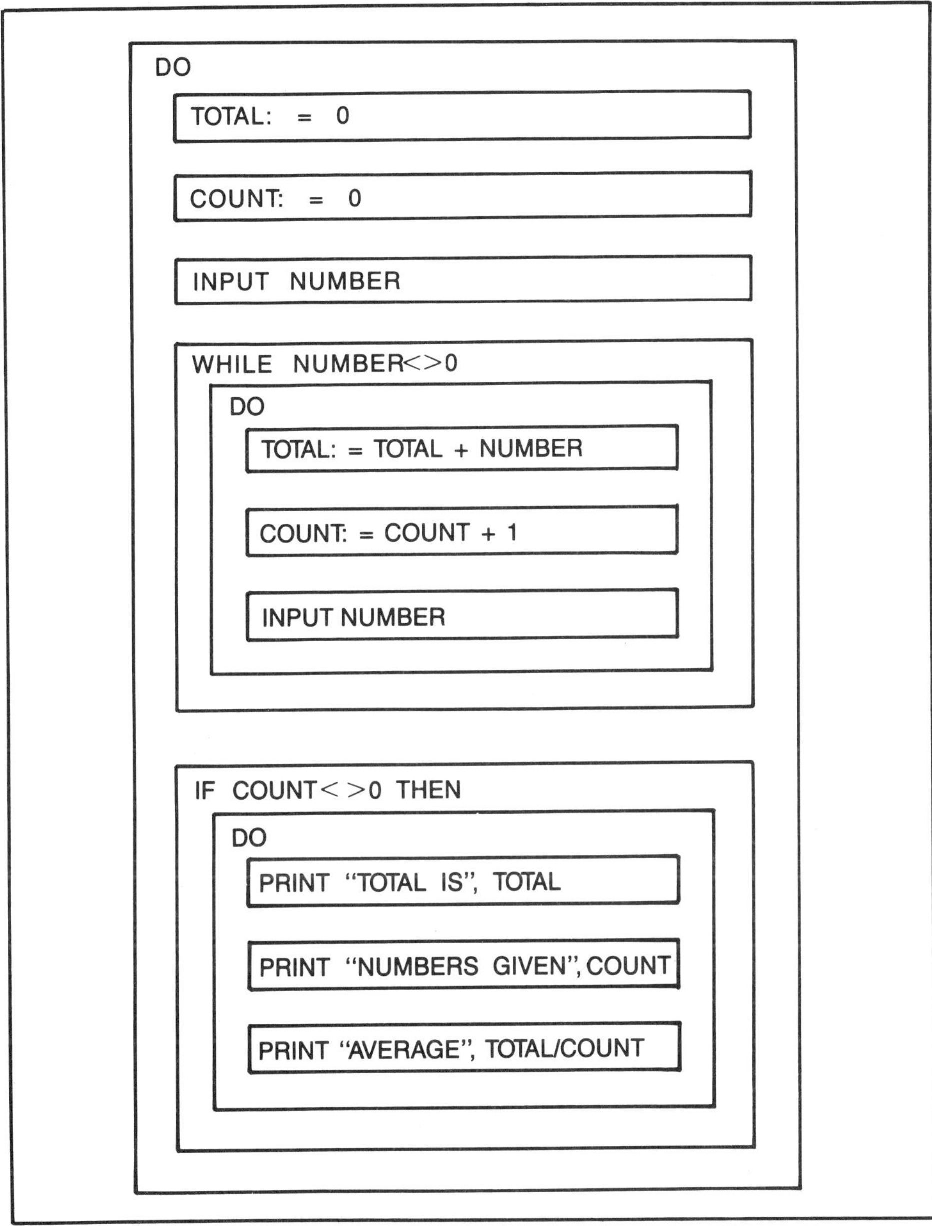

Fig. 7-5. An example using symbolic representation.

next symbol. Notice how the symbol wraps around the inner syntax symbols; it is able to control the inner syntax not only before, but after the inner syntax has executed. This is important later.

The second construct to look at is **WHILE**. Figure 7-7 shows how both flow lines of the inner syntax symbol are connected to the **WHILE** symbol. Because of this the **WHILE** symbol regains control every time the inner syntax statement finishes.

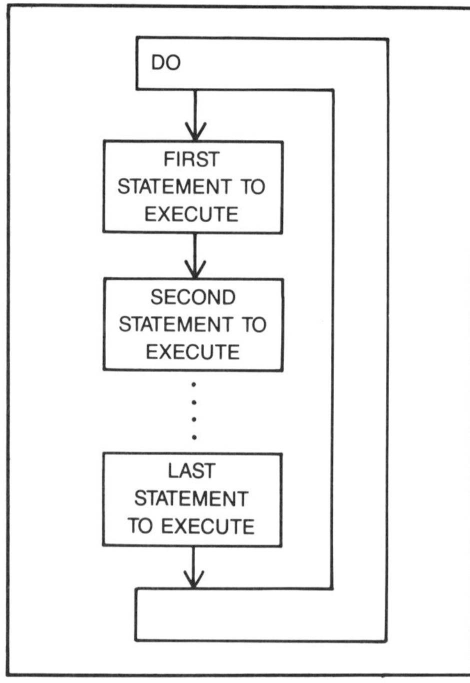

Fig. 7-6. Better symbolic representation of DO.

The **WHILE** symbol operates by sending control to the inner syntax symbol while a specified condition is true. When the condition becomes false, control is passed out the bottom of the **WHILE** symbol and on to the next. The **WHILE** symbol is *not* appropriate for a flowchart because it has two entry points. Entering through the top does not have the same effect as entering through the bottom. This will become evident when it is time to convert to standard flowchart symbols.

The **REPEAT** and **FOR** control constructs are represented in an identical manner, with the description of the construct in the claw symbol and the statements to be executed in the inner symbol.

The **IF** construct is similar to **WHILE**, except that it can control two different statements: one if the condition is true, and another if it is false. This leads to the crea-

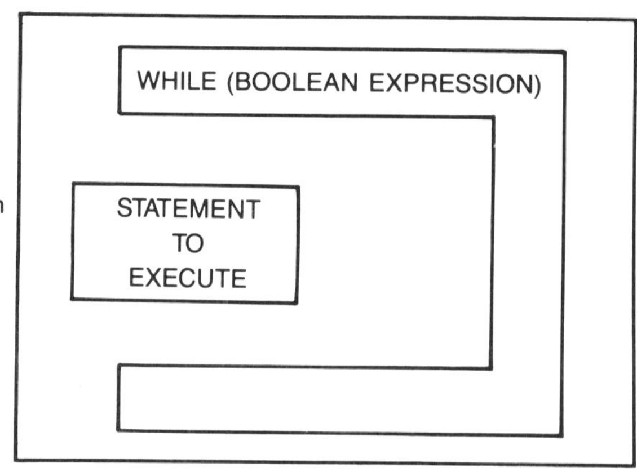

Fig. 7-7. Better symbolic representation of WHILE.

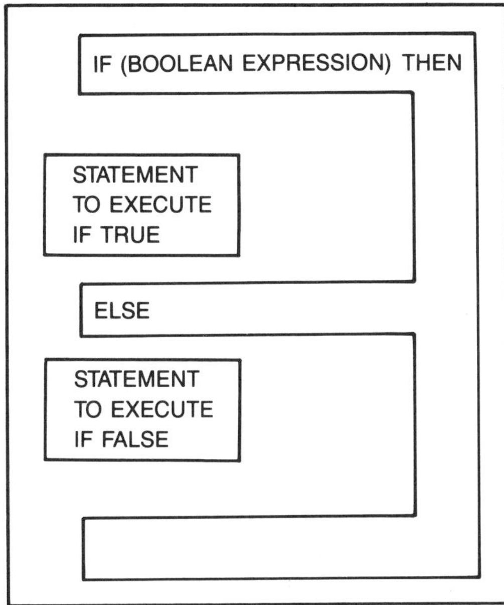

Fig. 7-8. Better symbolic representation of IF.

tion of the symbol pictured in Fig. 7-8. The top block is executed if the condition is true: otherwise the bottom block is executed.

These new symbols can be used to represent the PDL program shown earlier. The new diagram is shown in Fig. 7-9.

Representing PDL Control Structures

Now, we can create a method using legal flowchart symbols to represent our program. We will analyze the different control construct symbols developed in the previous section and emulate them with standard flowchart symbols.

The DO Construct. Because DO only serves to group together a set of symbols which share the same nesting, no symbols are needed which modify the flow of control. Therefore, the operation symbols can be just linked together as shown in Fig. 7-10. A merge symbol has to be added at the top as a reminder that it is not possible to jump to a location inside the DO; control must be passed to the first symbol. However, when converting a PDL program to a flowchart, the merge symbol would probably not be included.

The WHILE Construct. Let's go back and examine how WHILE was defined in the previous chapter. It can be summarized by the following steps: check condition; if condition is false, go to last step; execute statement; go to first step; and go to next statement. This summary spells out the structure needed to implement a WHILE construct. Compare it carefully with Fig. 7-11. Some thought will indicate that the flowchart does exactly what our definition requires it to do.

The REPEAT Construct. REPEAT is almost identical to WHILE. REPEAT accomplishes the following: executes the statement and, if the condition is false, returns to the first step. The flowchart associated with this control construct is shown in Fig. 7-12. Structurally it is simpler than WHILE, although it performs an analogous function.

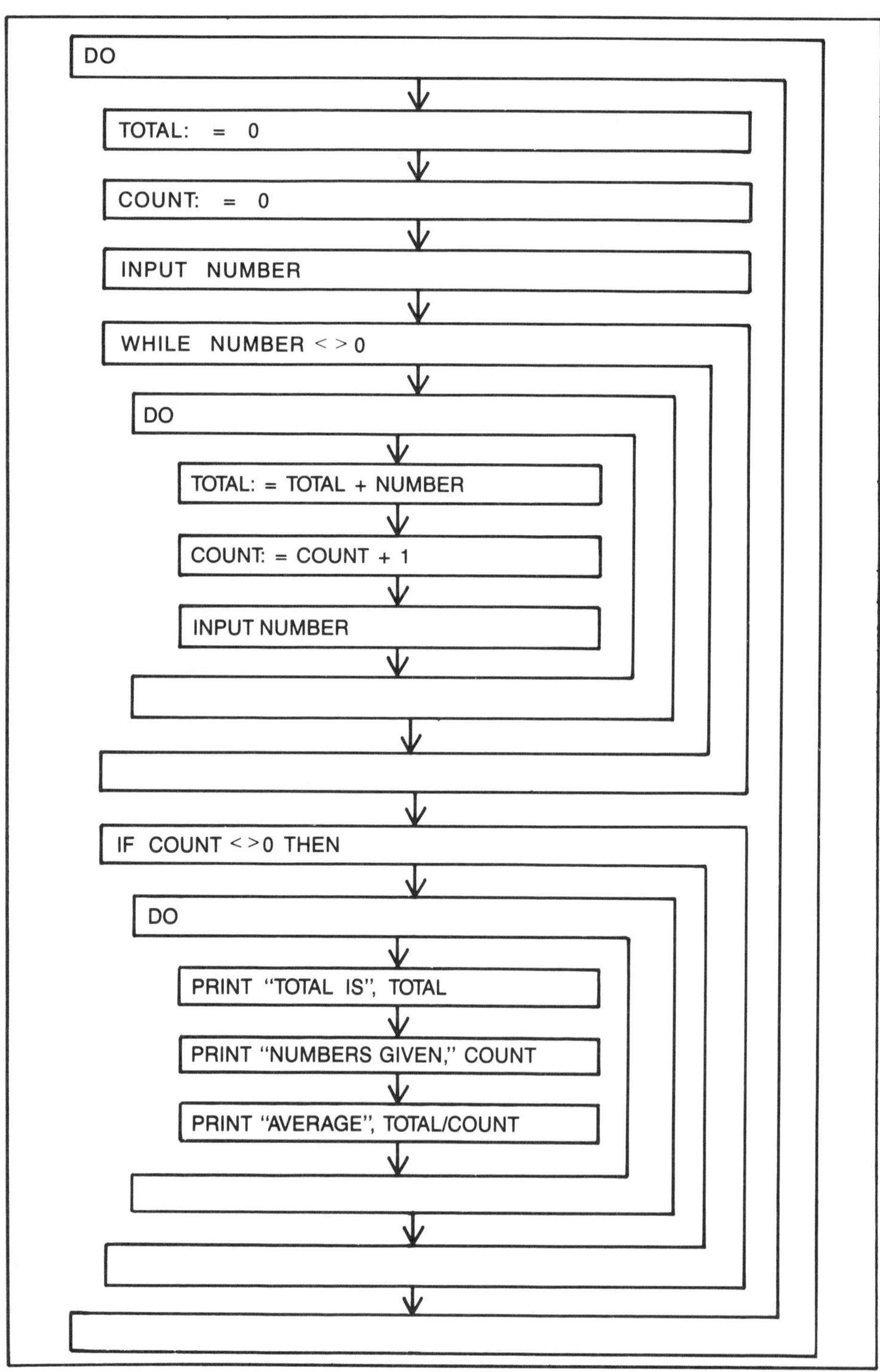

Fig. 7-9. An example using the better symbolic representation.

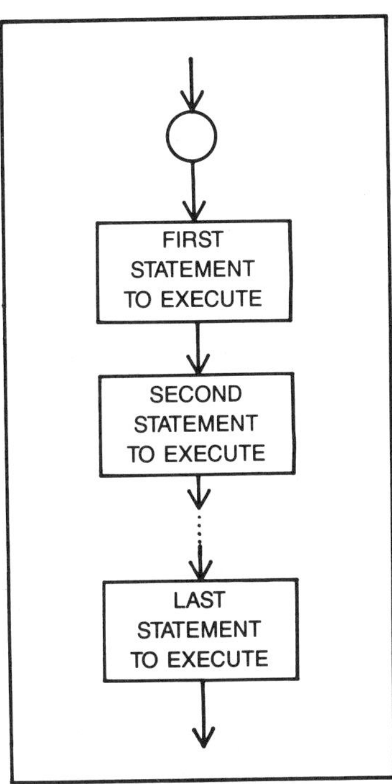

Fig. 7-10. A flowchart for DO.

The IF Construct. IF is slightly more tricky than WHILE or REPEAT because we must control two statement blocks. The logic of IF is summarized: if the condition is false, go to the fourth step; execute the first statement; go to the last step; execute the second statement; and go to the next statement. The flowchart is shown in Fig. 7-13.

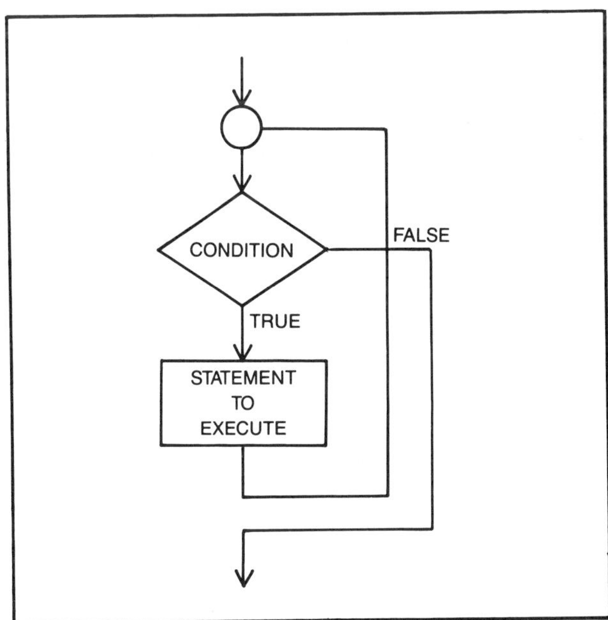

Fig. 7-11. A flowchart for WHILE.

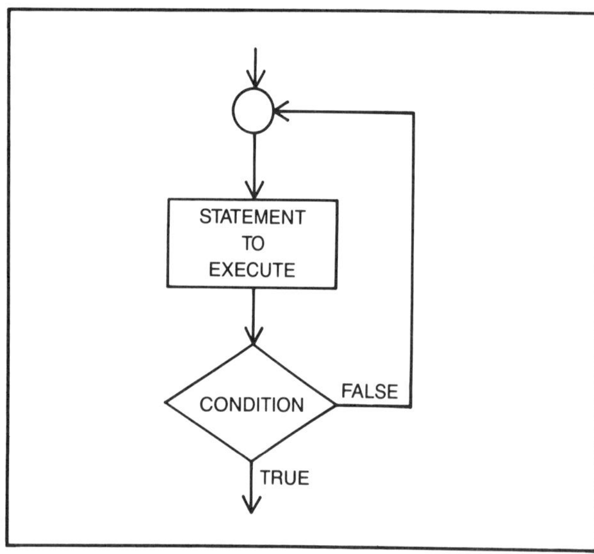

Fig. 7-12. A flowchart for REPEAT.

The FOR Construct. The most difficult construct to implement is FOR. Its logic is summarized as follows: Set the index to the initial value; execute the statement; add increment to the index; and if the increment is less than or equal to the final value, go to the second step. The flowchart is shown in Fig 7-14. Here you see the impor-

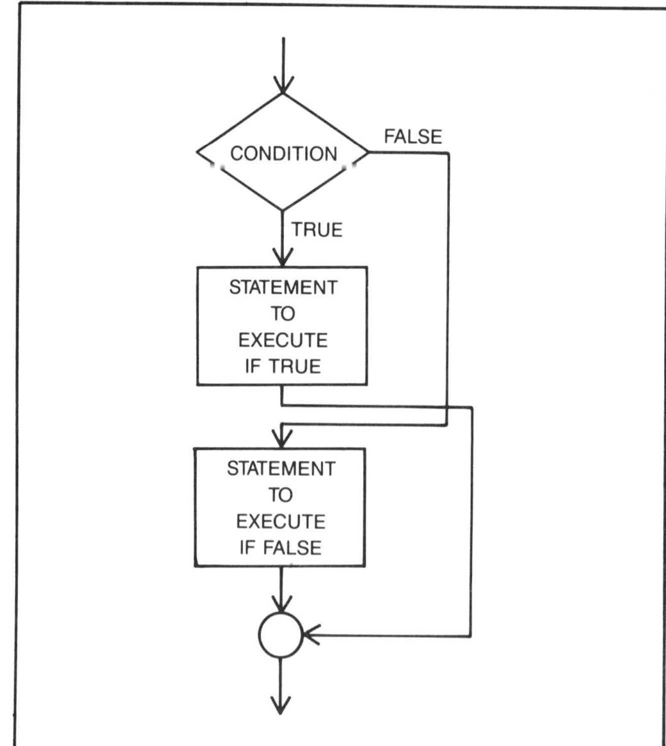

Fig. 7-13. A flowchart for IF.

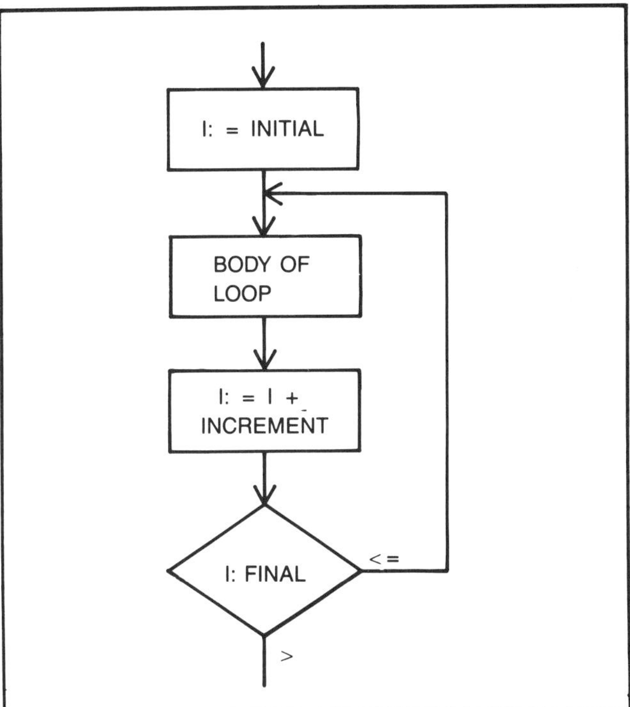

Fig. 7-14. A flowchart for FOR.

tance of having two entry points into the claw-like symbol. When control enters through the top, the index is initialized—a process which is not repeated when control enters through the bottom entry point.

CONVERSION OF PDL TO FLOWCHART

Our next task is to take a PDL program and convert it into a flowchart. Because flowchart symbols are separate from one another, the structure implied by the PDL program may not be easily seen in the flowchart.

```
do
  create universal flowchart by enclosing program in operation symbol and
  --connecting it to start and stop symbols
  while
     there is an operation symbol containing PDL
  do
     pick an operation symbol containing PDL
     replace outermost outer syntax statement with appropriate flowchart symbols
     place inner syntax statements in new operation symbols
  od
od
```

Fig. 7-15. Algorithm to convert from PDL to a flowchart.

The algorithm to convert from a PDL program to a flowchart is shown in Fig. 7-15. It creates a flowchart containing a single process symbol with the entire PDL program in it. Then, depending on outermost control construct, the symbol is refined into other symbols which perform the same function as the control construct they replace. The result of each refinement is a flowchart which may contain more symbols, but contains fewer control constructs in the process symbols. The process is repeated until no operation symbol contains an outer syntax statement.

This may be a little difficult to understand, so an example using the PDL program in Fig. 7-1 may be useful. The result of the first step, shown in Fig. 7-16, creates a flowchart with a start symbol leading into a operation symbol containing the PDL program to convert. A flow line leads from this symbol to a stop symbol. This may remind you of the "universal flowchart" mentioned in Chapter 2.

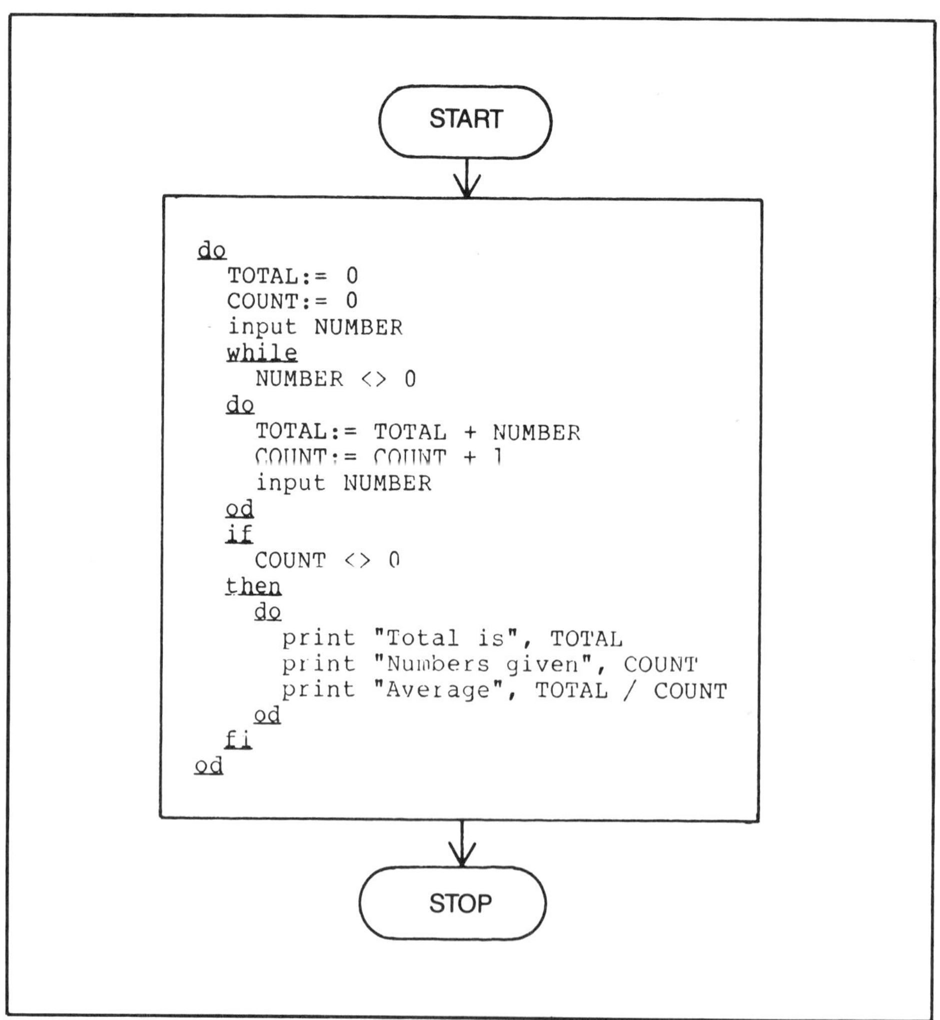

Fig. 7-16. An example of PDL conversion: Step One.

Now, process symbols which contain outer syntax statements must be refined into proper flowchart symbols. This process is shown in Figs. 7-17 through 7-19.

CONNECTORS

A flowchart describing a program of any complexity can be quite large. We can solve the problem by running the flow lines from page to page; however, this is hardly a solution to the problem. When a flowchart becomes much larger than a single page,

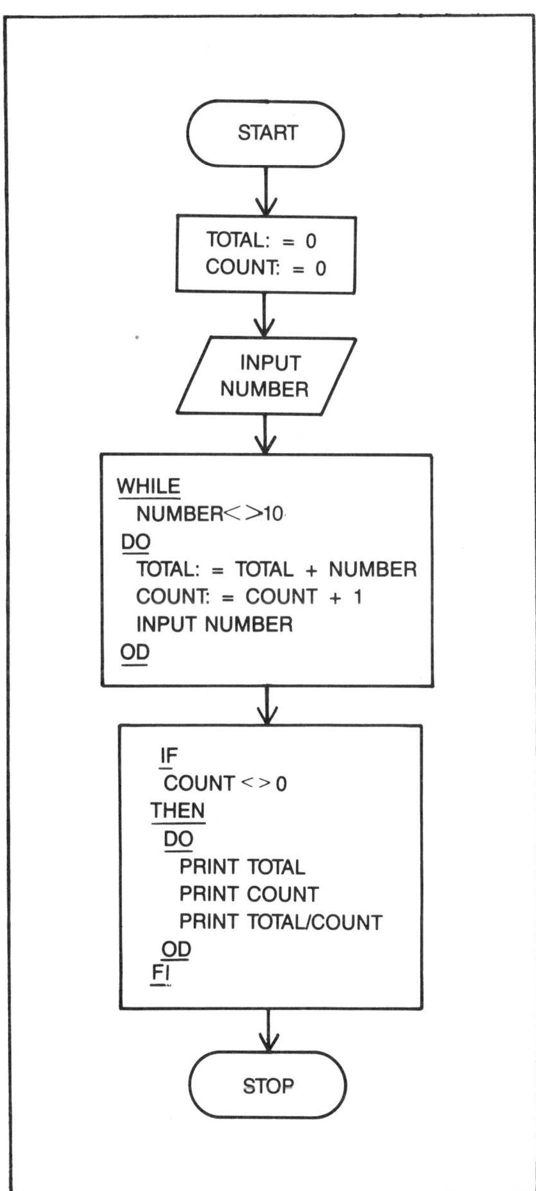

Fig. 7-17. First simplification of the PDL conversion process.

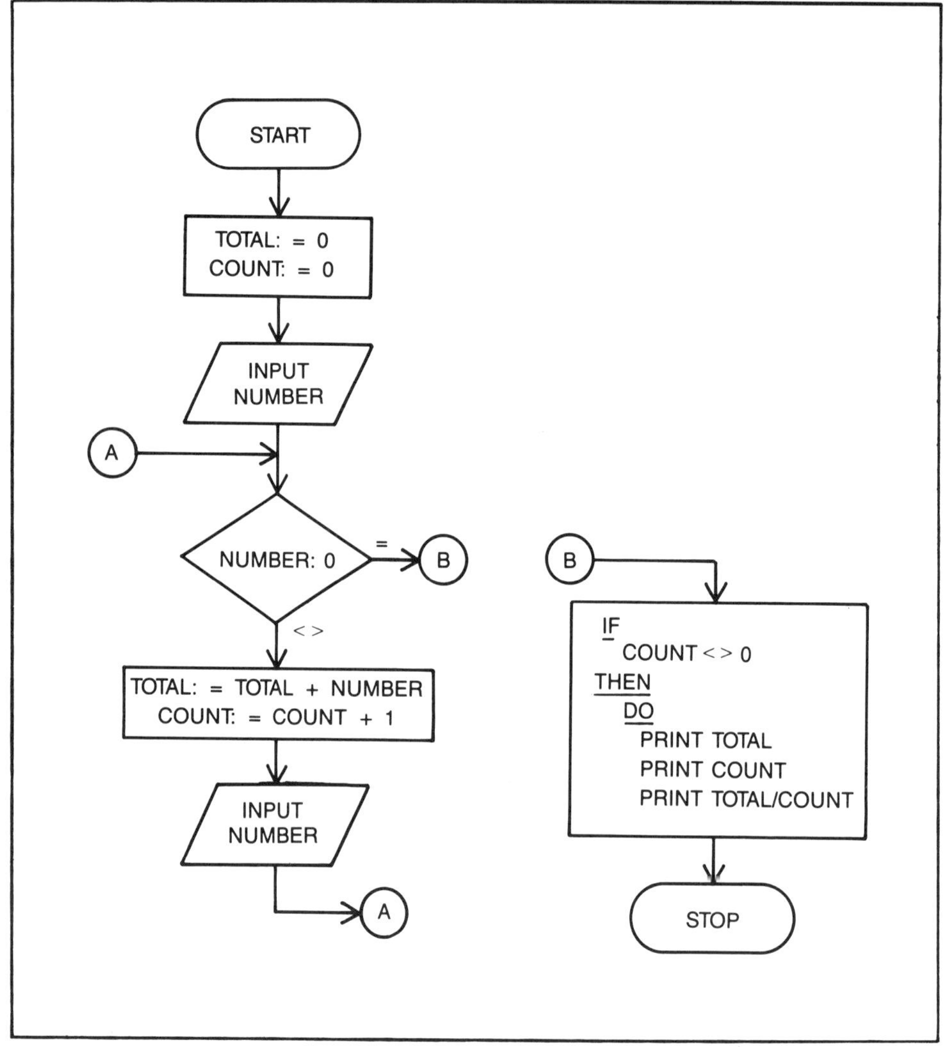

Fig. 7-18. Second simplification of the PDL conversion process.

connectors are often used. Connectors replace flow lines across page boundaries and over long distances on the same page, resulting in a cleaner, easier-to-read flowchart.

On-Page Connectors. The first type of connector to look at is the *on-page connector.* The on-page connector symbol is shown in Fig. 7-20. It is the same as the merge symbol. A merge symbol can be distinguished from a connector by the identifier inside the connector.

A connector can be used in one of two ways. A flow line leaving the connector identifies the declaration of the connector. A particular connector can be declared in a flowchart only once on a page. A connector with a flow line entering it is a reference to the connector.

A particular connector can be referenced more than once. When control enters a

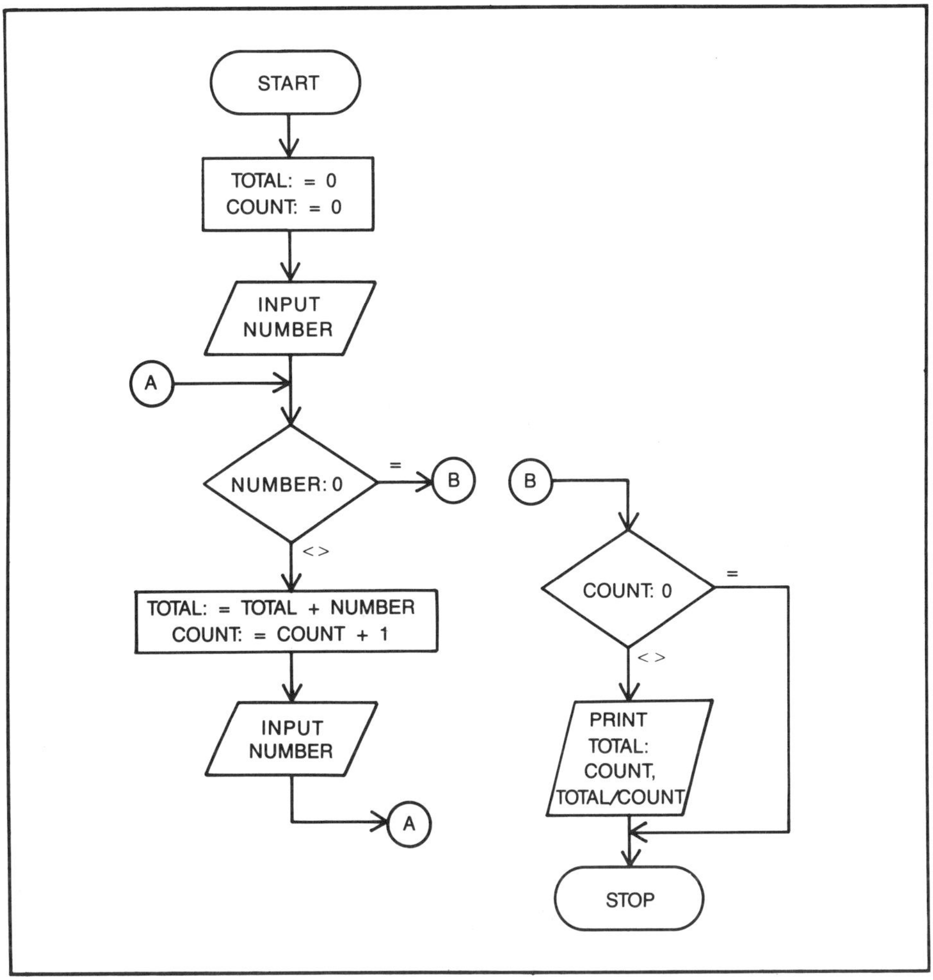

Fig. 7-19. Final simplification of the PDL conversion.

connector (a reference), control passes to the declared connector labeled the same. Control then passes on to the next symbol, whatever it may be.

Although connectors are really necessary when many flow lines are on a page and it is difficult to keep track of them, many programmers always use connectors to re-

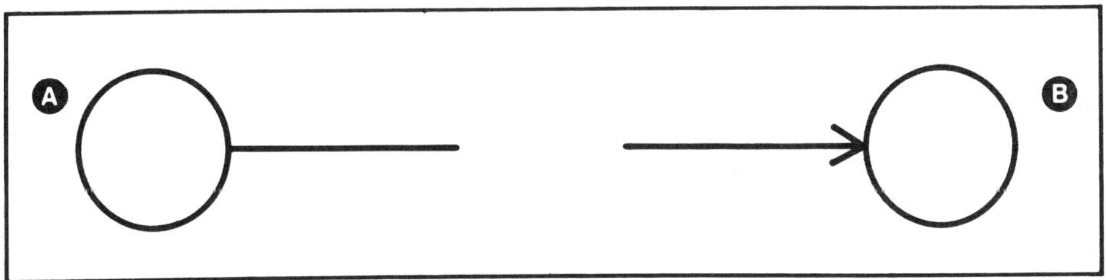

Fig. 7-20. On-page connector: (A) Definition (B) Reference.

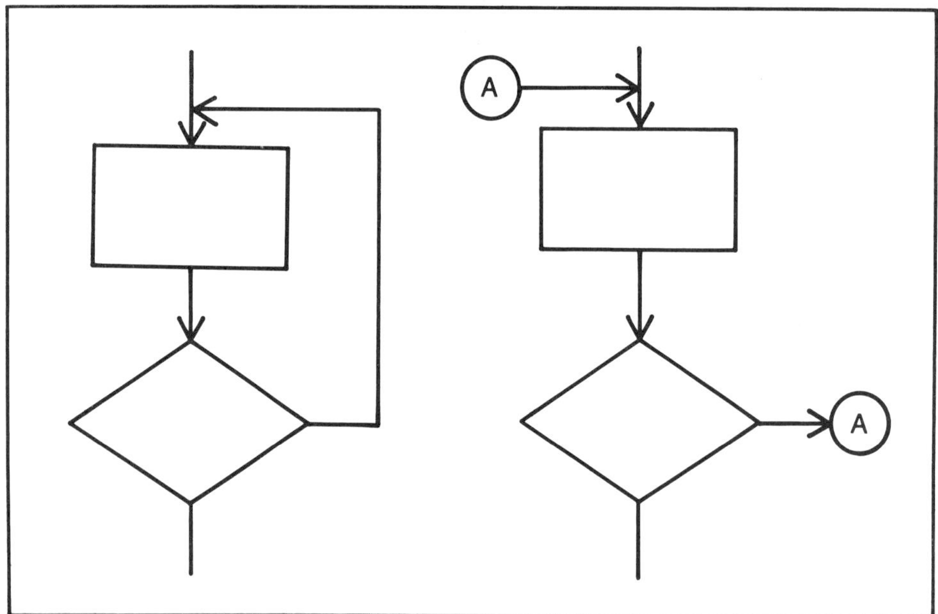

Fig. 7-21. Using on-page connectors.

place a flow line leading upwards. This way all flow lines lead down and connectors signal control passing to a point above. An example of the use of on-page connectors is shown in Fig. 7-21.

Off-Page Connectors. The second connector is the *off-page connector,* pictured in Fig. 7-22. Like on-page connectors, they identify control passing from one point in the flowchart to another, but are used when control passes between pages. The concepts of declared and referenced connectors are identical to those of on-page connectors, but their use is virtually mandatory. An example is shown in Fig. 7-23.

Connector Labeling Conventions. The connectors used in the preceding figures employed accepted labeling conventions to distinguish between them. Each connector is assigned a letter as an identifier; the connector declaration and all connector references to it use the same letter. Obviously, no two connector declarations have the same identifier (on the same page).

This rule also applies to off-page connectors. As an additional aid to someone reading the flowchart, page references are added to off-page connector references: The page number that the reference is made on, followed by a period, followed by the page number where the connector is declared.

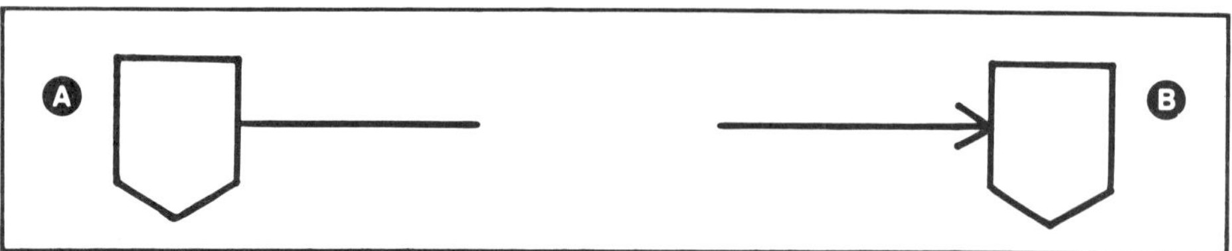

Fig. 7-22. Off-page connector: (A) Definition (B) Reference.

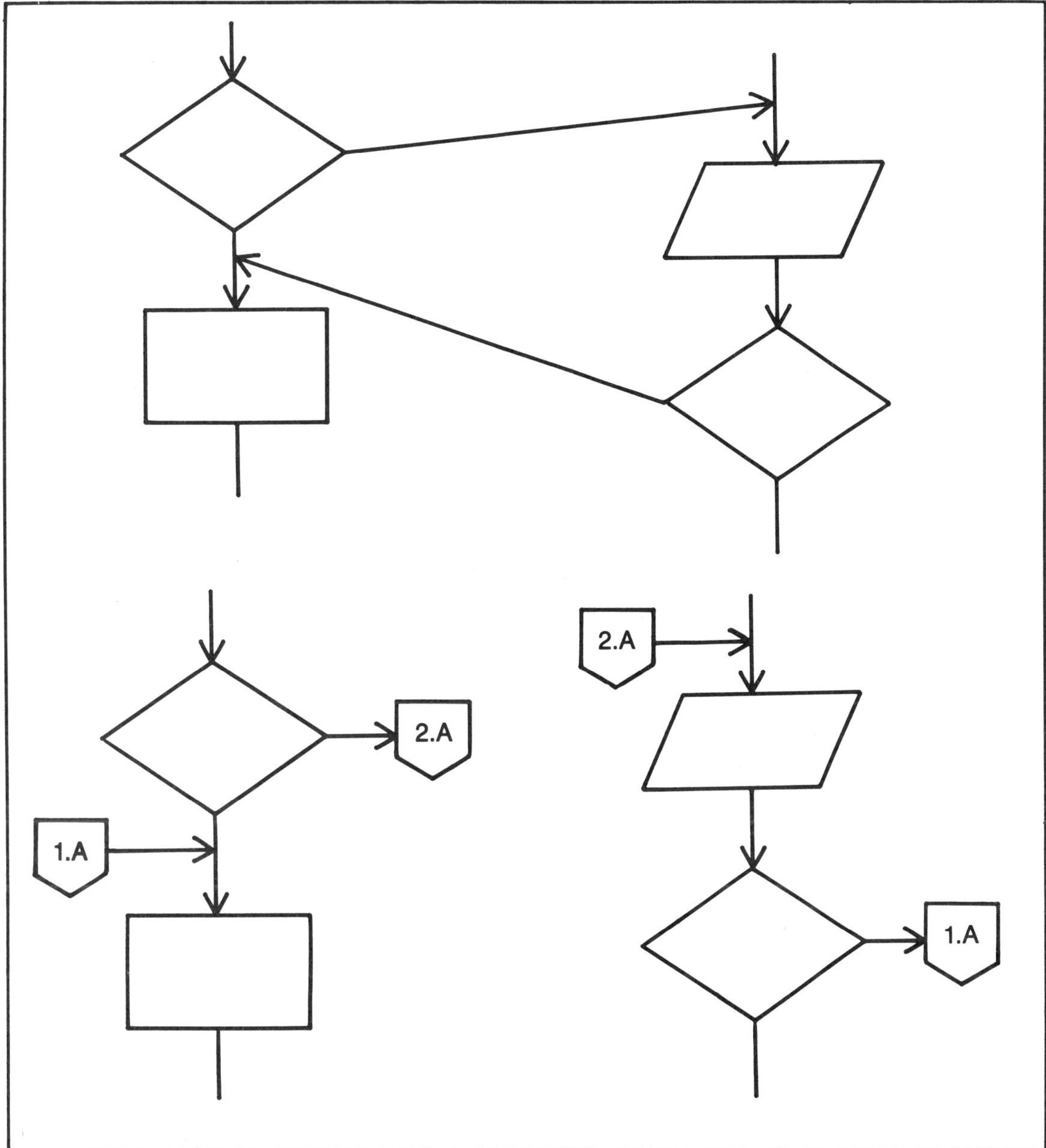

Fig. 7-23. Use of off-page connectors.

CONVERTING THE PHONE DIRECTORY PROGRAM

Let's look at the phone directory program from the previous chapter, second refinement. After enclosing the entire program in a single operation symbol and performing two simplification steps, Fig. 7-24 is obtained.

Now an important decision must be made. The simplification process could be con-

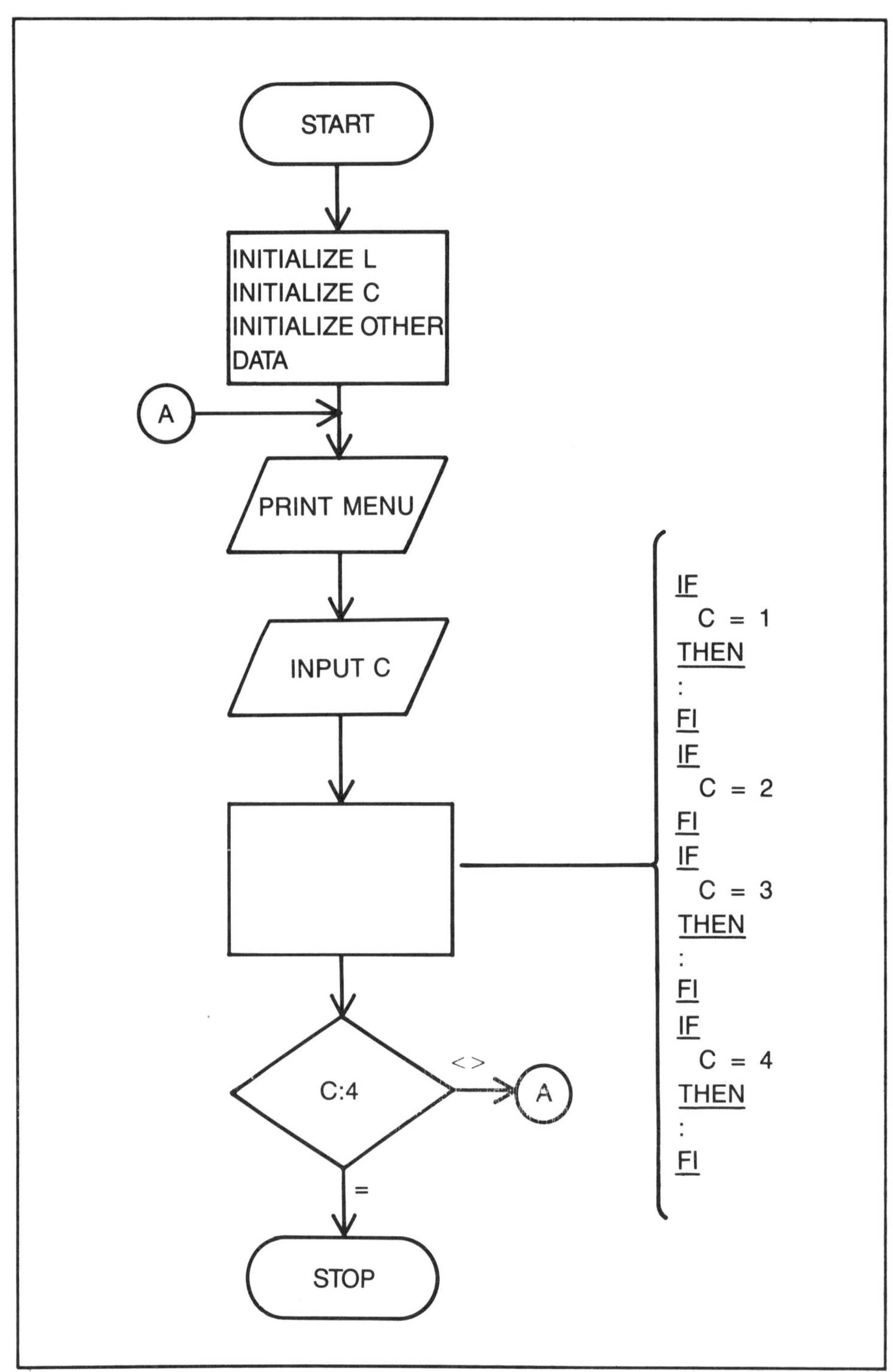

Fig. 7-24. Mid-point in conversion of phone directory program.

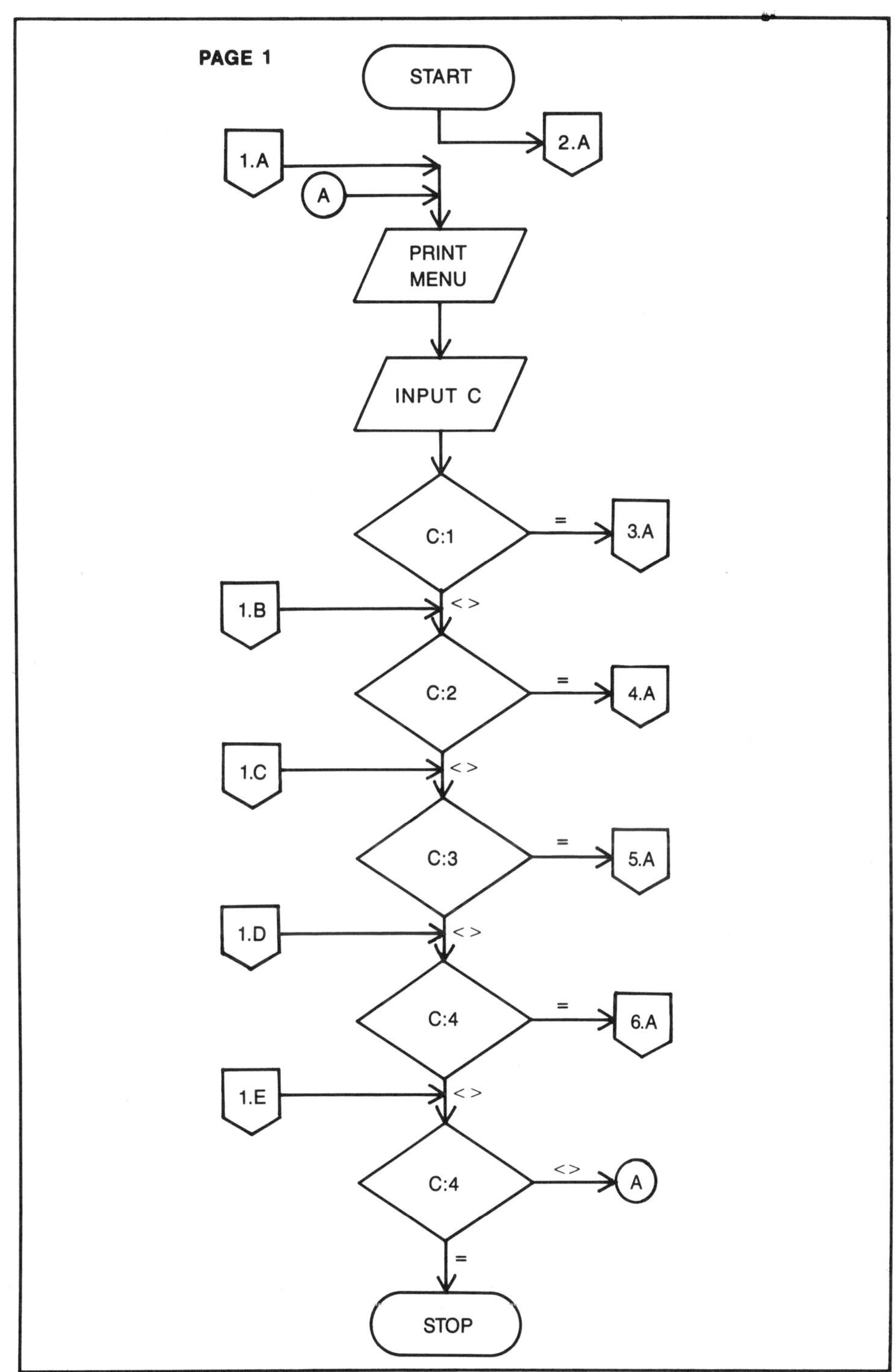

Fig. 7-25. First page of completed phone directory flowchart.

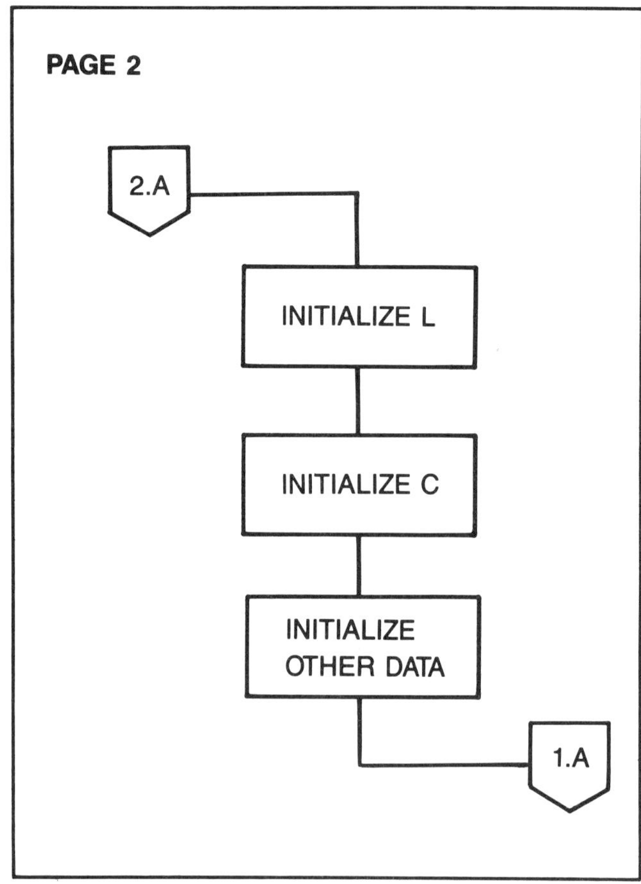

Fig. 7-26. Second page of the phone directory flowchart.

tinued blindly, producing a flowchart which runs from page to page. Or, by intelligently separating the program with connectors, portions of the flowchart which perform a common function can be placed on separate pages. We will use this latter option; the program will be split so the main program is on the first page, and the flowcharts for the four program functions, as well as the flowchart to initialize the data, are all on separate pages.

Now conversion can proceed normally. Figures 7-25 through 7-30 show the completed flowchart after performing the simplification steps.

Now that the phone list PDL program has been converted into a flowchart, it can be converted into a BASIC program. We face the same problem as we did in Chapter 4: not all the inner syntax commands represent valid BASIC operations. Even so, conversion into a pseudo-BASIC program will be instructive.

One way to convert this multipage flowchart is to convert one page at a time, leaving jumps caused by off-page connectors blank, just as any other jump does. After all pages have been converted, a second pass can be performed filling in all the necessary blanks. Figure 7-31 shows the BASIC program after the first pass. Lines 60 through 190 were generated by the first page. The code for the second page follows, starting at line 220.

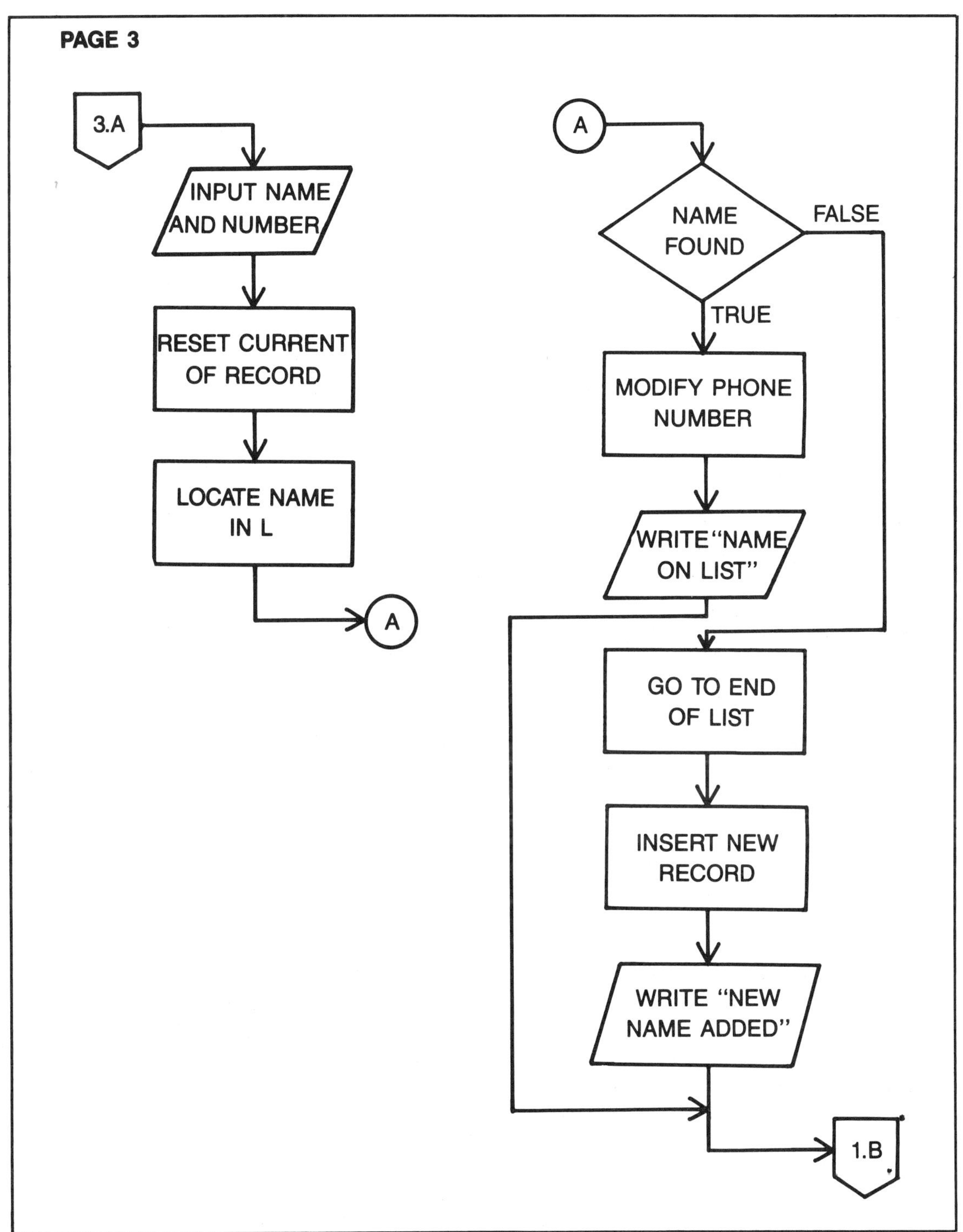

Fig. 7-27. Third page of completed phone directory flowchart.

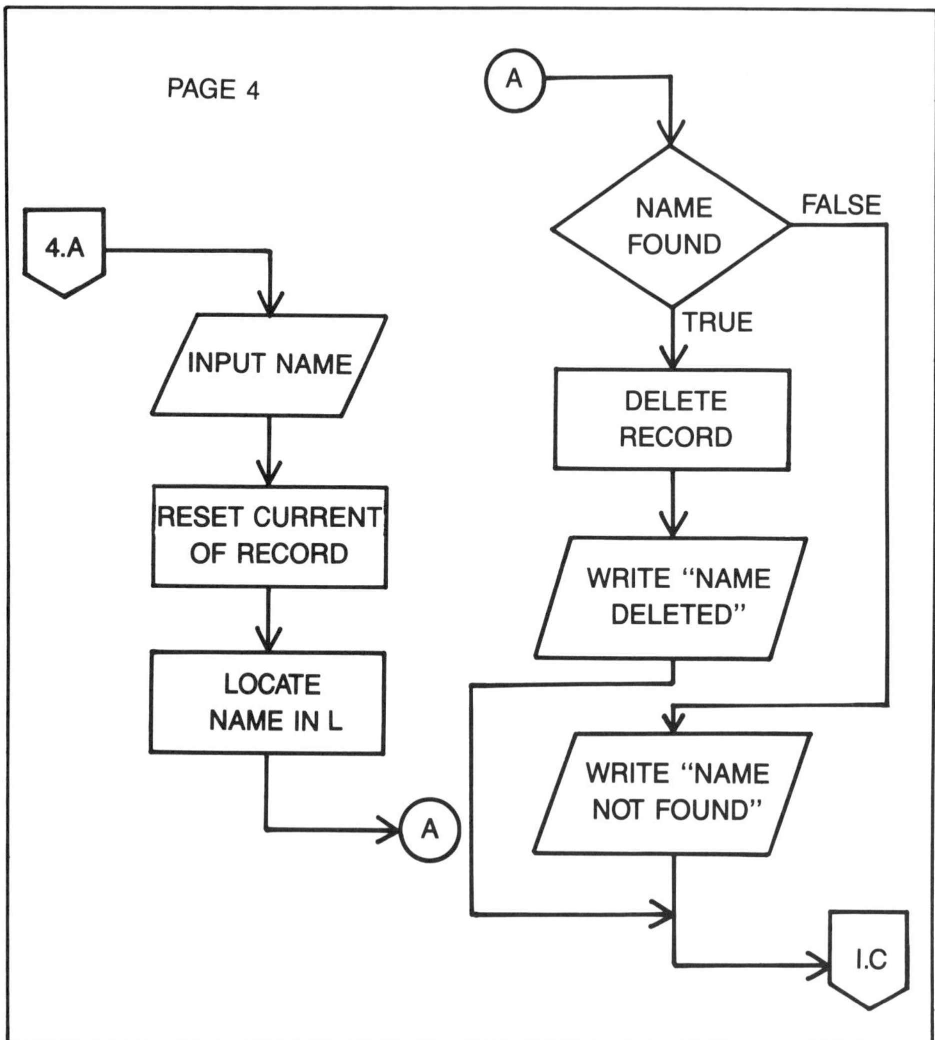

Fig. 7-28. Fourth page of the phone directory flowchart.

The rest of the program follows. Notice that the **REM** statements are used only for jumps caused by off-page connectors; their use elsewhere has been eliminated. The second pass operates the same as in previous examples, shown in Fig. 7-32.

Conversion of the final flowchart has been left as an exercise. It is done exactly as the example above, but uses more symbols.

SUMMARY

A PDL program can be converted into a flowchart by representing each control construct by appropriate flowchart symbols surrounding the flowchart symbols which represent the inner syntax of the construct.

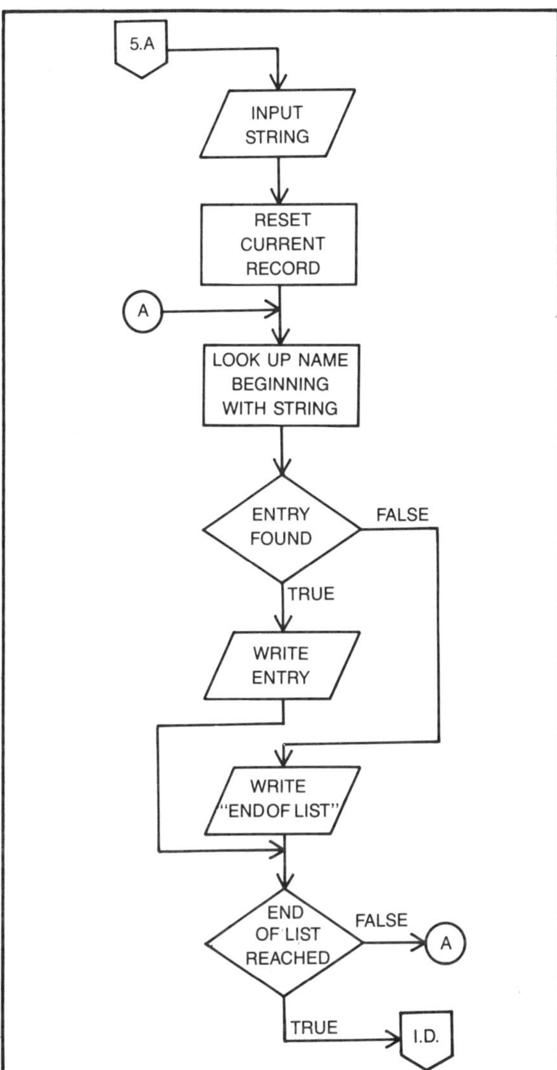

Fig. 7-29. Fifth page of the flowchart.

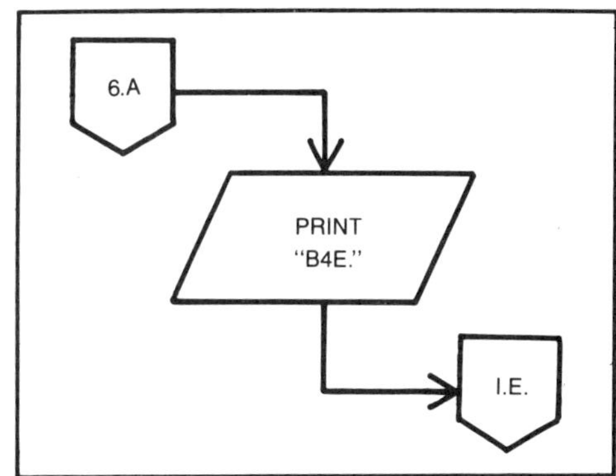

Fig. 7-30. Sixth and last page of the completed phone directory flowchart.

```
10 REM *********
20 PRINT "PHONE DIRECTORY PROGRAM"
30 REM *********
40 GOTO ***
50 REM <JUMP FROM LINE ***>
60 PRINT "1) Add a name"
70 PRINT "2) Delete a name"
80 PRINT "3) Print a name or names"
90 PRINT "4) Quit"
100 INPUT C
110 IF C = 1 THEN ***
120 REM <JUMP FROM LINE ***>
130 IF C = 2 THEN ***
140 REM <JUMP FROM LINE ***>
150 IF C = 3 THEN ***
160 REM <JUMP FROM LINE ***>
170 IF C = 4 THEN ***
180 REM <JUMP FROM LINE ***>
190 IF NOT (C = 4) THEN 60
200 END
210 REM <JUMP FROM LINE 40>
220 Clear L
230 Clear C
240 Initialize any other data
250 GOTO 50
260 REM <JUMP FROM LINE 110>
270 Input name and number
280 Reset current of record
290 Lookup name in L
300 IF NOT( name is found ) THEN ***
310 Change number
320 PRINT "Name already on list, number changed"
330 GOTO ***
340 Go to end of L
350 Insert new information
360 PRINT "New name entered"
370 GOTO 120
380 REM <JUMP FROM LINE 130>
390 Input name
400 Reset current of record
410 Lookup name in L
420 IF NOT( name is found ) THEN ***
430 Delete entry
440 PRINT "Name deleted"
450 GOTO ***
```

```
460 PRINT "Name not found"
470 GOTO 140
480 REM <JUMP FROM LINE 150>
490 Input string
500 Reset current of record
510 Lookup entry whose last name begins with string
520 IF NOT( entry is found ) THEN ***
530 Print out name and number
540 GOTO ***
550 PRINT "End of list reached."
560 IF NOT( end of list is reached ) THEN ***
570 GOTO 160
580 REM <JUMP FROM LINE 170>
590 PRINT "Bye."
600 GOTO 180
```

Fig. 7-31. Pass one through the phone directory flowchart.

```
10 REM *********
20 PRINT "PHONE DIRECTORY PROGRAM"
30 REM *********
40 GOTO 210
50 REM <JUMP FROM LINE 250>
60 PRINT "1) Add a name"
70 PRINT "2) Delete a name"
80 PRINT "3) Print a name or names"
90 PRINT "4) Quit"
100 INPUT C
110 IF C = 1 THEN 260
120 REM <JUMP FROM LINE 370>
130 IF C = 2 THEN 380
140 REM <JUMP FROM LINE 470>
150 IF C = 3 THEN 480
160 REM <JUMP FROM LINE 570>
170 IF C = 4 THEN 580
180 REM <JUMP FROM LINE 600>
190 IF NOT (C = 4) THEN 60
200 END
210 REM <JUMP FROM LINE 40>
220 Clear L
230 Clear C
240 Initialize any other data
250 GOTO 50
260 REM <JUMP FROM LINE 110>
270 Input name and number
```

```
280 Reset current of record
290 Lookup name in L
300 IF NOT( name is found ) THEN 340
310 Change number
320 PRINT "Name already on list, number changed"
330 GOTO 370
340 Go to end of L
350 Insert new information
360 PRINT "New name entered"
370 GOTO 120
380 REM <JUMP FROM LINE 130>
390 Input name
400 Reset current of record
410 Lookup name in L
420 IF NOT( name is found ) THEN 460
430 Delete entry
440 PRINT "Name deleted"
450 GOTO 470
460 PRINT "Name not found"
470 GOTO 140
480 REM <JUMP FROM LINE 150>
490 Input string
500 Reset current of record
510 Lookup entry whose last name begins with string
520 IF NOT( entry is found ) THEN 550
530 Print out name and number
540 GOTO 560
550 PRINT "End of list reached."
560 IF NOT( end of list is reached ) THEN 510
570 GOTO 160
580 REM <JUMP FROM LINE 170>
590 PRINT "Bye."
600 GOTO 180
```

Fig. 7-32. Pass two through the phone directory flowchart.

On-page and *off-page connectors* are used to replace flow lines within and across page boundaries. A connector is defined by a flow line leaving it, and is referenced by a flow line entering it. An on-page connector can be defined once per page, and an off-page connector once per flowchart. The effect of a connector is to transfer control when entered through a reference to the location where the connector is defined.

EXERCISES

1. Convert the third refinement of the phone directory program. Notice that change affects how the program is split between pages. Therefore, each page can be modified individually.

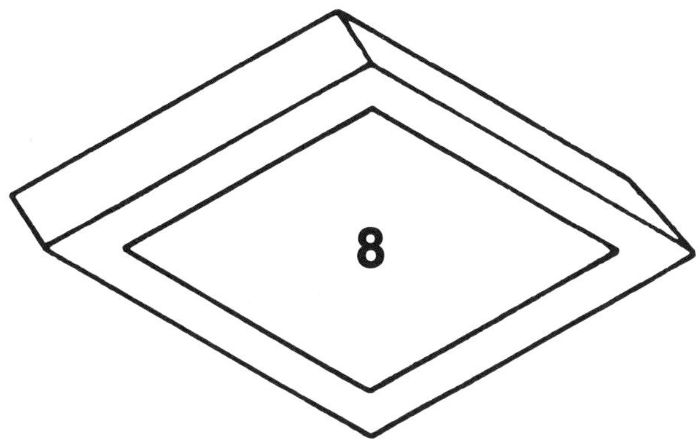

Subroutines

A *subroutine* is a program used within the context of another program. The first part of this definition (that a subroutine is a program) is very important. Although subroutines are "part" of another program, they still perform input, computation, and output functions. Because they are used within another program, input and output functions are often performed differently. While subroutines can and often do perform I/O with terminals, printers, etc., they perform I/O with the main program as well, through memory variables which "transmit" data between the main program and the subroutine. Once the subroutine begins, the program loses *all* control until the subroutine finishes. This means that data must be transmitted in an organized way.

PARAMETERS AND SIDE EFFECTS

Ideally, a subroutine should operate independently from the program that uses it. This may be difficult to understand until we discuss parameters.

In many programming languages, the memory variables that contain data to be sent to the subroutine are specified by *parameters.* Conceptually, the subroutine can be thought to have its own separate section of memory which the subroutine, and only the subroutine, can use. When the program with data in its own memory variables intended for the subroutine calls the subroutine, the data is copied into the subroutine's memory variables. When the subroutine ends, the data in the subroutine's memory variables is copied back into the program's memory variables. Sometimes the program does not need the new data created by the subroutine; it is able to specify exactly which memory variables are to be copied back when the subroutine is done.

Figure 8-1 shows part of a Pascal program which uses a subroutine, and the first line of the subroutine. The line shown in the main program causes the subroutine **TEST** to be executed. In addition, three memory variables are specified: **A**, **B**, and **C**.

We don't know what will be done with the data in these variables until we read the *declaration* of subroutine **TEST**. The phrase **X, var Y, Z** is the key: **X**, **Y**, and **Z** are three memory variables for **TEST**. These are totally different from any **X**, **Y**, or **Z** appearing in the main program. When the subroutine is called from the program, the value in **A** is copied into **X**, **B** is copied into **Y**, and **C** is copied into **Z**. Then the subroutine begins, using the data in **X**, **Y**, and **Z**. When the subroutine is finished, only the values of the variables preceded by **var** in the subroutine declaration are copied back into the main program's variables. In this case, whatever is in **Y** is copied back into **B**. The program then continues with the next instruction.

This method of passing data has many advantages. First and foremost, it lets a subroutine be easily used with many different programs. Besides what the subroutine does, you need only know what parameters are used and what they are used for. The programmer who writes the program does *not* need to know what memory variables are used in the subroutine, and the programmer who writes the subroutine does *not* need to know what memory variables are used in the program. Neither programmer need worry about inadvertently using or destroying data used by the other program/subroutine. Since the main program and its subroutines keep separate variables, copying values between them, this methodology is often referred to as *call by value.*

Call-by-value methodology for passing data is accepted as the "right" way of doing things. There is also a "wrong" way—which is unfortunately, the only way BASIC

```
Section of Pascal Main Program
    •
    •
    •
    A:= 10;
    B:= 15;
    C:= A + B;
    TEST( A, B, C );
    •
    •
    •

----------

First Line of TEST Subroutine

    PROCEDURE TEST( X, VAR Y, Z );
    •
    •
    •
```

Fig. 8-1. Calling a subroutine in Pascal.

Fig. 8-2. A side effect in Pascal.

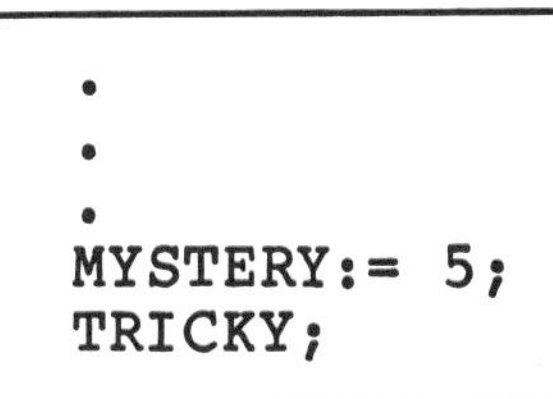

can handle subroutines.

I said a subroutine maintains a totally distinct region of memory to store memory variables. However, subroutines can still access variables from the main program. This poses some problems. Refer to the two Pascal lines shown in Fig. 8-2, and try to guess what the variable **MYSTERY** will contain after the subroutine **TRICKY** is executed (the first line assigns the value 5 to **MYSTERY**).

Did you say five? Well, you could be right. You might very well be wrong, though, since **TRICKY** might have changed **MYSTERY** during execution. Such a change to a memory variable not used as a parameter is called a *side effect.*

Side effects, if not used properly, can cause many problems. If programmer A is responsible for maintaining the main program, and programmer B maintains **TRICKY**, there would have to be constant communication between the two. If programmer A changes the name of a particular variable or decides to use it in a different way, he would have to contact the other programmer so he, in turn, could make the proper corrections in his program.

The way programs and subroutines maintain data is shown in Fig. 8-3. Diagram A illustrates the method used by languages like Pascal. Remember that the subroutine can access data the main program uses. The opposite is not true, since subroutine data does not exist until the subroutine is called (and the main program loses control), and is cleared when the subroutine ends. The arrows represent data copied from one memory area to another. This data transfer occurs automatically in Pascal.

Diagram B shows how memory is maintained when the side effect scheme is used. All memory used for variables is lumped into a common area where the main program and all its subroutines store their data. The data area is divided only by conceptual boundaries; it is possible for main programs and subroutines to gain direct access to the same memory addresses. For this reason, the side effect scheme is often described as *call by location.* The programmer—not the language processor—is responsible for deciding which variables belong to the main program and which belong to the subroutines, and for keeping them separate. Any data transfer that occurs must be expicitly requested in the program.

To see how these methodologies work, consider a problem relating to maintaining the list for the telephone directory program. One of the functions that must be performed several times throughout the program is setting the current record to the next occurrence of some name. In order for a subroutine to do this, three pieces of data need to be used: the list of names, the current record, and the name to be found.

Three methods could be used to pass the data between the program and subroutine.

☐ Parameters—Three separate parameters for each piece of data are used. The parameters for the name to be located and the list to search would not need to be **var** parameters; the subroutine does not need to change them. The third parameter, the current record, does need to be **var** since the new value for the current record must be copied back so that the program may use it. This method is the most flexible procedure, compared to the following methods.

☐ Side Effect—When the subroutine is called, the subroutine uses the variables the program has created to store the three necessary values, searches for the name, and changes the variable for the current record to the location of the new record. The subroutine must be designed not to change the other two variables (unless such a change is expected). If for some reason the subroutine needs to change either the list of names or the name to be found, the data should be copied into a different variable, which can be modified by the subroutine without having the undesired side effect. While this method has the disadvantage of requiring the programmer to take responsibility for seeing that the data is manipulated in the correct manner, it has the advantage of requiring the least effort on the computer's part to oversee that the data is used in the proper fashion. (Computer effort meaning more memory and longer execution time than would otherwise be necessary.)

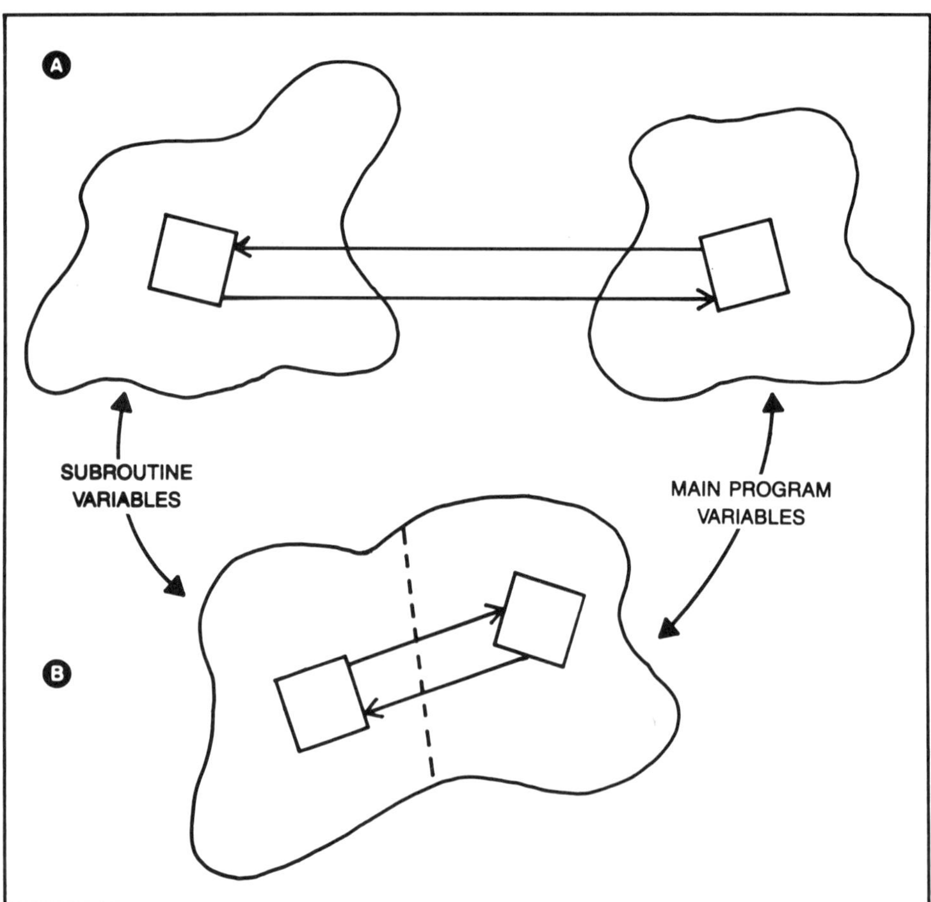

Fig. 8-3. How memory is managed with subroutines: (A) Pascal (B) BASIC.

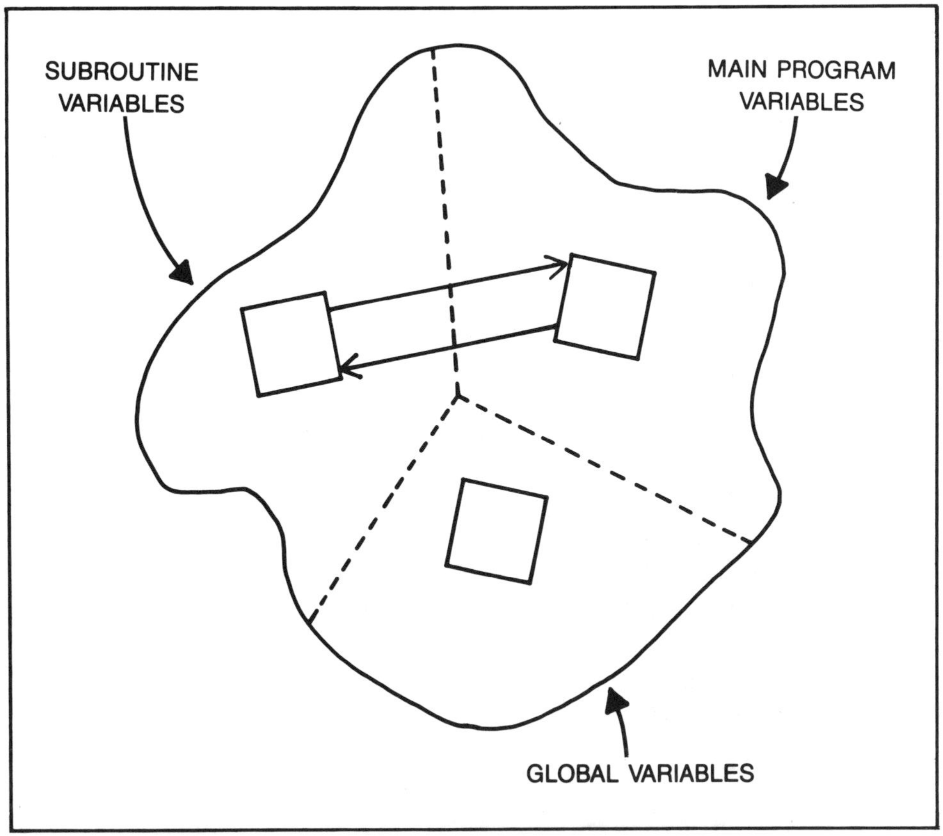

Fig. 8-4. A combined approach to managing memory in BASIC.

☐ Combined—Some information is passed by parameters, and the rest is accessed directly by the subroutine (i.e., a call-by-location side effect). For example, in our telephone directory program we will have procedures which process the list of names and the current record. Since the program uses only one list of names and current record, it would be repetitious and unnecessary to pass these pieces of data as parameters. Thus, any changes to them would be done as a side effect by the subroutine. On the other hand, a parameter such as a name to be searched for might be stored in different variables each time the subroutine is called (or might even be a constant, such as "Jones" or "Smith"). In this case one would not design a subroutine which expects the name to be stored in the same place every time. Therefore, this data would be passed as a parameter.

The combined approach leads to a different concept, pictured in Fig. 8-4, of how memory is used to store data. It is most similar to Fig. 8-3B), except that there is a separate area of memory directly accessible to both the main program and its subroutines. This is the approach that will be taken in our discussion of subroutines. Although BASIC does not support parameter passing, we will see later how we can simulate this technique.

A PROGRAMMING EXAMPLE

Our discussion of subroutines will revolve around a program to print a histogram. A *histogram* consists of a series of bars whose length is proportional to some quantity. The program will read ten values into an array, and then print a ten-bar histogram. Each bar will be made up of asterisks, the number of which will equal the number read.

The flowchart is shown in Fig. 8-5. The following describes the design of two subroutines used in this program. One reads the values of the array, the other prints a single bar, given its length.

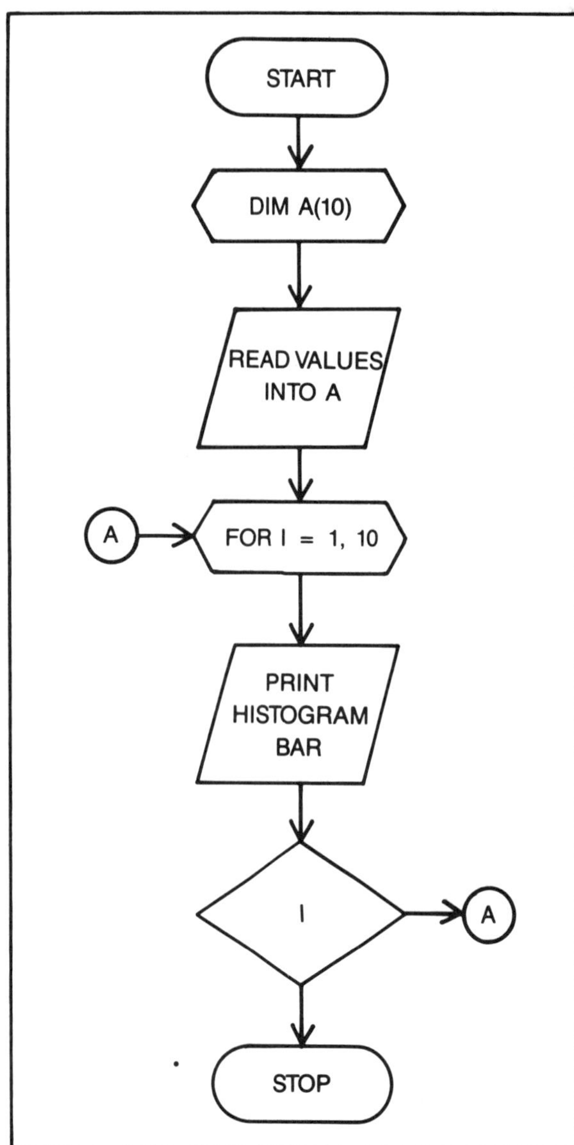

Fig. 8-5. A histogram flowchart requiring subroutines.

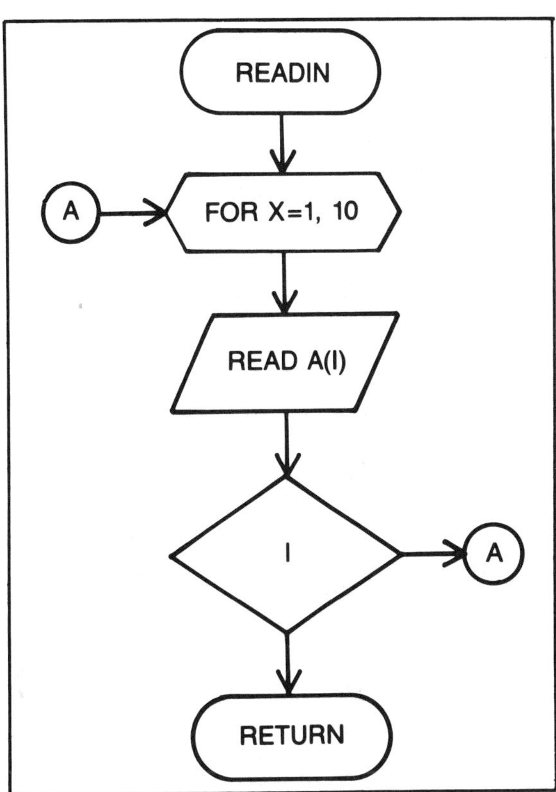

Fig. 8-6. A subroutine to read in data: READIN.

SUBPROGRAMS WITHOUT PARAMETERS

As we look at how subroutines are designed, the first subroutine we will study does not require parameters to be passed. The subroutine will read ten values into the **A** array, using only global data so no other data need be passed to the subroutine.

Figure 8-6 is a flowchart for the subroutine. We can identify it as a subroutine in two ways: first, **READIN** appears in the start symbol, instead of **START. READIN** is the name of the subroutine, and will call it from the main program. Also, the word **RETURN** appears in the stop symbol, because the program returns to the main program when it finishes the subroutine. This micro-flowchart contains a variable table.

A subroutine is invoked using a special form of the operation symbol, shown in Fig. 8-7. The name of the subroutine being called is placed above the horizontal line. Below the line is placed a short synopsis of what the subroutine will do (the same type

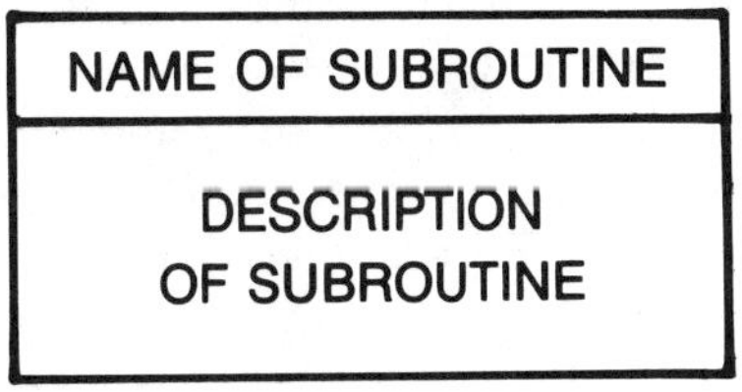

NAME OF SUBROUTINE

DESCRIPTION
OF SUBROUTINE

Fig. 8-7. Flowchart symbol to invoke a subroutine.

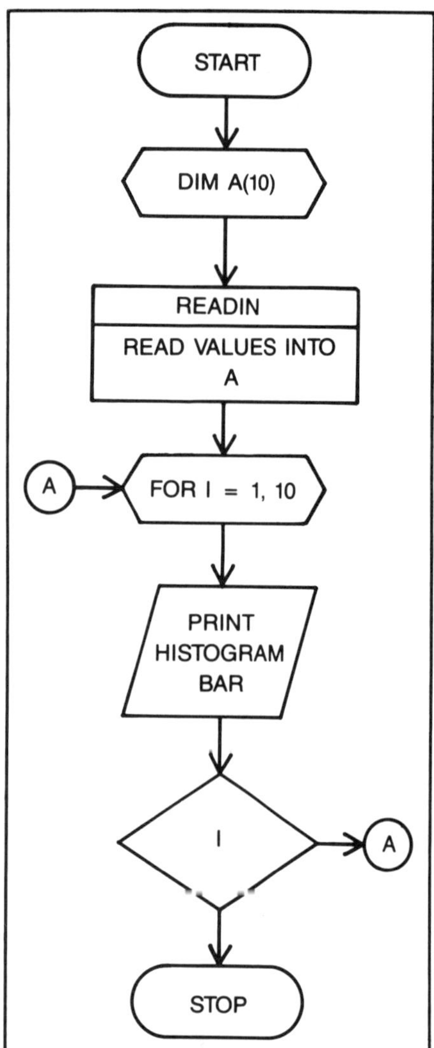

Fig. 8-8. Calling READIN from the main program.

of phrase would appear in a normal operation symbol). The main program which uses **READIN** is shown in Fig. 8-8.

PASSING PARAMETERS IN BASIC

The second subroutine needed for the histogram program requires a single parameter: the length of the bar. The flowchart for the subroutine is shown in Fig. 8-9.

BAR is in the start symbol, but the symbol also contains the name of the parameter it requires. The subroutine operates by printing an asterisk the required number of times. The semicolon causes the asterisks to be placed next to each other. The **PRINT** statement following the loop ends the line so the next **PRINT** statement can write the next line.

Since BASIC does not support parameter passing, a way to simulate the passing of parameters will have to be devised. One way is to use a standard set of variables used solely to pass data between the main program and the subroutine. For example, the variables **P1, P2, P3, . . ., P9** could be reserved for passing numeric data and **P1$, P2$, P3$ . . . , P9$** for string data. If the subroutine uses two numeric parameters and a single string parameter, **P1** and **P2** would be used for the numeric parameters and **P3$** for the string parameter. Thus, up to nine parameters can be passed this way.

Parameters can also return data to the main program. Consider a subroutine to add two numbers. It requires three parameters: two input parameters, which contain the two numbers to be added, and one output parameter, which contains the result. If the sum of 5 and 12 needs to be printed, the numbers 5 and 12 would be stored in **P1** and **P2**, respectively. The subroutine would be called and when executed, 17 (the result) would be in **P3**.

If this method is used, the single parameter for **BAR** will be contained in **P1**. When **BAR** begins, it has only to copy **P1** into **X**. Because **X** is not used to return data to the main program, its value does not have to be copied into **P1** before the subroutine ends. Figure 8-10 shows the flowchart for **BAR** which performs this transfer.

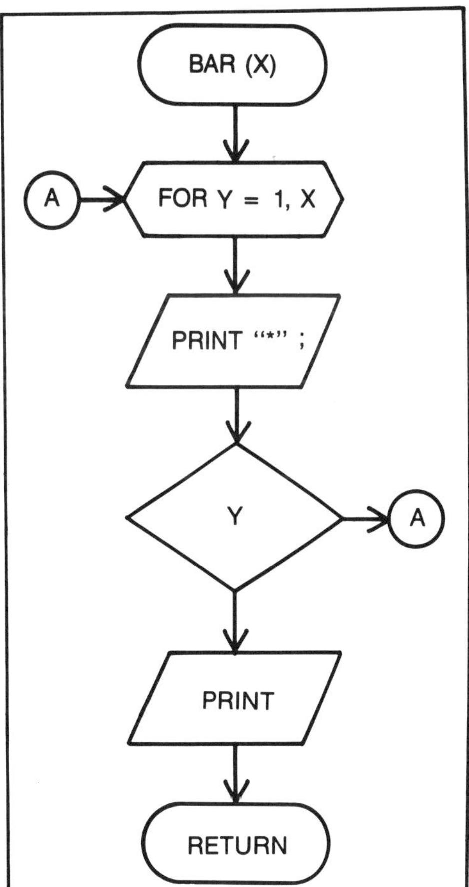

Fig. 8-9. A subroutine to print a histograph bar: BAR.

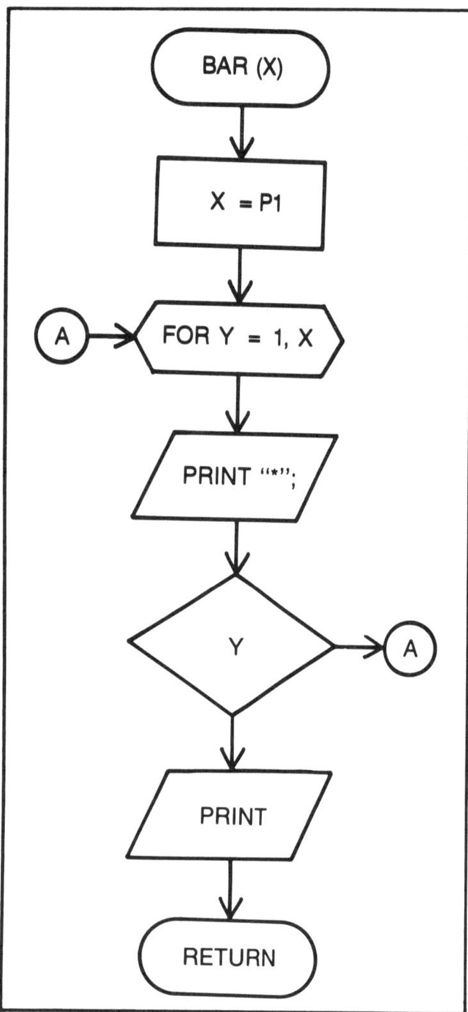

Fig. 8-10. BAR with simulated parameter passing.

The flowchart in Fig. 8-11 shows the flowchart for the main program using **BAR**. The extra operation symbol copies the length of the bar into **P1** before calling the subroutine.

IMPLEMENTING SUBROUTINES

Now that we have flowcharts for the main program as well as the two subroutines we can begin to write a program. Suppose for a moment that instead of writing **GOTO 100** in a program, the programmer could write **L = 100** and **GOTO L**; the **GOTO** would branch to the line number stored in **L**. How might subroutines be invoked in this manner?

The program in Fig. 8-12 shows how the line number after the jump to the subroutine is stored in L before the subroutine is called when a subroutine is invoked. When the subroutine ends, it simply jumps to the line number stored in L. Consider

Fig. 8-11. Calling BAR from the main program.

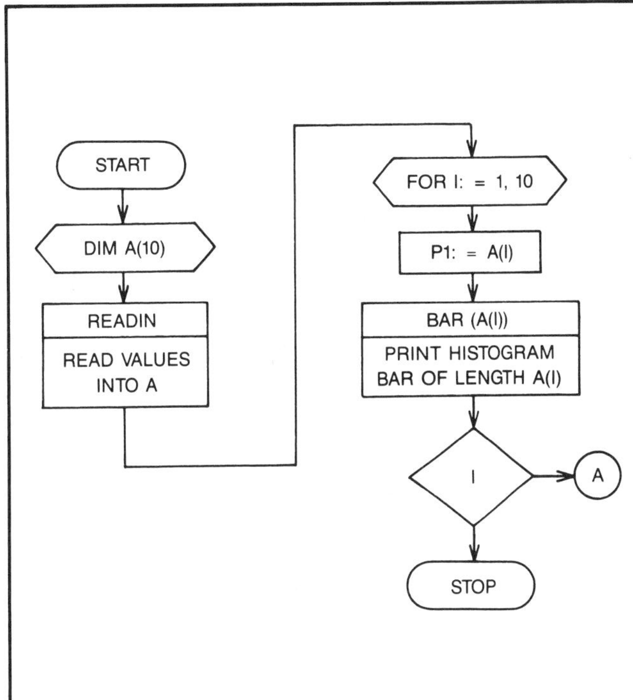


```
10 REM ********
20 PRINT "READ IN AND DISPLAY HISTOGRAM"
30 REM ********
40 DIM A(10)
50 LET L = 70
60 GOTO 130
70 FOR I = 1 TO 10
80 LET P = A(I)
90 LET L = 110
100 GOTO 210
110 NEXT I
120 END
130 REM ********
140 REM READIN:  SUBROUTINE TO READ IN DATA INTO ARRAY A
150 REM ********
160 FOR X = 1 TO 10
170 PRINT "ENTER A NUMBER"
180 INPUT A(X)
190 NEXT X
200 GOTO L
210 REM ********
220 REM BAR(X):  SUBROUTINE TO PRINT HISTOGRAM BAR OF LENGTH X
230 REM ********
240 X = P
250 FOR Y = 1 TO X
260 PRINT "*";
270 NEXT Y
280 PRINT
290 GOTO L
```

Fig. 8-12. One method of calling a subroutine.

```
10 REM ********
20 PRINT "READ IN AND DISPLAY HISTORGRAM"
30 REM ********
40 DIM A(10)
50 LET L = 70
60 GOTO 150
70 FOR I = 1 TO 10
80 LET P = A(I)
90 LET L = 110
100 GOTO 230
110 LET L = 130
120 GOTO 230
130 NEXT I
140 END
150 REM ********
160 REM READIN:  SUBROUTINE TO READ IN DATA INTO ARRAY A
170 REM ********
180 FOR X = 1 TO 10
190 PRINT "ENTER A NUMBER"
200 INPUT A(X)
210 NEXT X
220 GOTO L
230 REM ********
240 REM BAR(X):  SUBROUTINE TO PRINT HISTOGRAM BAR OF LENGTH X
250 REM ********
260 X = P
270 FOR Y = 1 TO X
280 PRINT "*";
290 NEXT Y
300 PRINT
310 GOTO L
```

Fig. 8-13. A subroutine called in two places.

```
10 REM ********
20 PRINT "READ IN AND DISPLAY HISTORGRAM"
30 REM ********
40 DIM A(10)
50 GOSUB 200
60 FOR I = 1 TO 10
70 LET P = A(I)
80 GOSUB 400
90 NEXT I
100 END
200 REM ********
210 REM READIN:  SUBROUTINE TO READ IN DATA INTO ARRAY A
220 REM ********
230 FOR X = 1 TO 10
240 PRINT "ENTER A NUMBER"
250 INPUT A(X)
260 NEXT X
270 RETURN
400 REM ********
410 REM BAR(X):  SUBROUTINE TO PRINT HISTOGRAM BAR OF LENGTH X
420 REM ********
430 X = P
440 FOR Y = 1 TO X
450 PRINT "*";
460 NEXT Y
470 PRINT
480 RETURN
```

Fig. 8-14. Using GOSUB and RETURN to call a subroutine.

for a moment if the subroutine is used twice in the program, as shown in Fig. 8-13. Standard **GOTO**s cannot be used here since the **BAR** subroutine has to jump to different locations, depending on where it is called.

Subroutines can be handled in this fashion, but BASIC provides two instructions which simplify the process. **GOSUB** replaces the two statements to call the subroutine. **GOSUB** acts like **GOTO**, except that before it jumps it remembers the next line number.

The **RETURN** instruction is used to end the subroutine properly. **RETURN** also acts like **GOTO**, but needs no line number. It jumps to the line number the last **GOSUB** "remembers." Figure 8-14 replaces Fig. 8-12 by using **GOSUB** and **RETURN**. The first subroutine begins on line 200, and the second on 400; by separating the subroutines and main program, it is possible to modify one without disturbing the other.

MULTIPLE SUBROUTINE NESTING

Until now all subroutines have been accessed by the main program. Many times, however, subroutines use other subroutines, which in turn can use other subroutines. The subroutines are *nested.*

When designing the phone list program, a subroutine to increment the current record might have been written. This subroutine would have been used by all the subroutines to locate a name, delete a name, etc.

In a structured language, nesting subroutines poses no real problem; each subroutine has its own memory area, and there is no danger of a subroutine modifying the main

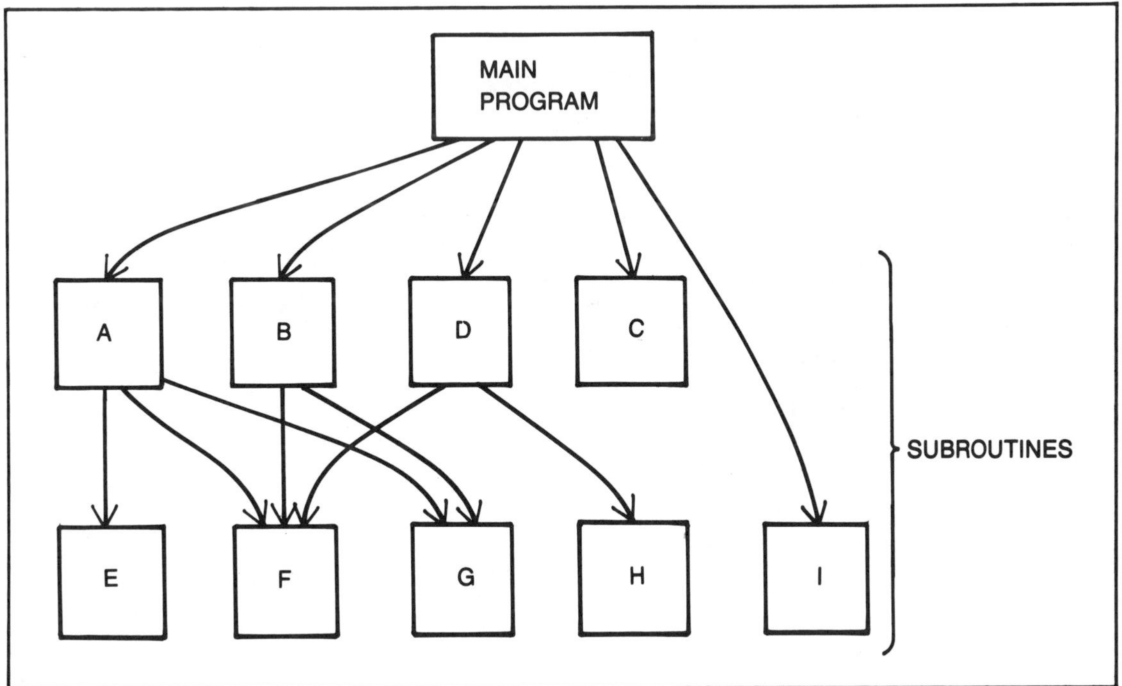

Fig. 8-15. A subroutine hierarchy.

program's or another subroutine's data. This danger *does* exist in BASIC. Not only that, but the method of passing parameters using an established set of variables becomes less effective.

Suppose subroutine A needs three numeric parameters: P1, P2, and P3. If A calls subroutine B, which needs two numeric parameters, P1 and P2 must be saved before B is called if A will need their values when B has ended. Solutions to this problem can be formulated after we take a closer look at subroutine nesting.

The graph in Fig. 8-15 shows the relationship between a main program and a set of eight subroutines. An arrow is used to connect the main program or subroutine to another subroutine it calls. Thus, the main program calls subroutines A, B, C, D, and I. A calls E, F and G. B calls F and G. D calls F and H. The other subroutines do not use subroutines.

As shown, the main program and subroutines make up a *hierarchy.* That is, if a path (a series of arrows) can be found from subroutine X to subroutine Y, then there

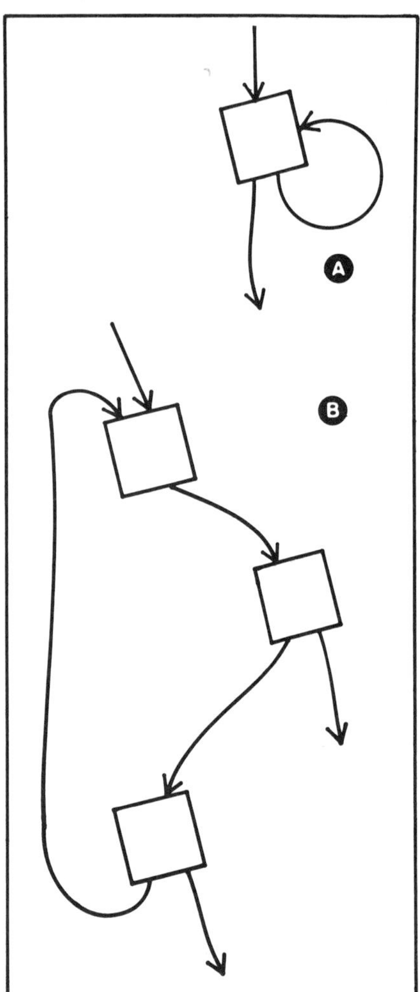

Fig. 8-16. Types of recursion.

must *not* be a path from Y to X. This eliminates the two types of connections shown in Fig. 8-16. The path in (A) shows a subroutine which calls itself. This is known as *recursion.* Recursion can be a powerful tool, but it is not supported in BASIC , although it can be simulated. Path (B) represents what is called a *cycle*, related to another form of recursion.

Because the graph in Fig. 8-15 does not contain recursion, certain conclusions can be drawn. If there is a path from subroutine X (or the main program) to subroutine Y, then Y is able to modify any data used by X. Therefore, the programmer must make certain Y does not modify data X is using. The easiest way to check for this is to compare the variable tables for the two subroutines. If both use the same variable, there is a good chance Y might change valuable information in X. One solution is to make sure Y uses no variables belonging to X. This solution becomes impractical in very large programs. If that is the case, the programmer must see where Y is called in X and make sure Y does not change data that is important to X. For example, X might use variable A, but not have anything of value in it when Y is called. Therefore, Y can modify A with no effect on X. But, if X were using A when Y was called, Y or X would have to be modified to not use A. Or X or Y might store A in another variable not being used, and then restore the value of A later.

SUMMARY

A *subroutine* is a program used within another program. It performs I/O with the main program through *parameters* and *side effects.* A parameter allows a copy of the value of a variable in the main program to be used in a variable in the subroutine, and is often termed a *call by value*. When a side effect is used, the subroutine directly modifies data from the main program; this is termed a *call by location.* The BASIC language supports only side effects.

To call a subroutine, an operation symbol with a horizontal line is used. The subroutine itself places the name of the subroutine in the start symbol and the word **RETURN** in the stop symbol. In BASIC, the **GOSUB** instruction calls the subroutine and **RETURN** places execution back in the main program.

Subroutines may also call subroutines. As a rule, a subroutine cannot call itself nor be called by a subroutine which it called directly or indirectly, a process called *recursion.*

EXERCISES

1. For the phone list program, design and incorporate subroutines to do the following:

   a) Print out a range of names. Accept two parameters: P1$ (first name in range) and P2$ (last name in range).
   b) Print out entries based on first name.

2. Modify BAR to accept a second parameter: the character from which to make the bar. Thus BAR(7,#) would print #######.

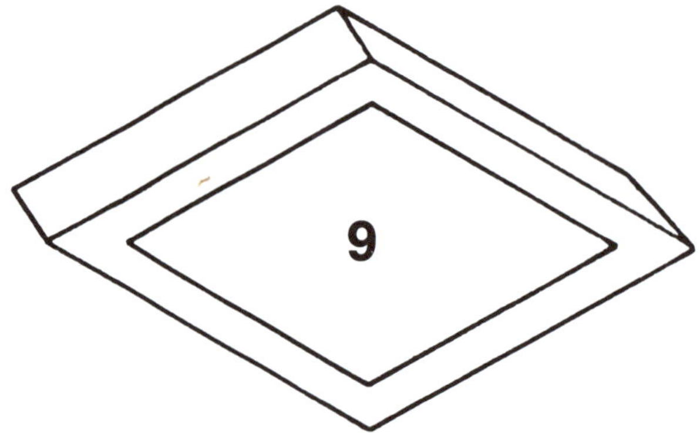

Data Manipulation and Data Flowcharts

The purpose of any program is to perform computations on some data to produce new data. Many times no new data results, but the old data is reorganized in some fashion. In this chapter we will discuss three typical data manipulation functions: *merging, extracting,* and *sorting.*

THE WORKING ENVIRONMENT

Data manipulation can occur during the three phases of a program: input, computation, and output. For example, input data from two devices can be merged before use. Data which is already stored, in a list for instance, can be sorted. During an output operation certain data rather than the entire collection of data can be extracted and sent to a device.

All operations take data from a source (either an input device or memory) and send it to a destination (either an output device or memory). Memory usually is, and often must be, either the source, destination, or both.

SORTING

The process of sorting embodies a large collection of algorithms which take a set of data items and produce another set, in which the order of the data has some property. Any process of sorting requires a "less-than" function: a function taking two data items and indicating which one is less than the other. If a list of names had to be sorted alphabetically, the function would indicate that "Jones" is less than "Small," which in turn would be less than "Smith."

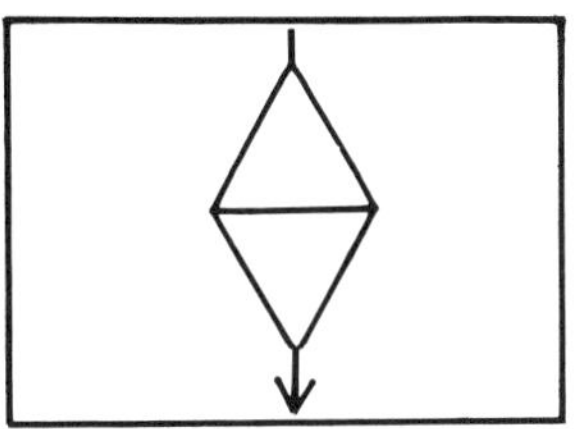

Fig. 9-1. The sort symbol.

Sorting can be a simple or complicated process depending on the speed required. The symbol for sorting is shown in Fig. 9-1, and an example using sorting is shown in Fig. 9-2. The sorting symbol can have an annotation symbol connected to it to document what data is being sorted and into what form it is being sorted. The program reads ten numbers into an array, sorts them into ascending order, and then writes them out.

Sorting is often used in business applications. Because such programs are quite large, it is difficult to show an example of sorting in proper context. The task now is to devise an algorithm which will perform the contrived sort shown in Fig. 9-2.

The algorithm we will examine is called the *selection sort.* The idea is to find the smallest number and move it to the beginning of the list. Then the next smallest number is found and moved to the next position, until the list is in order. Since numbers are being sorted, the relational less-than operator (<) can be used.

An example of how this algorithm would sort a list is shown in Fig. 9-3. The ar-

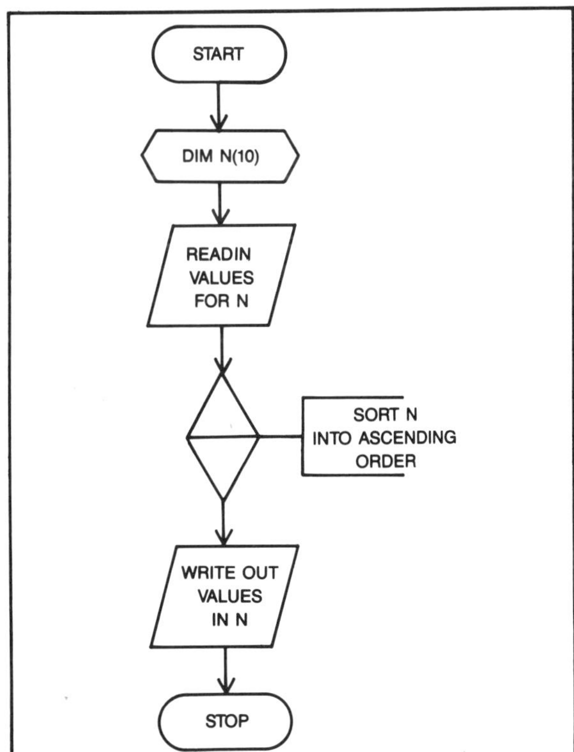

Fig. 9-2. A flowchart using sorting.

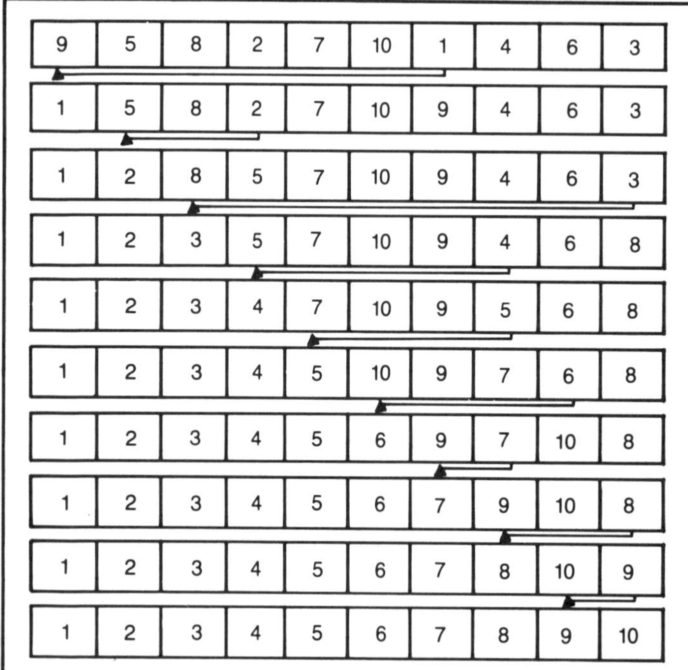

Fig. 9-3. An example of the selection sort at work.

rows show the switches are made to the list by the program. Each switch causes the next smallest number to be placed in its proper location. The algorithm to perform a selection sort is shown in Fig. 9-4. The program to perform the sort is Fig. 9-5.

An important attribute of a sorting algorithm is its stability. A stable sort does not alter the ordering of equivalent items. For example, consider a school's enrollment record. If the list was first sorted alphabetically and then by grade level, we would expect

```
The following algorithm sorts the ten elements in the array
A into ascending order.
 for
   I:= 1 to 9                  ——> for each location in array
 do
   X:= I                       ——> find smallest valve
   for
     J:= I + 1 to N
   do
     if
       A(J) < A(X)
     then
       X:= J
     fi
   od
   switch A(X) and A(I)        ——> place it in position
 od
```

Fig. 9-4. The selection sort.

```
10 REM ********
20 PRINT "SORTING PROGRAM"
30 REM ********
40 DIM A(10)
50 FOR I = 1 TO 10
60 PRINT "ENTER A NUMBER"
70 INPUT A(I)
80 NEXT I
90 FOR I = 1 TO 9
100 LET M = I
110 FOR J = I + 1 TO 10
120 IF NOT( A(J) < A(M) ) THEN 140
130 LET M = J
140 NEXT J
150 T = A(M)
160 A(M) = A(I)
170 A(I) = T
180 NEXT I
190 PRINT "HERE ARE THE SORTED NUMBERS:"
200 FOR I = 1 TO 10
210 PRINT A(I)
220 NEXT I
230 END
```

Fig. 9-5. A program using the selection sort.

the names within each grade to remain alphabetized; a stable sort would ensure this, while a non-stable sort would not.

In large business applications, the computer often does not have sufficient memory to store all the information that needs to be sorted at one time. In this case an *external sort* is used; portions of the data must be sorted and saved in a disk file and then merged or combined to preserve the sorted order. (Merging is the next topic of discussion.)

Sometimes a list containing two or more fields must be sorted. The sort is usually based on the contents of only one field. For example, consider an inventory list in which each entry contains the name of an item, cost, and quantity available. Suppose the list needs to be sorted so the names are in alphabetical order. If the list were stored using the array method described in Chapter 6, switching data items in the name array would require the associated costs and quantities to be switched in their arrays as well. The algorithm that does this sort is shown in Fig. 9-6. The only modification that needs to be made is two additional switch instructions.

MERGING

Merging is a process whereby two collections of similar data items are placed together. The process is often performed when the two data sets are in some sorted order.

```
The following algorithm sorts the ten elements in the arrays
A, B, and C based on the values of A.

 for
   I:= 1 to 9
 do
   X:= I
   for
     J:= I + 1 to N
   do
     if
       A(J) < A(X)
     then
       X:= J
     fi
   od
   switch A(X) and A(I)
   switch B(X) and B(I)
   switch C(X) and C(I)
 od
```

Fig. 9-6. Sorting a multi-field list.

The merge process combines the data so that the criterion for sorting is maintained.

The flowchart symbol that denotes merging is shown in Fig. 9-7. As with the sorting symbol, an annotation symbol can be used to explain the conditions of the merge. Figure 9-8 shows two lists, each containing a set of alphabetized names, and the list created by merging the two.

To merge two lists, it is necessary to have a less-than function. This is usually the same function used to sort the data being merged. An algorithm for merging is shown in Fig. 9-9. It simply looks at the first item in each list, picking off whichever is less than the other, and places it in a third list until the first two lists are empty. When one of the lists is emptied, the remaining elements are simply moved to the new destination.

USING SORTING AND MERGING

Sorting and merging are powerful tools, especially when used together. One common

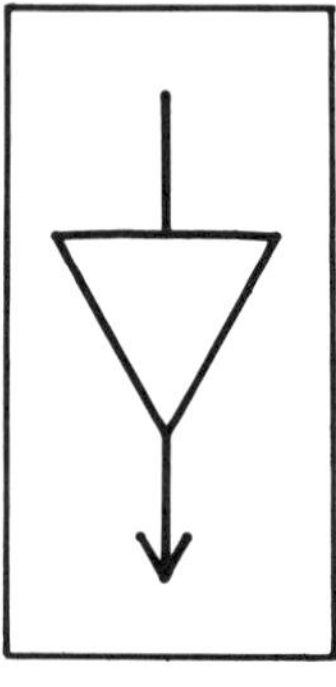

Fig. 9-7. The merge symbol.

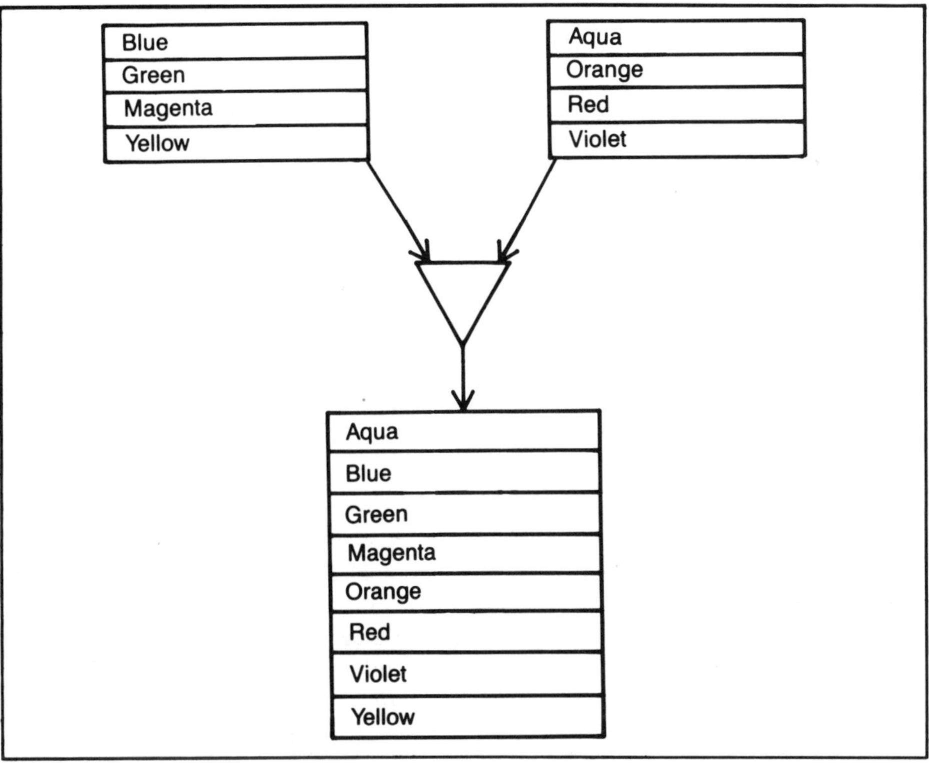

Fig. 9-8. An example of merging.

```
The following algorithm merges the two lists L1 and L2 into M.


while
  L1 and L2 are not empty
do
  if
    L1 is empty
  then
    I:= next item from L2
    remove item from L2
    add I to M
  fi
  else
    if
      L2 is empty
    then
      I:= next item from L1
      remove item from L1
      add I to M
    else
      I:= smaller item from L1 or L2
      remove item from appropriate list
      add I to M
    fi
  fi
od
```

Fig. 9-9. A merging algorithm.

situation is when a small amount of data must be added to a large sorted collection. One way to add the data is to simply append it to the end of the sorted data and then resort the entire list, a rather inefficient method, especially if an external sort must be done. A much better method is to sort the new data and then merge this with the old data. This results in great savings of time and computer resources.

The external sort is another use of merging. Figure 9-10 diagrams one of the ways an external sort takes place. An external sort divides the data into pieces small enough to fit in memory at one time. Then each segment is read and sorted. The segments are then merged together, in one of many different ways. The process shown first pairs the segments; a pass is made over the data during which each pair of segments is merged. The segments are then re-paired and theprocess repeated until only one segment is left.

EXTRACTING

Sorting does not change the total amount of data. This is also true of merging. *Extracting* lets data be removed, leaving data that possesses some quality.

In the phone list program, extraction occurred when names that began with a specified sequence of letters were printed. Extraction requires a selection function that indicates what data items to extract. The extraction symbol is shown in Fig. 9-11.

How extraction is performed depends on how the information is stored. If the data is in random order, the entire set must be checked to make sure all the required data is obtained. If the data is already sorted, extraction can often be simplified.

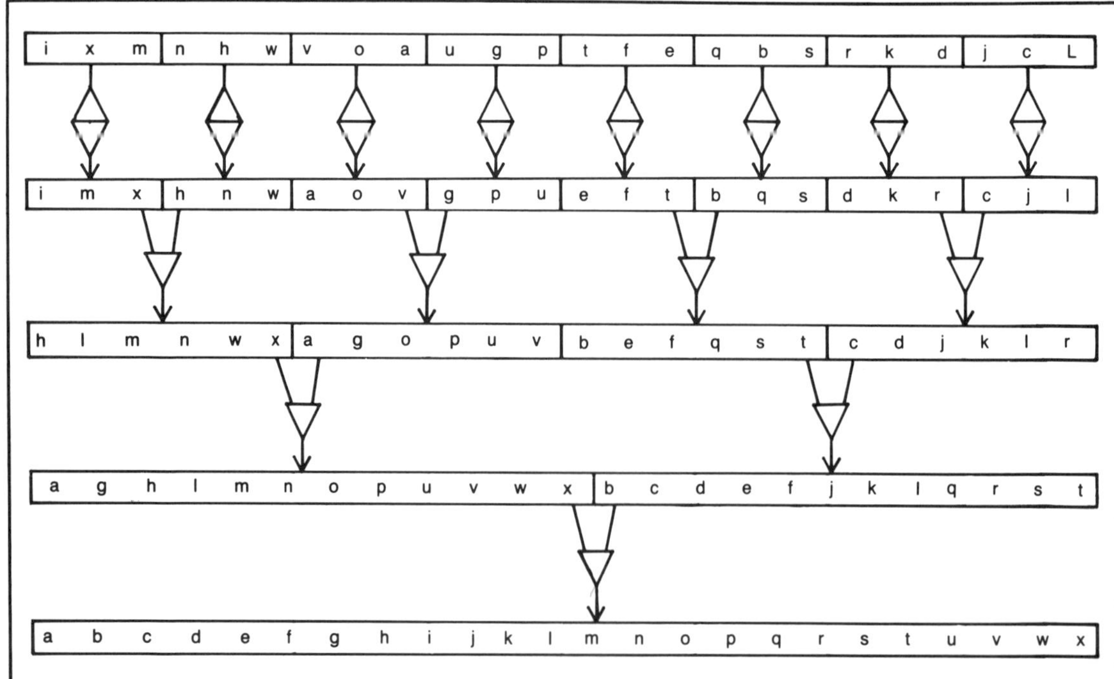

Fig. 9-10. An external sort at work.

Fig. 9-11. The extraction symbol.

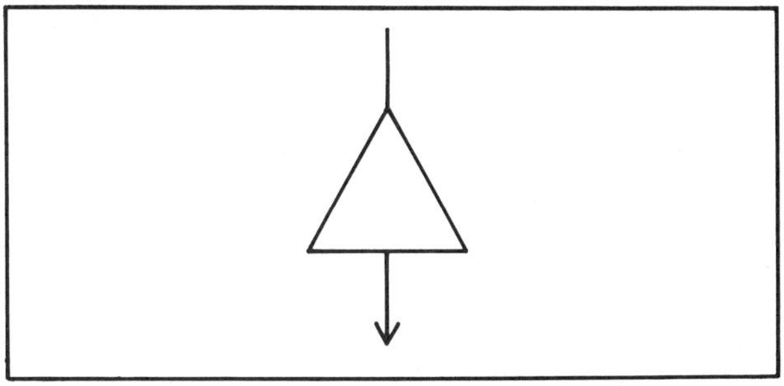

For example, consider a list of integers. If the integers are sorted in increasing order and all the numbers between 10 and 20 are to be printed, the program would skip to the first number in the range and continue to print entries until it reaches the first number exceeding that range.

An example of extraction is shown in Fig. 9-12. The procedure takes a set of integers stored in an array and prints all even numbers. The selection function takes advantage of the fact that an even integer divided in half is another integer, while an odd number halved is not. Therefore, 10 would be extracted because **10 / 2 = 5** and **INT(10 / 5) = INT(5) = 5**. However, 9 would not be extracted, because **9 / 2 = 4.5** and **INT(9 / 2) = INT(4.5) = 4.**

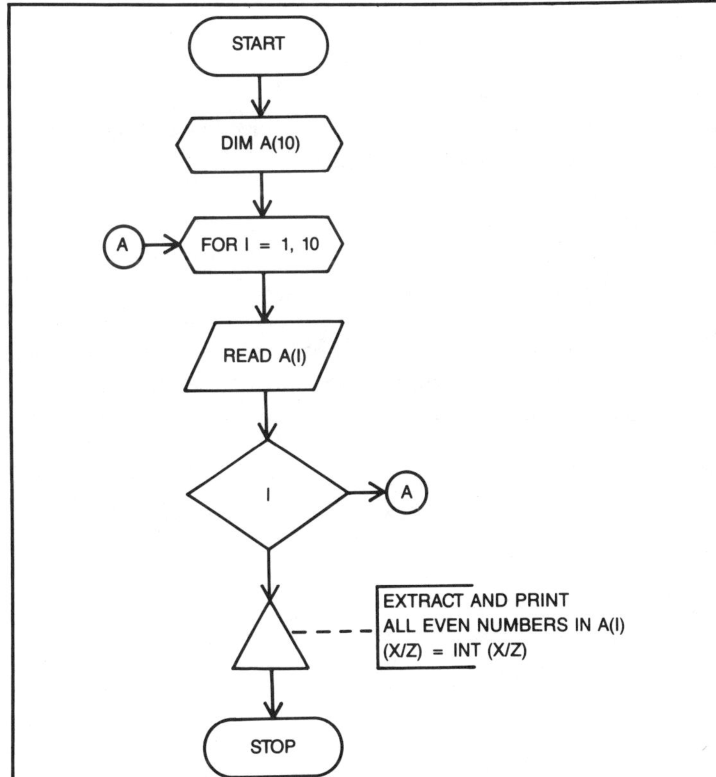

Fig. 9-12. A flowchart using extraction.

SUMMARY

There are three typical data manipulation functions which can be performed on a set of data: *sorting, merging,* and *extracting.* Sorting rearranges the data in the set so the ordering of data has some property. Merging combines two sorted sets of data so the final set has the same ordering property as the two smaller sets. Both sorting and merging make use of a "less-than" function. Extracting scans a data set and picks out only those items which have a desired property.

The *selection sort* is one example of a sorting algorithm. Basically, it finds the smallest element and places it at the beginning, then finds the smallest of the remaining elements and places it next, etc.

External sorts are performed when the data to be sorted cannot be contained in memory at the same time. The data is broken into smaller segments which can be sorted, and then the segments are merged.

EXERCISES

1. The selection sort can be easily modified to sort strings, since the "<" operator can be used on strings. That is, "**apple**" < "**banana**" is true while "**melon**" < "**cherry**" is false. Design a program which reads ten strings into an array and sorts them. Note: To switch **X** and **Y**, the following three instructions can be used:

```
LET T = X
LET X = Y
LET Y = T
```

(If you are lucky, your version of BASIC might have a statement called **SWAP** to perform this task. Check your manual.)

2. Modify the above program to read a quantity of each fruit into another array (for instance, 5 grapefruits, 10 lemons). Then sort the list alphabetically, keeping the array of quantities updated as well.

3. The phone list program from Chapter 6 uses a list of three arrays. Write a procedure to sort the three arrays based only on the last name. Keep the first name and phone number arrays updated accordingly.

4. Modify the procedure in problem 3 so that if the two last names are equal, the first names are checked to decide which is less than the other.

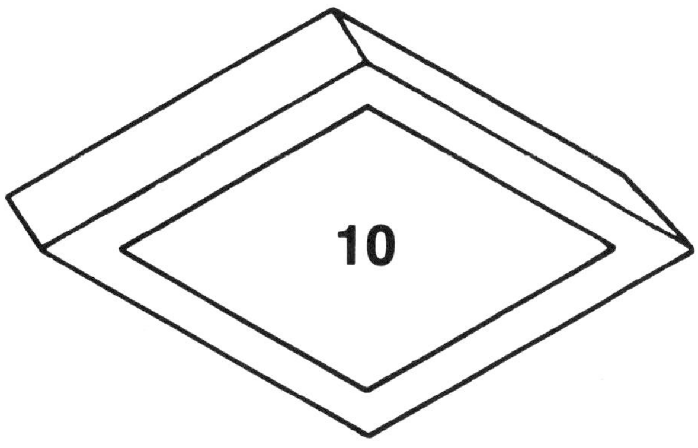

Special I/O Devices

Input and output (I/O) devices can be divided into two categories:

□ Information acquisition and display—These include devices such as printers, terminals, graphic tables, joysticks, light pens, etc. It is through these devices that data becomes available to the computer and data created by the computer is presented to the user.

The many different input devices are suited for different requirements. Input and output requirements can be split into graphic and alphanumeric categories. The graphic type requires devices such as light pens, graphic tables, joysticks, paddles, and to a lesser extent, keyboards. Alphanumeric data can be input via keyboards and such exotic devices as bar code readers, and scanners which "read" written material. We will look at the following output devices: display devices, printing devices, and plotting devices.

□ Mass storage—These devices store large quantities of data in a format from which it can be retrieved quickly and easily. The data can be stored on paper (card readers or paper tape) or on magnetic media. Cards are primarily used in situations where they must be handled by non-computer users, like payroll systems where cards are kept by employees who fill in their hours. Most mass storage devices use some sort of magnetic media: cassette tape, floppy disks, hard disks, and real tape.

OUTPUT DEVICES, OUTPUT NEEDS

Output devices take data from the computer and present it in an understandable way to the user, using letters, numbers, and symbols. Other features, such as graphics and color, can often increase the amount of data conveyed to the user.

Video Displays. Different types of displays are available for the wide variety of applications in which they are used. Two major types are *raster displays* and *vector* or *stroke displays*. A raster display forms an image by arranging dots in a rectangular grid. A vector display creates an image composed of line segments. The following are important attributes of display devices.

Resolution—The resolution of a display is the number of distinct locations which can be displayed in horizontal and vertical directions. A typical display can display up to 300 × 250 points. In a raster display, this would mean being able to display a dot anywhere in a 300 × 250 point grid. In a vector display, each line segment would have to begin and terminate on a point in a 300 × 250 point grid.

Color—Black-and-white displays are useful for word processing and other business applications, and usually give a sharper display (dollar for dollar) than color displays. Color displays vary as to the number of colors that are available. Some displays let the user select and display a fixed number of colors, such as eight, from a *palette* of several thousand to several hundred thousand colors.

Graphics—The ability to display graphics is inherent in vector displays. In raster displays graphics can be achieved in ways that depend on control over individual pixels. A *pixel* is a single point on a raster display. Some displays only display characters selected from a predefined character set containing letters, numbers, and characters such as @, #, &, and so on.

Some displays have special graphics characters which let the user create simple pictures. Figure 10-1 is an example of character graphics. This method is acceptable for applications where detailed graphics are not needed. Pixel graphics are needed to produce detailed graphics, by turning each dot on or off independently from those around it. Pixel graphics let you draw lines in any direction, as shown in Fig. 10-2. Notice the stair-step effect, inevitable when drawing angled lines on a raster display.

Printers. The printer is the most common device used to obtain a "hard copy" of computer output. The *dot-matrix* printer is the analog of the raster display; its output is formed by dots. "Character" printers form letters more like a conventional

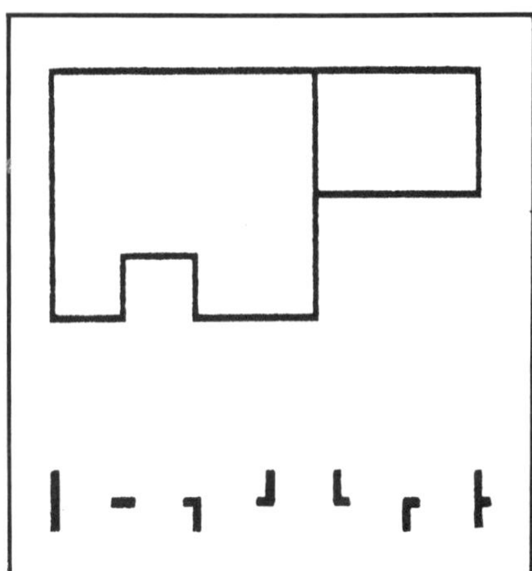

Fig. 10-1. Creating graphics with graphic characters.

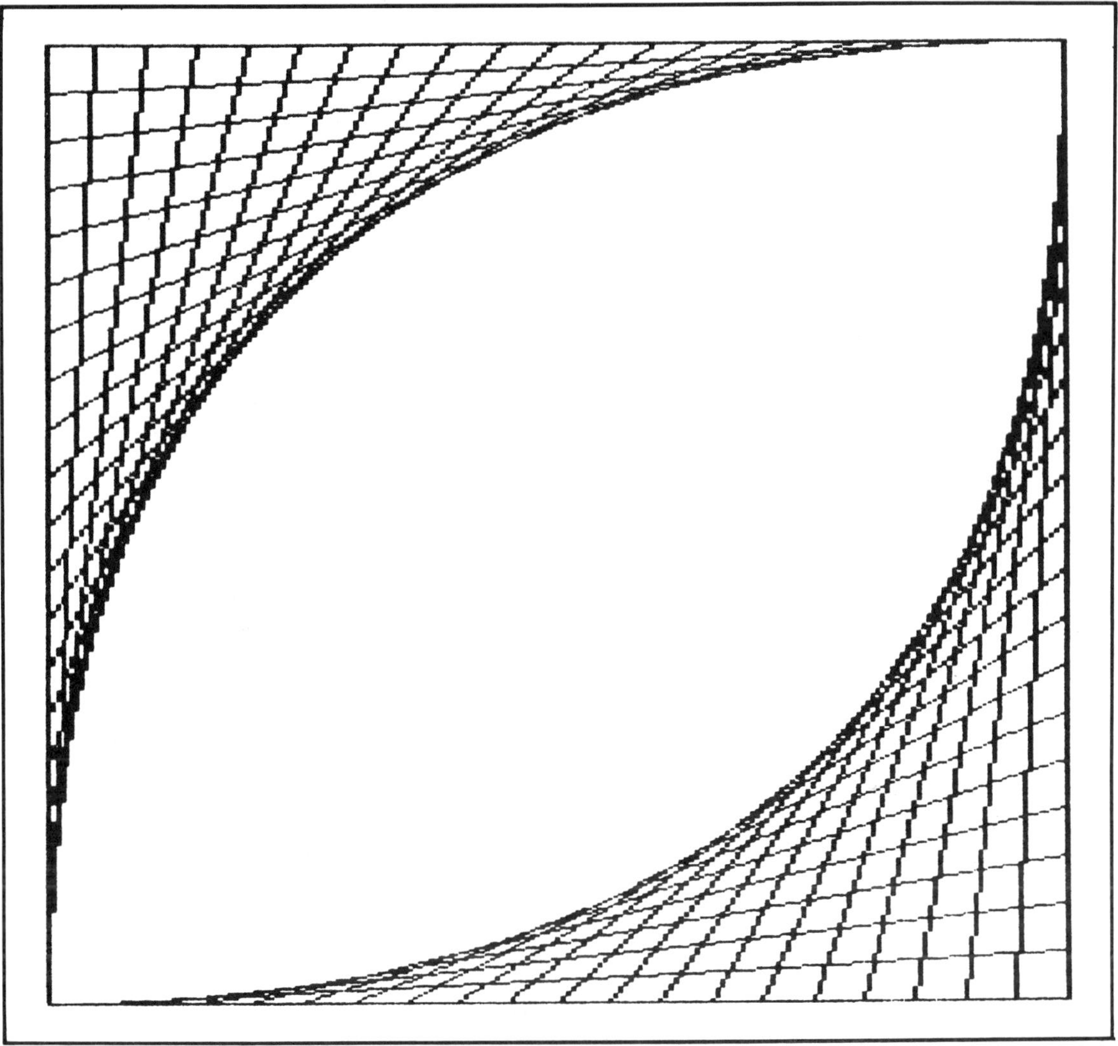

Fig. 10-2. An example of pixel graphics.

typewriter, although the actual mechanics of the process vary greatly. The following are important features of printers:

Speed—Small printers for home and small business uses will print from 30-150 characters per second. Larger, more expensive printers can produce up to 500 *lines* per second.

Graphics—This feature is often available on dot matrix printers. By letting the user control which dots are printed as the print head travels over the page, pictures and charts can be created.

Letter Quality—Letter quality refers to print of quality acceptable in business letters, reports, etc. All character printers tend to be letter quality, but tend not to be able to display graphics, and vice versa.

Color—In addition to graphics, some dot-matrix printers can print in different colors. However, the range of hues is often limited.

Plotters. Plotters are often indispensable when graphs and line drawings are needed. Plotters are to hard-copy devices what vector displays are to video devices. A plotter uses a pen which can be raised, lowered, and moved over the surface of a sheet of paper. Features include multiple pens which can be changed automatically, and microprocessors that let you plot characters and geometric figures automatically.

More important than knowing what types of output devices are available, is understanding how they can be used. Many problems can be defined in terms of output needs; a programmer must decide the content and appearance of the information being output. Output can be divided into two categories, *alphanumeric* and *graphic*.

Alphanumeric Data. Many programs present data as words and numbers:

Text—This category includes output which is read, such as business letters and reports. Such output is often created by word processors. When using a word processor, text is displayed on a video device as it is entered and edited and is printed when finished.

Tables—Many programs generate tables, such as income tax tables and tables of scientific data.

Spreadsheets—Basically, a spreadsheet is a grid of entries in which the values of some entries are computed using the values from other entries. The computer ensures that all entries are up-to-date, so if one entry is changed all entries that depend on it are changed automatically.

Graphics. Some types of graphic output are listed below:

Diagrams—Pictures such as line, bar, and pie charts are used in many business and scientific applications. Line charts display data which is dependent on other information (air pressure with respect to altitude). Pie charts show the distribution of a fixed quantity. Bar charts can be used to show a quantity with respect to different things (population with respect to country).

CAD—CAD stands for *computer-aided design.* CAD systems are used to design electronic circuits, automobiles, bridges, etc. These systems graphically display the item being designed.

Instruments—Computers are often used as control devices for such things as nuclear reactors. In such cases, the computer must display information about the different systems it monitors.

INPUT DEVICES AND NEEDS

We will look at the two most common of the countless input devices: the keyboard and the joystick.

The Keyboard. Keyboards represent a type of selection device: the data input must be selected from the keys available. Keyboards are most commonly used with terminals, but are also found on cash registers and similar data entry equipment.

The Joystick. This is a device that allows you to send a large quantity of data to a computer. Simple switch-type joysticks indicate whether the stick is being pushed in one of 16 directions. Other joysticks can indicate the angle in which the stick is positioned. In many applications it would take a three- or four-digit number to indicate the angles in the x-axis (side-to-side direction) and in the y-axis (up - and - down direction); the joystick alleviates the need to type cumbersome numbers on a keyboard. The joystick is often used as a positioning device to move data on a video tube. The computer repeatedly reads, or *polls*, the position of the joystick many times per second, updating the video display accordingly. Input devices fulfill the various input needs of a program:

Text—The need to input large quantities of text is most obviously met by using a word processor. Beyond that, text input is usually limited to short phrases: a program which maintains library records might require the user to input the title and author of a book when it is checked out. Or, you might need to input different phrases used to label a graph.

Numeric information—Includes accounting programs which require input of many numeric figures; or arcade games in which the player steers a car—the input device is a steering wheel, and the position of the steering wheel is converted into a number the computer uses to guide the car.

Measurements—Computers receive measurements from devices called *sensors*. There are sensors which can measure speed, direction, amount of fluid flow, etc. Measurements are usually necessary in computer systems that perform some sort of control.

Graphic Input—Used in programs that include CAD systems, which usually let the user input graphic data by using a joystick or light pen coupled with a video capable of displaying graphics. The user uses the input device to draw new shapes, move them, modify them, etc.

INTERFACING I/O DEVICES

All I/O devices must be interfaced to the computer system by one of two methods. Hardware interfacing connects the device electronically by a means mutually acceptable to the computer and the I/O device. Software interfacing transmits data between the user and the computer in a manner understandable and useful to both.

When text information is transmitted, most devices use *ASCII* as a format. ASCII (pronounced "AS-key") is used by many input and output devices and by most personal computers.

Information must also be interpreted correctly. If a program was expecting to read the time of day but received a date instead, it would attempt to process the information as the time of day. A user prompt would avoid this problem arising from human interaction. A similar problem exists with mass storage devices. If a program saves information using a certain format, the information must be read using the same format, or erroneous results will be produced.

FLOWCHART SYMBOLS FOR I/O NEEDS

Additional flowchart symbols are used in addition to the read/write symbol for I/O operations. The symbols are shown in Fig. 10-3.

The manual input symbol is used whenever a user is required to enter information. Although the outline of a keyboard is implied, input through any type of device

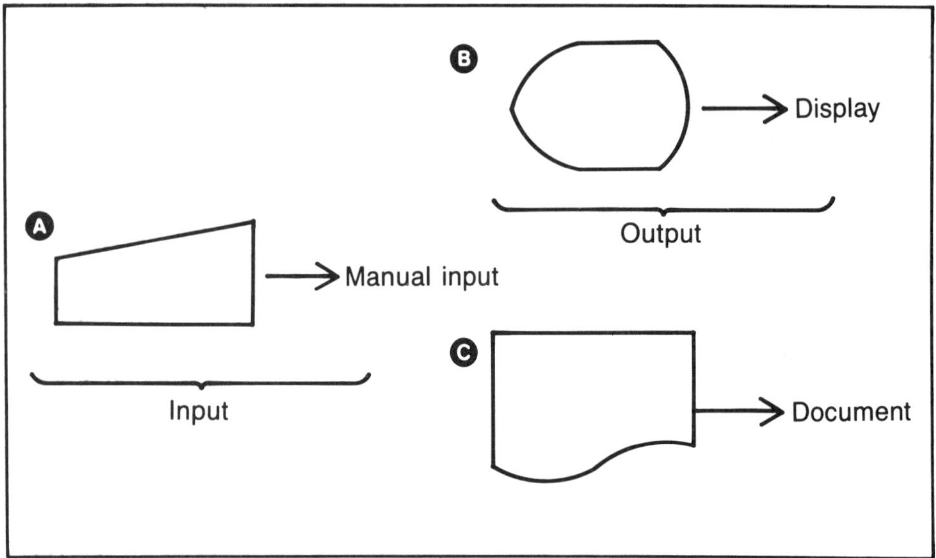

Fig. 10-3. Symbols for input and output needs: (A) manual input (B) display (C) document.

is valid. If a keyboard is not the device used, an annotation symbol is best included to clarify the process.

The document output symbol is used to show hard copy output. Plots, charts, and documents are all valid.

The display output symbol is used when output is directed to a device such as video display, etc. These output symbols are used exactly the same as the read/write symbol, with regards to connecting it to other symbols and the descriptions placed inside them.

USING THE I/O SYMBOLS

Let's look at a problem which requires us to make different I/O decisions. The problem will deal with analyzing the profits of a small company for a business year. The program must read expenses and gross income for each month, and then must compute the profit for that month and the total profit for the year up to that point in time. The profit for a month will equal the net income minus the expenses incurred. Figure 10-4 is a macro-flowchart which reads the data and computes the desired values. We must now decide how to output the information.

One way to display data is in a tabular format. An example of this type of output is shown in Fig. 10-5. To do this, two write symbols have to be added to Fig. 10-4. One write symbol placed before the loop prints the heading of the table. Another, inside the loop, writes each line of data as it is computed. A complete flowchart is shown in Fig. 10-6.

The flowchart we just developed isn't perfect. Data is read and written alternately; if the same device is used for input *and* output, the lines of input will be mixed with the table being output. Many small computer systems use dual I/O lines, so another

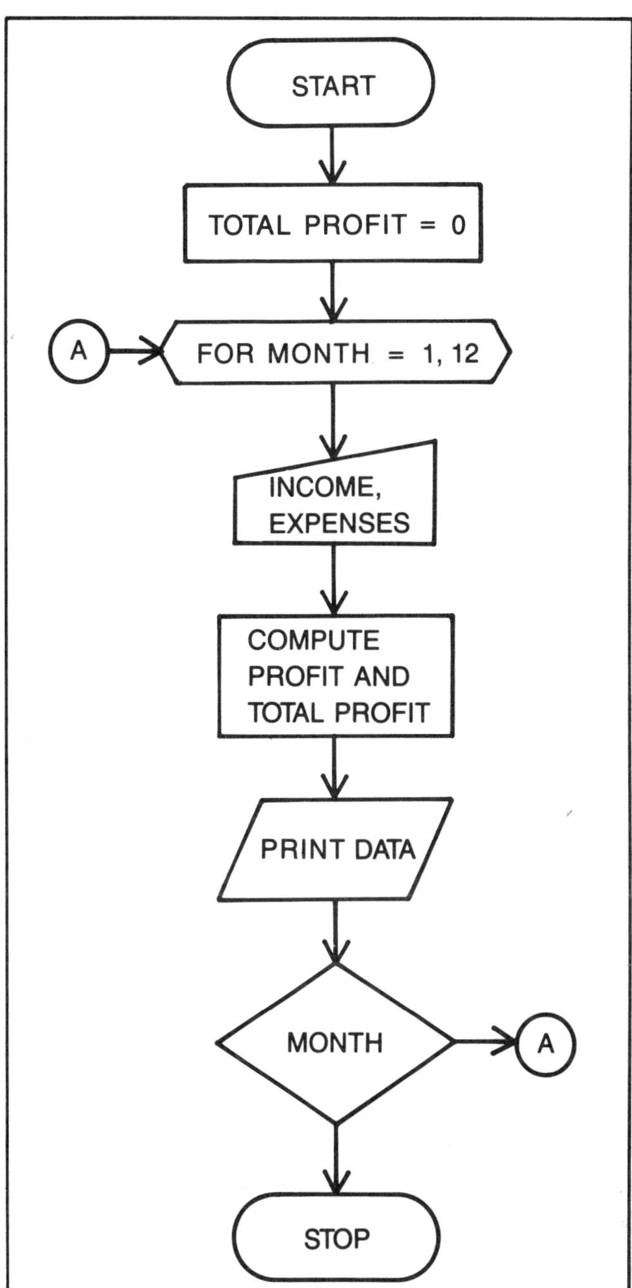

Fig. 10-4. Macro-flowchart for profit program.

solution must be found. The solution is to first read the data into an array and then usc thc data in thc array to produce the table. Figure 10-7 shows how arrays would be used for this purpose.

Flowcharting I/O symbols only represents the medium being used; that does not convey how the information is to be read or what the output will look like.

Month	Income	Expenses	Profit	Total Profit
=====	======	========	======	============
1	1200	800	400	400
2	1400	850	550	950
3	1500	925	575	1525
4	1550	950	600	2125
5	1800	1000	800	2925
6	1750	1100	650	3575
7	1825	1050	775	4350
8	1700	1000	700	5050
9	1600	950	650	5700
10	1450	975	475	6175
11	1300	900	400	6575
12	1225	850	375	6950

Fig. 10-5. A table of profits.

SUMMARY

There are many different input and output devices, suited to a variety of applications. What devices are used depend on the requirements of the situation.

Output devices include video displays, printers, and plotters. The choice of which device to use depends on whether a type of alphanumeric data or graphic data is needed.

Input devices include light pens, joysticks, keyboards, etc. Input requirements include text, numeric information, measurements, and graphic data.

There are three special flowchart symbols for I/O. One symbol is for input, and the other two are for display and hard copy output. These symbols only indicate what device is being used; they do not indicate the how the data looks.

EXERCISES

1. Convert the flowchart in Fig. 10-7 into a BASIC program.

2. Based on the program above and the **BAR** subroutine in Chapter 8, develop a program which displays both a table and a histogram.

3. The phone directory program in Chapter 6 used a menu to read a command. Another method is to read a command word. For example, the program would print:

Command?

and the user would enter one of four words:

ADD, **DELETE**, **PRINT**, or **QUIT**.

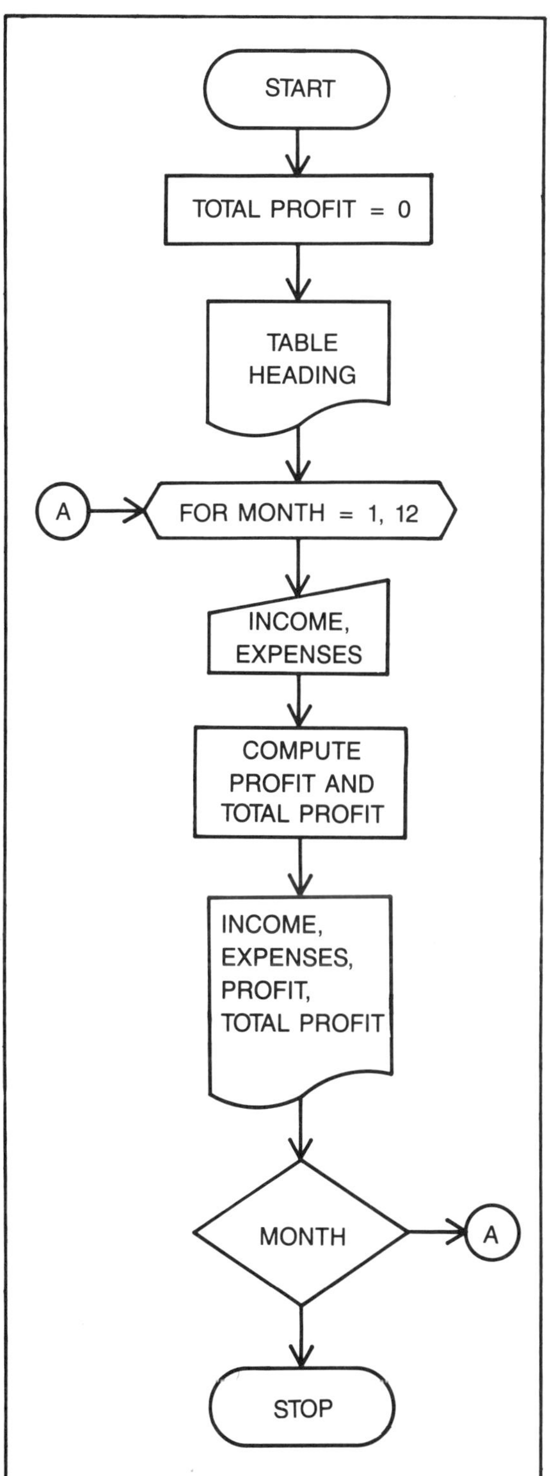

Fig. 10-6. Flowchart to create table of profits.

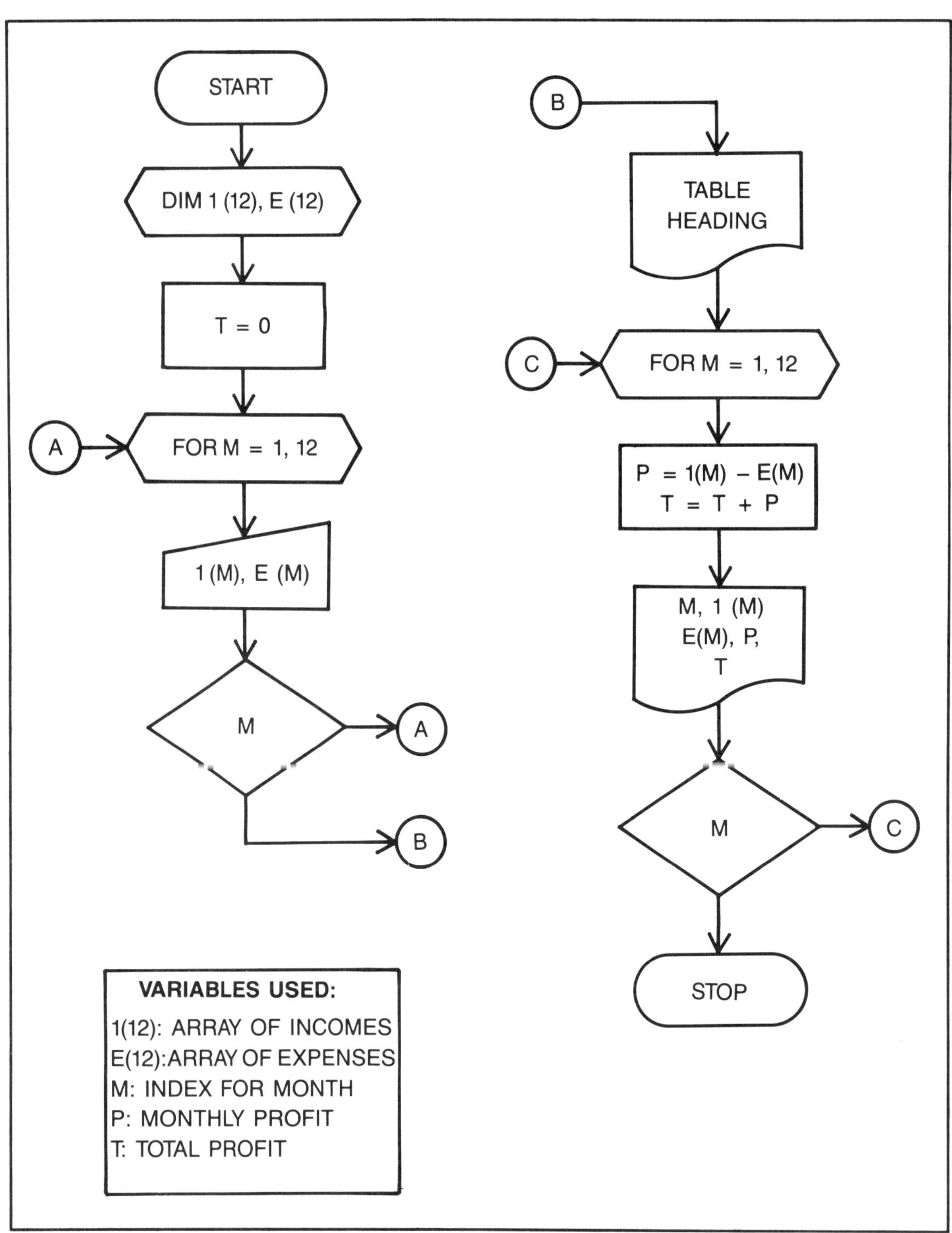

Fig. 10-7. Using arrays to separate input and output.

Modify the program to use this method of input.

4. Another way to modify the phone directory program is to let the user include "operands" to a command. Modify the program so the print command will look like:

```
PRINT MAC
```

which will print all the names beginning with the letters MAC. Then modify the other commands in a similar fashion.

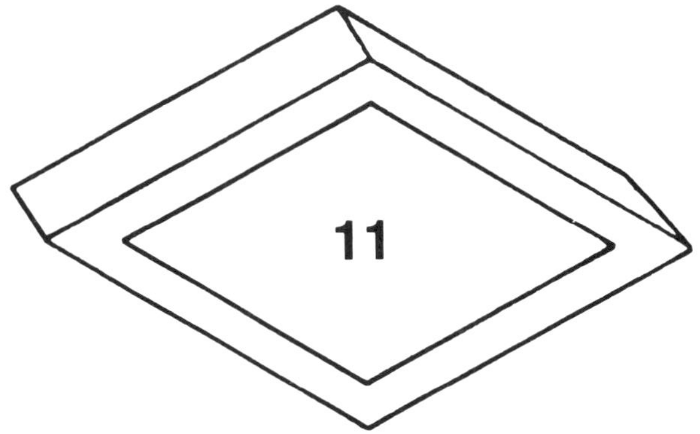

Mass Storage Devices

Mass storage devices are indispensable; they store large amounts of data the computer can access and modify quickly.

STORAGE CONCEPTS

At the most elemental level, data is stored as a sequence of bytes. The bytes are grouped into larger elements, called *fields.* A field is considered to be a single piece of data—a numeric value, for instance—which can be placed into a variable. It is very inefficient to transfer a single field between a computer and a mass storage device, so the fields are grouped together into *records.*

The format of a record is a description of the type and order of each of its fields. A record format might be a numeric field, followed by a string field, followed by a second numeric field.

A *file* is a collection of records. All the records in a particular file must have the same format. Files let a computer handle large quantities of data to be copied, erased, and transferred. Programs can also manipulate individual records within a file many different ways. The divisions of a file are shown in Fig. 11-1, except for the byte level; different computers store numbers and strings differently at this level.

FILE OPERATIONS

Programs perform various operations on files. Although BASIC often treats the following operations differently than described, programmers must solve problems conceptually as if the descriptions presented here held true in BASIC.

```
The following codes are used:
A, B, C, D, E:  different types of fields
      M, N, O:  different records
      X, Y, Z:  different files
FIELD LEVEL              RECORD LEVEL              FILE LEVEL
===========              ============              ==========

     A
     C                        N
     D

     A
     C                        N
     D
                                                       Z
     A
     C                        N
     D

     A
     C                        N
     D

     E
     C                        O
     D
     B

     E
     C                        O                        X
     D
     B

     E
     C                        O
     D
     B

     A                        M
     D
                                                       Y
     A                        M
     D
```

Fig. 11-1. Components of a file.

Opening. Opening must be performed before data can be added to or read from a file. When a file is opened, the format of the data must be given. This format, or *template,* indicates the name of each field and the type of data it can contain.

A section of memory is set aside for template variables. Template variables are similar to memory variables, but their purpose is to hold data being transferred to and from the file. Also, a current record is established. The current record keeps track of where the next record is to be read from or written to. How the current record is used will be discussed shortly.

In multi-user computer systems, opening a file often has the effect of preventing other users from using the file; when they attempt to open the file they receive an error message. Opening a file which does not exist usually causes it to be created.

Writing. Writing to a file lets new information be stored. To add a new record, the new information is first stored in the file template. Then a write command transfers the data from the template to the file. The record is inserted at the location of the current record.

Reading. Reading, the inverse of writing, lets data be transferred from the file to the computer. To read data, a read command transfers the information stored in the record pointed to by the current record to the file template. The data in the template can then be referenced and used.

Closing. When a program is finished using a file, the file is closed. Certain housekeeping operations are performed and the record template is removed from memory. In a multi-user system, the file is made available to other users.

METHODS OF FILE ACCESS

There are two methods by which data in files can be accessed. The main difference is the programmer's control over the current record.

Sequential Mode. When a file is opened in sequential mode, it is restricted to *either* reading or writing. As a further hindrance, the programmer has no control over the current record. Rather, when a file is opened for reading it is set to the first record in a file. When a file is opened for writing, it is set to the end of the file after the last record. Whenever a read or write operation is performed, the current record is incremented to the next position. The effect is that the data must be accessed one piece at a time, and it isn't possible to skip back to a previous record.

Random Access Mode. When a file is opened in random access mode, its current record can be modified. Also, both reading and writing may be performed. When using a random access file, an additional command, *locate,* is needed. The locate command lets the current record be changed. Records are usually labeled numerically with the first record in a file being record 1. Thus, a LOCATE 10 operation would set the current record to the tenth record.

Figure 11-2 gives general instructions for programming sequential and random access files.

BASIC AND FILES

The file-handling capabilities of BASIC vary depending on the version being used. Some do not support files at all. If files are supported, they are usually sequential. The follow-

Instructions for Sequential File Input

OPEN n,"file name",INPUT	—Prepares file for input
INPUT n,variables	—Reads data from file
CLOSE n	—Closes file

Instructions for Sequential File Output:

Open n,"file name",OUTPUT	—Prepares file for output
PRINT n,variables	—Places data in file
CLOSE n	—Closes file

Instructions for Random Access Files:

OPEN n,"file name",RANDOM,field variables	—Prepares file
LET field variable = data	—Places data in field variable
PUT n	—Writes record to file
GET n	—Reads record from file
CLOSE n	—Closes file

Note: n is a number used to identify the different files being used.
Only one file may be open at a time with the same file identifier.

Fig. 11-2. BASIC I/O instructions.

ing is a brief description of how sequential files might be supported by BASIC. Typically, when BASIC opens a sequential file, no record templates are used. Instead, the user writes to a file using a version of the PRINT statement, and reads from a file using a similar version of the INPUT statement.

EXAMPLES OF MASS STORAGE DEVICES

Probably the most simple mass storage device is the cassette tape recorder. Because it is inexpensive, it is used with many personal computers. However, slow speed limits its use to non-business applications; and only sequential files are permitted, and often they must be read or written all at once.

Magnetic tape drives are analogous to cassette tape but are much faster, can store much more on a tape (which is much larger than a cassette), and are more flexible with regard to file control. However, like cassette players, they are sequential in nature—the tape must be scanned until the right location is found.

The floppy disk drive uses a circular piece of magnetic medium, shown in Fig. 11-3; information is recorded on it in concentric circles called *tracks.* The floppy disk is a random access device because the recording head is able to move directly to the location of a particular piece of data.

The big brother of the floppy disk is the hard disk. A hard disk uses rigid plates of magnetic medium. Hard disks are used in computer installations where high storage capacity and fast data transfer is needed.

MASS STORAGE NEEDS

From a programming point of view, the mechanics of a mass storage device is often irrelevant. Depending on the device, the access modes available will differ. But once the access mode is chosen, the device remains "hidden" behind the different file operations available. For example, a write operation is usually the same no matter what device is being written to, but the programmer still must decide what device will best suit the program application.

It is not as easy to categorize mass storage needs as it is to categorize input and output requirements. It is often more important to look at the quantity of data and the speed at which it is needed.

Data Quantity. When the quantity of data grows large, the cost of storing it becomes a predominant factor. When data is very numerous, as with the government's Social Security files, magnetic tape is used. With smaller amounts hard disk drives become feasible. For small storage needs, floppy disk drives are a good choice.

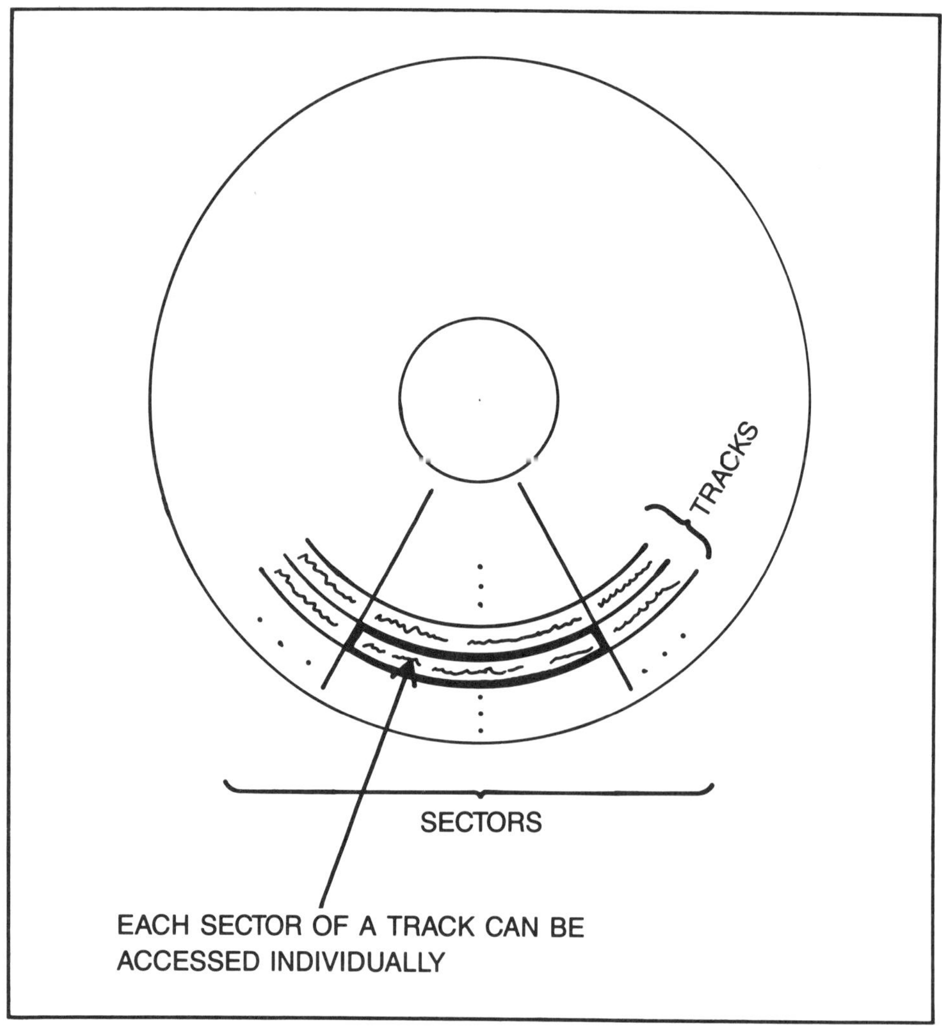

Fig. 11-3. How data is stored on a floppy disk.

Access Time. Balanced against the cost of data storage is the cost of finding and transferring data quickly. Hard disks are quickest, followed by tape drives and floppy disks.

FLOWCHART SYMBOLS FOR MASS STORAGE

A variety of special symbols represent different mass storage devices; Fig. 11-4 shows

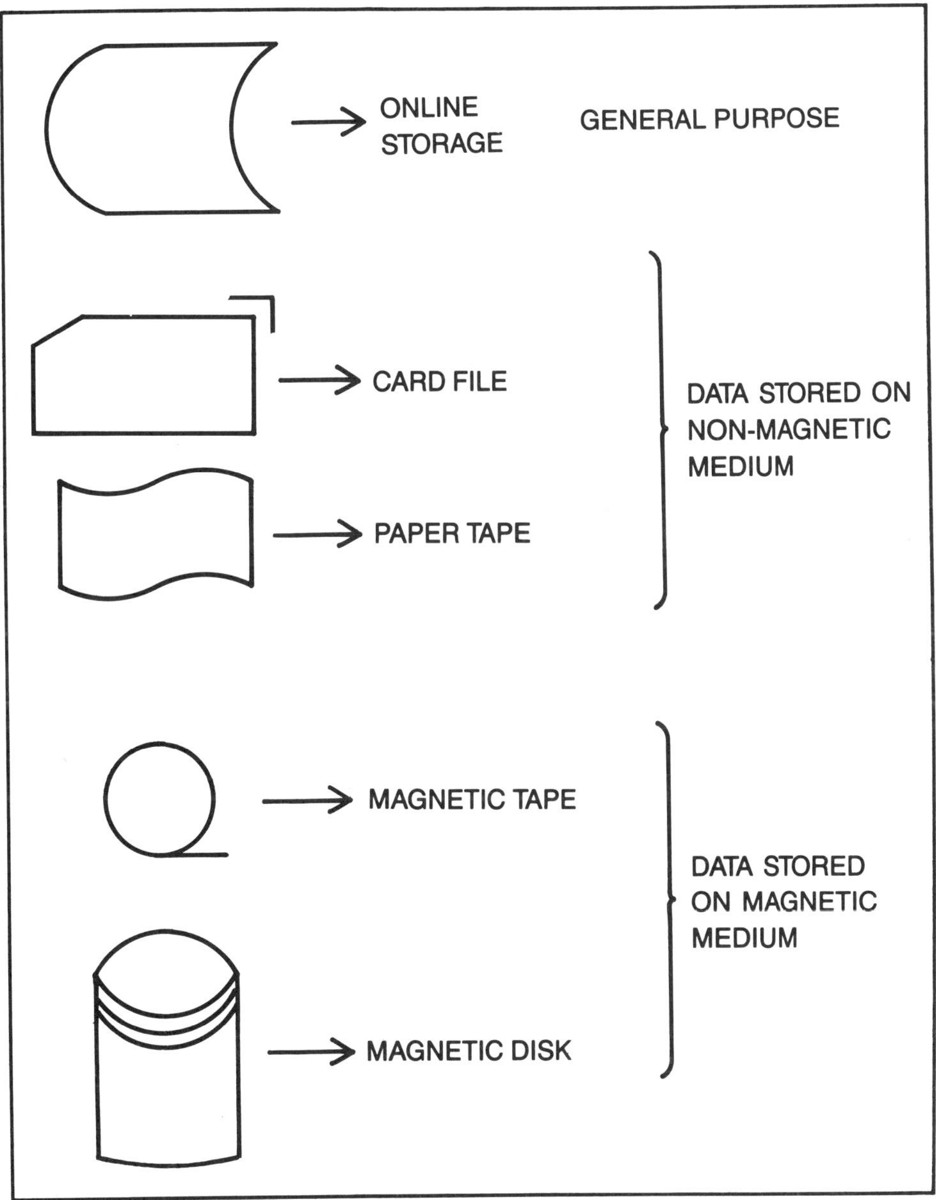

Fig. 11-4. Flowcharting symbols for mass storage devices.

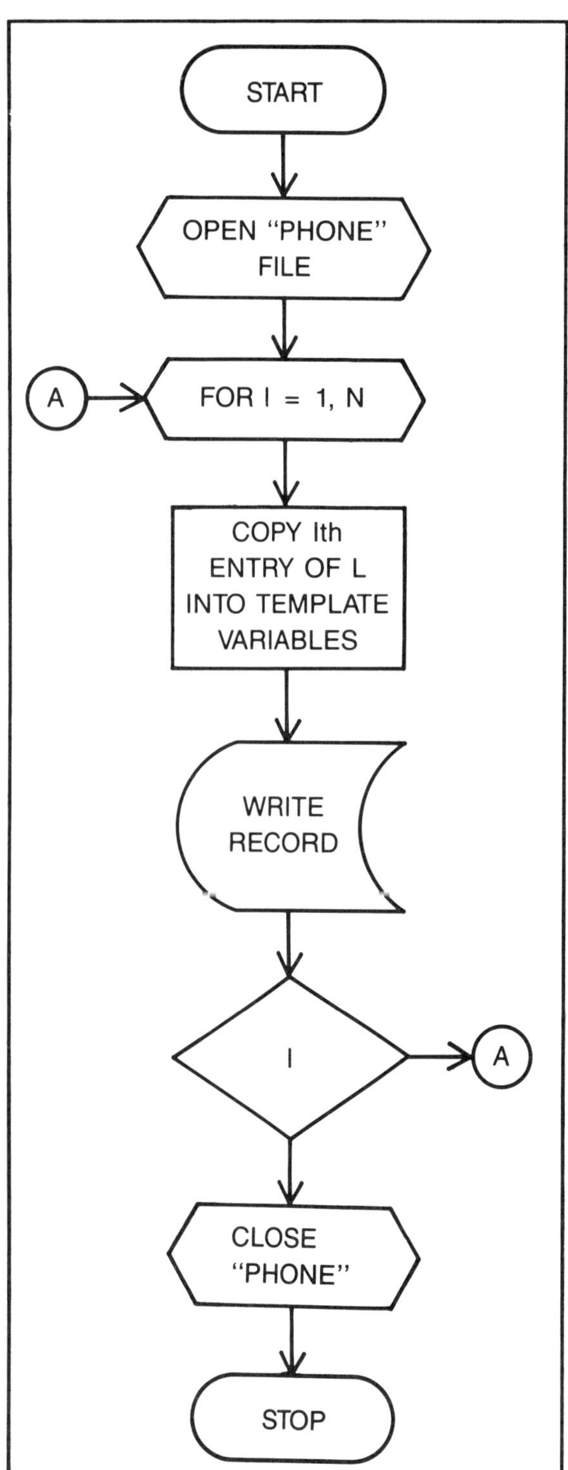

Fig. 11-5. Algorithm to save a list with template variables.

some of them. The symbols are used in place of the read/write symbol, to show I/O with the device they represent. The off-line storage symbol is a generic symbol, appropriate for cassette tape or floppy disks.

Mass storage symbols only show what the data is stored on, they do not show the format of the data. The symbols usually aren't used for operations such as opening

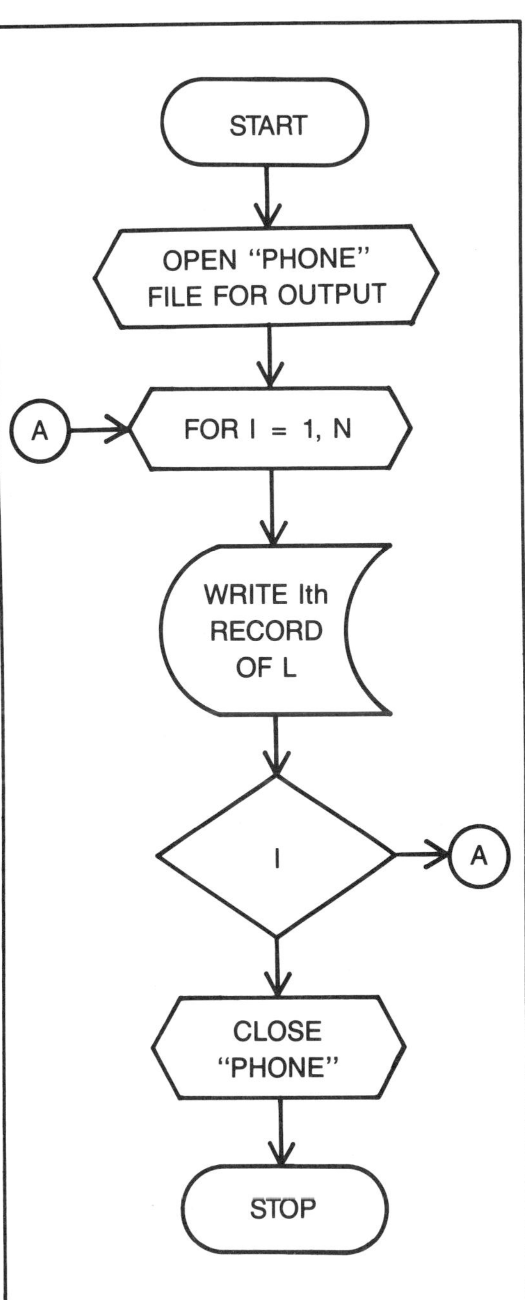

Fig. 11-6. Algorithm to save a list without template variables.

or closing; the preparation symbol is more appropriate for that purpose. When a file is opened, the format of each record should be noted.

AN EXAMPLE

The phone directory program is not useful because it is incapable of saving the list of entries and reading them back. Let us now solve the first problem: saving the list.

The list is stored in memory in the same way it will be stored in a file, so creating the file template is easy. It will consist of three fields: the last name, first name, and phone number.

A subroutine saving the names in the file "phone" is shown in Fig. 11-5. After opening the file, each entry is copied into the template variables and a write operation is performed to write the data into the file. Finally, the file is closed.

On BASIC systems which do not use template variables, the flowchart would look like Fig. 11-6. Data is written directly into the file from the arrays.

Typical subroutines using these methods are shown in Fig. 11-7. The one using template variables is used with random access files; the one which doesn't is used with sequential files. In both cases, the number 1 identifies the file in the file operation instructions.

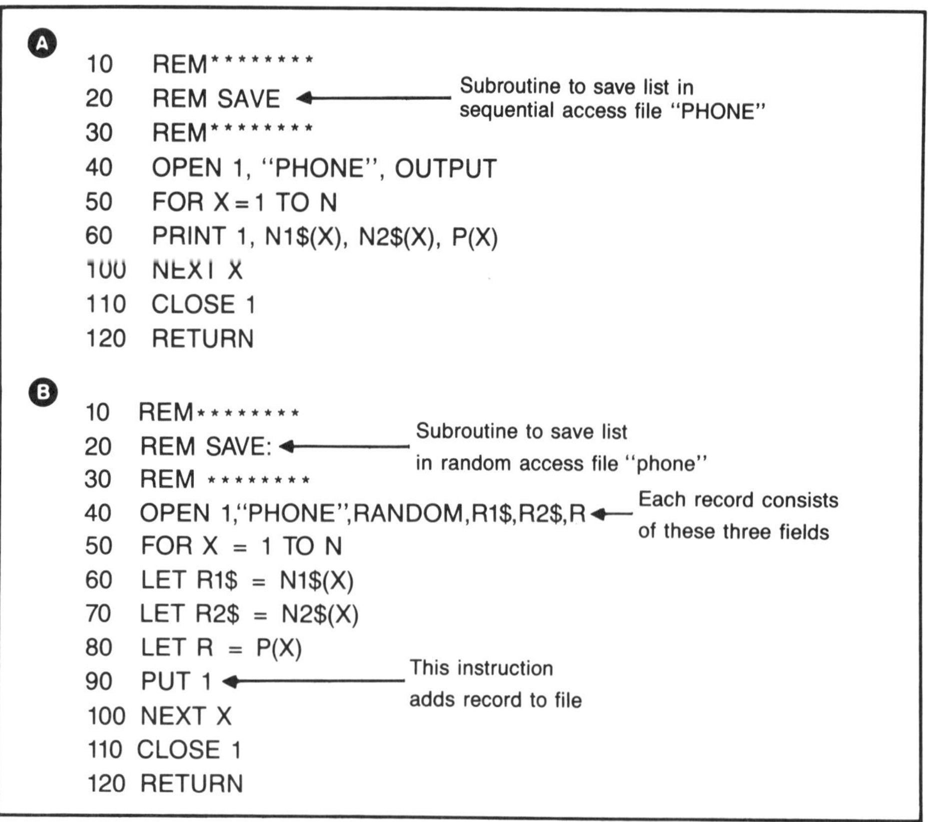

(A)

```
10   REM********
20   REM SAVE  <-------  Subroutine to save list in
                         sequential access file "PHONE"
30   REM********
40   OPEN 1, "PHONE", OUTPUT
50   FOR X=1 TO N
60   PRINT 1, N1$(X), N2$(X), P(X)
100  NEXT X
110  CLOSE 1
120  RETURN
```

(B)

```
10  REM********
20  REM SAVE: <-------  Subroutine to save list
                        in random access file "phone"
30  REM ********
40  OPEN 1,"PHONE",RANDOM,R1$,R2$,R <--  Each record consists
                                         of these three fields
50  FOR X = 1 TO N
60  LET R1$ = N1$(X)
70  LET R2$ = N2$(X)
80  LET R = P(X)
90  PUT 1 <-------  This instruction
                    adds record to file
100 NEXT X
110 CLOSE 1
120 RETURN
```

Fig. 11-7. BASIC subroutines for saving a list: (A) sequential (B) random access.

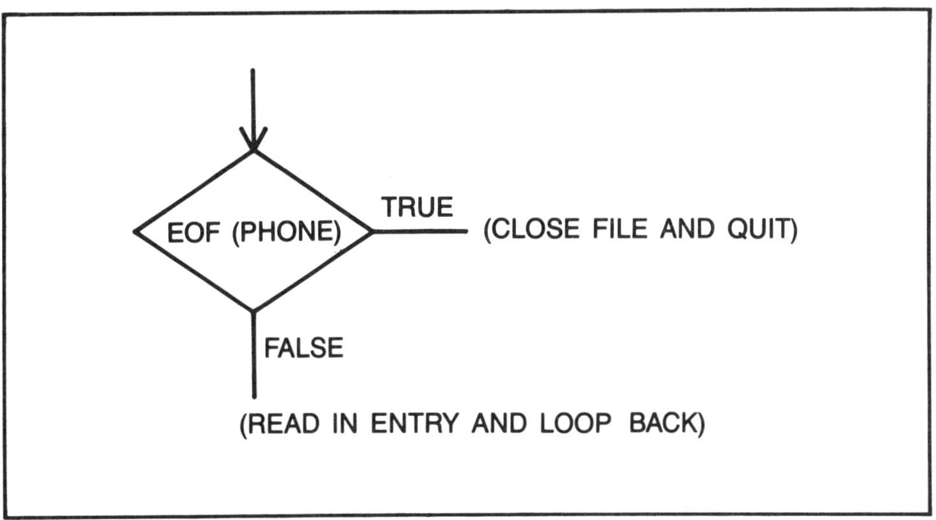

Fig. 11-8. Decision symbol to test for end of file.

SUMMARY

A *file* is a set of records which contain *fields.* The concept of a file is similar to that of a list. Four operations can be performed on a file: *opening, writing, reading,* and *closing.* There are two types of files. *Random access files* allow the current record to be modified by the user. In *sequential files,* the current record cannot be changed; it scans the file one record at a time.

Mass storage needs are quantified by the amount of data stored and the speed at which it needs to be accessed. There are a variety of flowcharting symbols to represent the different mass storage devices.

EXERCISES

1. Most versions of BASIC provide a function called **EOF(file)** (**file** is the name of the file), which is true if the end of the file has been reached, and false if it hasn't. Using the **EOF** function, write a subroutine to read data from the "phone" file into the list. Before reading, initialize the list. The decision symbol in Fig. 11-8 will be needed.

2. Translate the flowchart above into BASIC, using the following instructions: **GET 1** to read a record into template variables; **INPUT 1** to read directly into memory variables; and **OPEN 1, PHONE, INPUT** to open a sequential file for input.

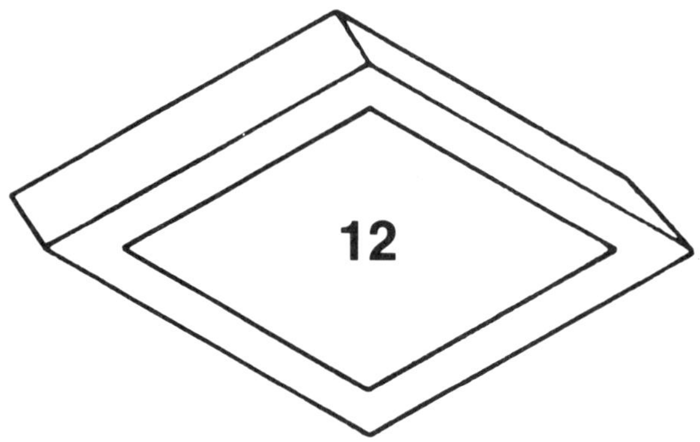

System Flowcharts

I have alluded to an additional use for flowchart symbols. The allusion is to *system flowcharts*, which treat programs as a whole. They show the relationships between a program, or programs, the input data needed, and the output data produced.

PREPARING A SYSTEM FLOWCHART

When preparing a system flowchart, four basic components must be identified. Three components relate to the three functions of a program: input data, programs (computation), and output data. The fourth component is data files.

Data files can be treated as both input data and output data by one or more programs. However, unlike input or output data, which is concerned with data communication with humans, data files represent the ability to store and send information between different programs through mass storage devices.

We will consider theses components within the example of a record-keeping system for a library.

Identifying System Needs

First we need to identify the requirements of the system as a whole. For a library system, some desired functions might be lending books—the system should perform the record-keeping necessary to keep track of which books are signed out, and be able to report the status of any book or books. Also, preparing overdue notices should be a system function.

Data Files

It is usually best to identify the data files that will be needed in a particular situation, since many times the other components are designed around the data files. For example, storing often-used information in a data file can sometimes reduce input needed from a user.

One data file implied by the system requirements we decided on is a record of all the books in the library (which will be referred to as the **BOOK** file). For each book, information such as the title, author, subject, and data of publication should be stored. One other piece of information, called a *key*, would be needed. A key is a unique value assigned to each entry in the file. For the **BOOK** file, the key can simply be a number which is different for each book. The value of the key assigned to each book would be printed on the book itself.

Another useful file is a collection of all people who have a library card (which will be called the **MEMBER** file). The address and phone number of each person, along with a unique key for each, would be stored. Unlike the **BOOK** file, the key for the **MEMBER** file would not have to be arbitrary; a Social Security number would do nicely.

A third file that will be needed, called the **LEND** file, will store records identifying books that have been signed out, and the borrower. Each record in this file will identify a book, a person, and a due date. As with the **BOOK** and **MEMBER** files, keys play a role in the **LEND** file, but their function is different. Each record will have a key referring to a book in the **BOOK** file, and a second key referring to a person in the **MEMBER** file. This combination of book key and member key serves as the key; there is no need to create another. It is perfectly legal to say "I want to search for a record in the **LEND** file with a book key of 38492 and a person key of 111-11-1111."

To represent a data file in a system flowchart, the name of the data file is placed inside the symbol which stands for the mass storage device that will be used to read or write the data. Since the quantity of information described by these data files is large, a hard disk system would probably be used. Thus, each data file is represented by placing the file name inside the disk I/O symbol shown in Fig. 12-1.

Program Needs

Often a system flowchart will deal only with a single program. Large systems are broken down into a collection of programs which work together. The rules for flowcharting a single program system are the same.

The library system will be broken into three programs. The lending program, will

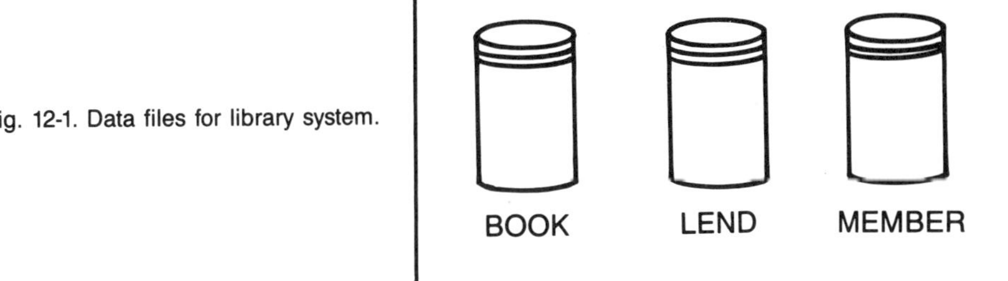

Fig. 12-1. Data files for library system.

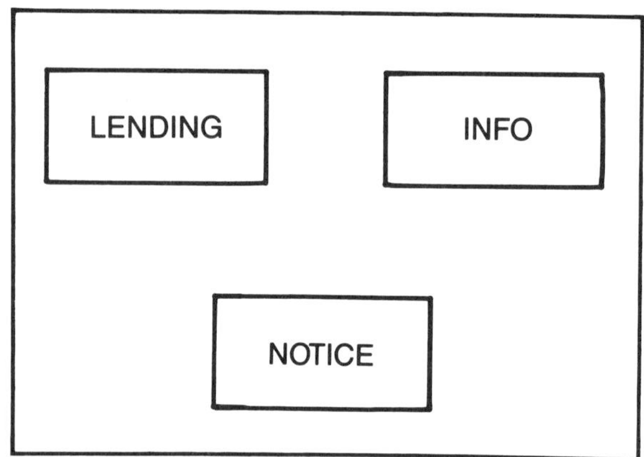

Fig. 12-2. Programs in library system.

add and remove data from the **LEND** file. The info program will search the three data files and print information, such as whether a particular book is signed out, what books a borrower has, etc. The notice program will generate overdue notices.

To represent a program in a system flowchart, the operation symbol is used, with the name of the program placed inside. Figure 12-2 shows the program symbols for the three programs in the library system.

Input Data

Now we will identify the input requirements of the library system, by isolating the input needs of the three programs in the system:

Lending—To sign a book out, the book number (they key used to identify the book in the **BOOK** file), and the borrowers Social Security number are needed. The program might keep track of the due data automatically. If not, this too would also have to be read.

Info—This program needs a command that indicates what information is needed.

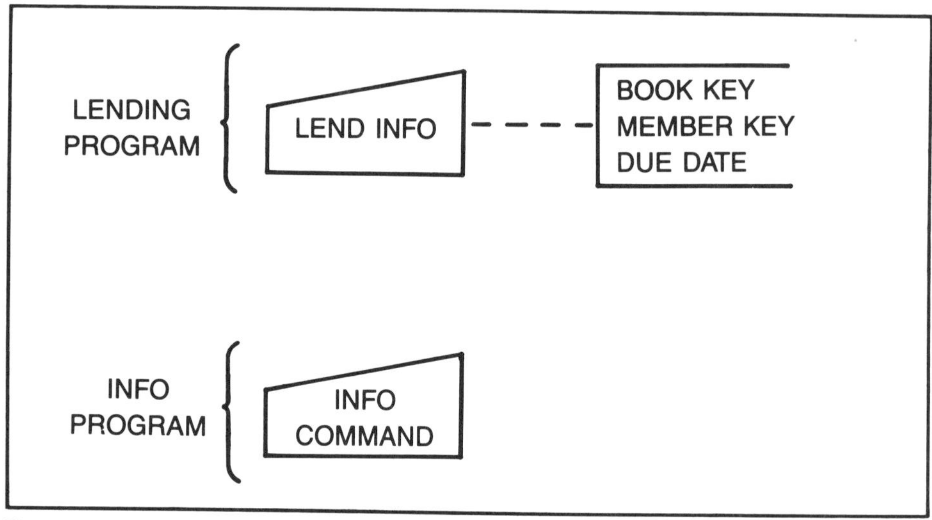

Fig. 12-3. Input needs in library system.

Additional information might then be requested, depending on the command. Also, depending on the functions supported, data from one or more of the data files will be needed.

Notice—This program might have no input needs (other than the data files it uses). However, if features such as printing notices for borrowers with more than a certain number of books is included, that information would be noted in the flowchart. Data from all three data files will be needed.

Input data is shown by the symbol which describes the type of equipment used to obtain the data. Since a keyboard will probably be used for all input needs, the manual input symbol can be used without modification. However, an annotation symbol describing the data to be input is very useful. The symbols describing these input needs are shown in Fig. 12-3.

Output Data

The last flowchart component is output data. The type of output that will be required was touched on when we discussed the programs in the system.

Lend—There is no real output "requirement" associated with the lending program. While it is true the program will display prompts and messages to the user, most programs do this. It is superfluous to indicate this type of output. Remember, though, that the program will output information to the **LEND** file in the true sense of the word.

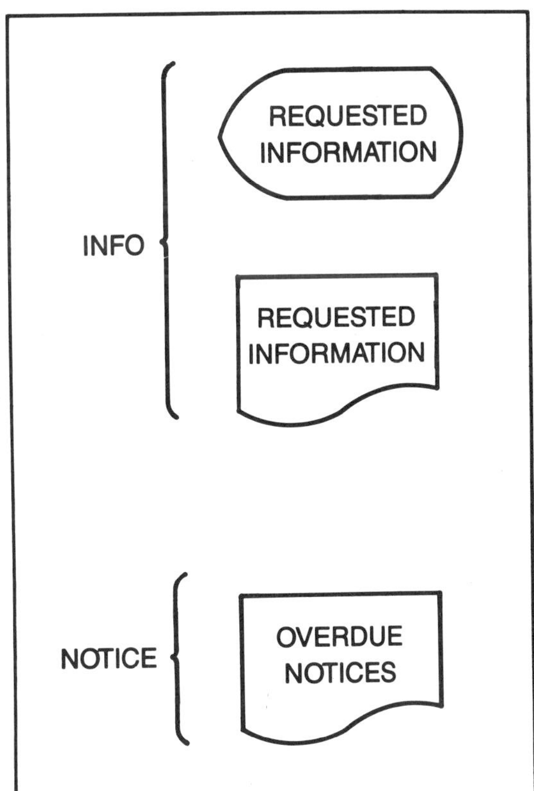

Fig. 12-4. Output needs in library system.

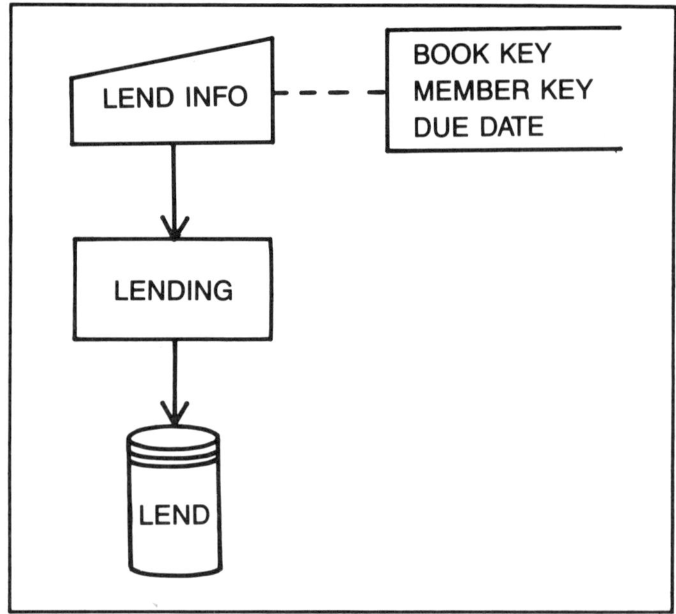

Fig. 12-5. System flowchart for lend program.

The program will also write to the LEND data file.

Info—The main purpose of the program is to display information. This will be done most often through a display device. However, it might sometimes be useful to have a printed copy when lots of data is presented. Thus, two symbols are needed here: the display symbol and the document symbol, to indicate the devices to which output will be directed.

Notice—This program will direct its output to a printer. Therefore, only the document symbol is needed.

As with the input symbols, it is useful to have annotation symbols indicating what information is being displayed or printed. The symbols to be used in this example are shown in Fig. 12-4.

CONSTRUCTING THE SYSTEM FLOWCHART

Now that the different flowchart components have been identified, they must be connected in an organized and clear fashion. The general strategy is to create "layers" which alternate between data (input data, output data, and data files) and programs. This idea is illustrated in Fig. 12-5, which shows a system flowchart in which only the LEND program has been included. Input data describing the facts about a loan are sent to the loan program. The loan program writes the information into the loan file. In systems consisting of programs which run in order, a flowchart resembling Fig. 12-6 might be the result.

The programs in the library system are not designed to be run in a particular order, so the idea of layers is not readily adaptable to this situation. One method that *can* be used is to create three separate flowcharts in which a different program is shown. Figure 12-7 shows the system flowchart for the info program; Fig. 12-8 is the notice

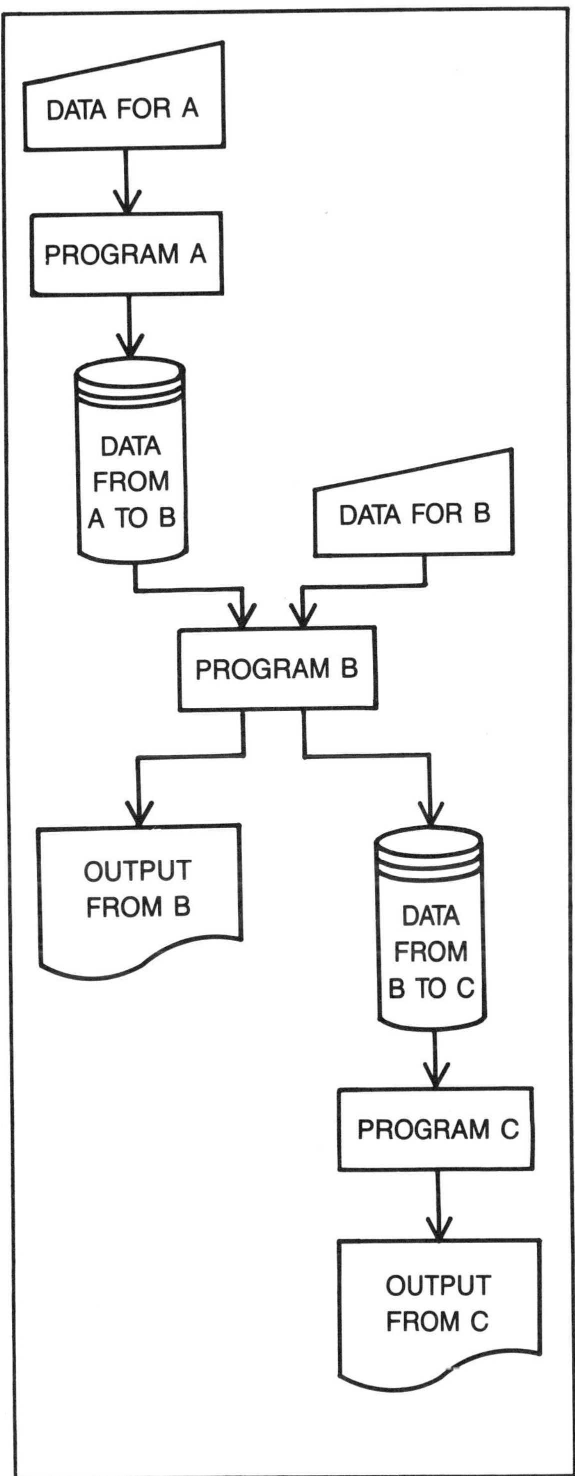

Fig. 12-6. System flowchart where three programs are run in order.

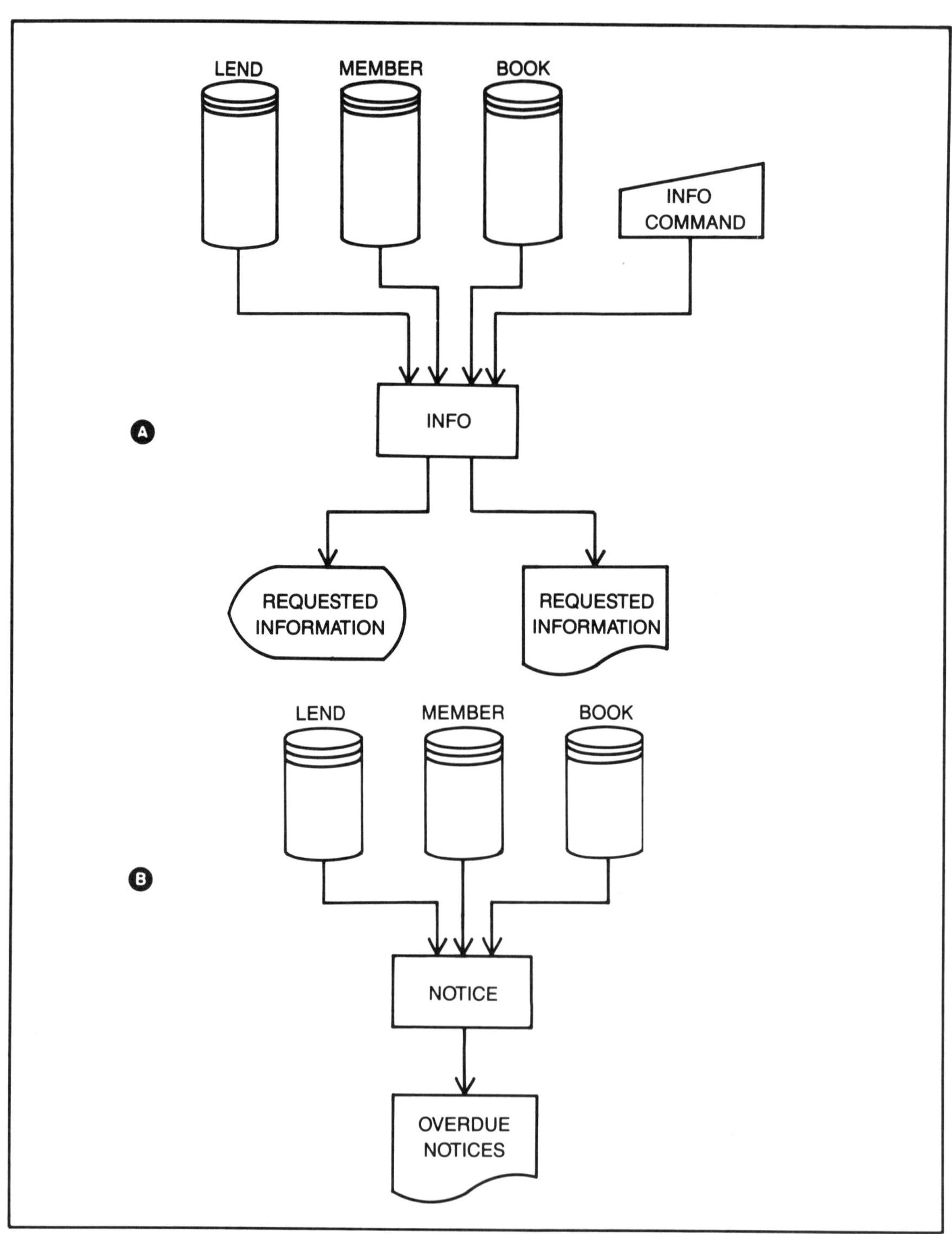

Fig. 12-7. System flowcharts for: (A) info and (B) notice programs.

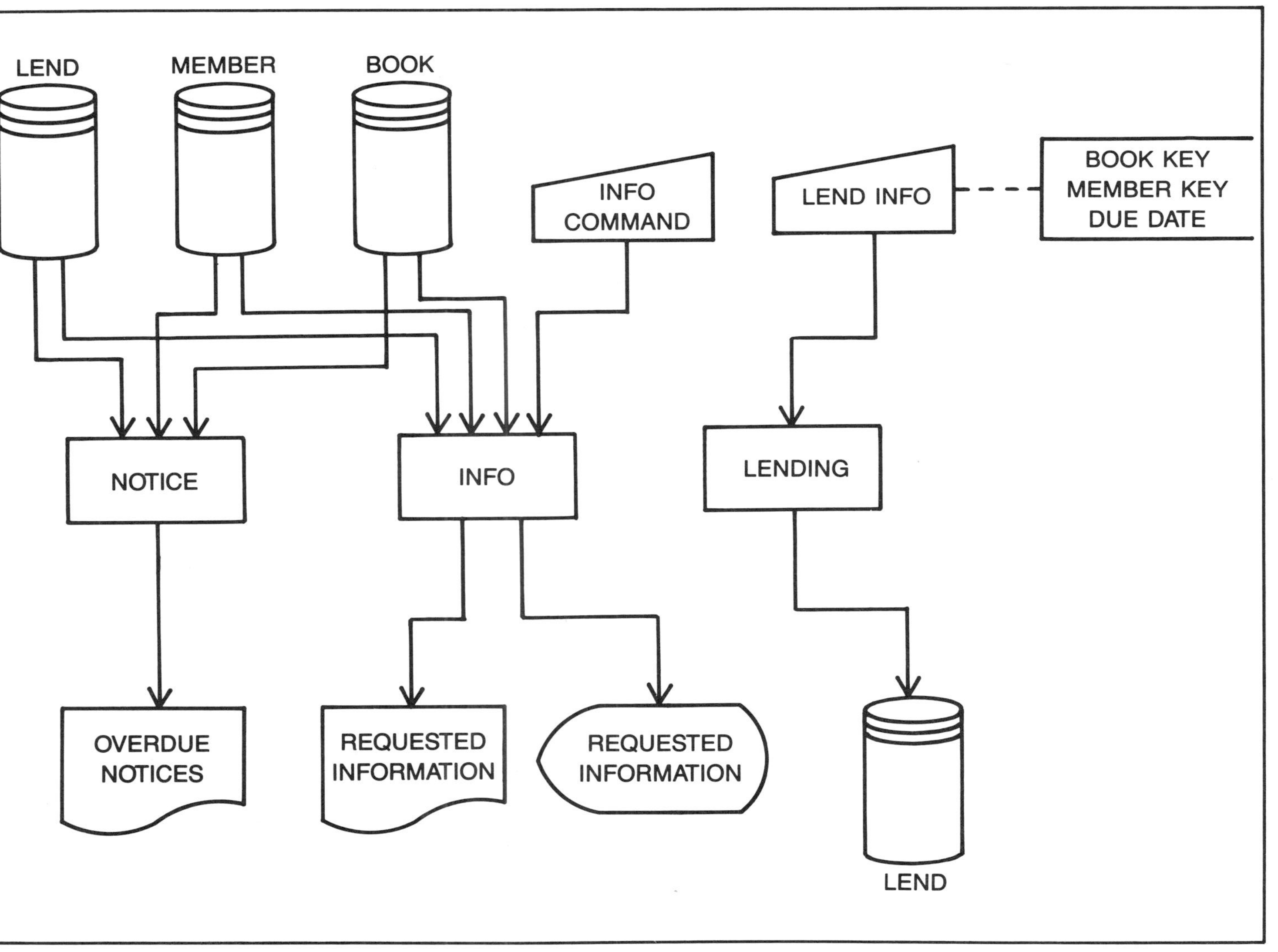

Fig. 12-8. Combined system flowchart for library system.

chart. These flowcharts can be viewed as a whole, with the understanding that identical symbols refer to the same thing. For example, the three **LEND** file disk symbols all refer to the same disk file, each symbol showing how the file is used in a particular example. It is possible to try to lump everything together, but the results are not very clear.

USING THE SYSTEM FLOWCHART

It's a good idea to construct a system flowchart early in the problem-solving process. Not only can it help a programmer remember ideas, but the different parts of the flowchart necessitate important design decisions. For example, the program symbols force the programmer to identify what functions the system should perform. In a small system, where the program symbols represent either the main program or various subroutines; the effect is the same. The input and output symbols require that the input and output needs of the system be evaluated. And the data file symbols, if they are needed at all, make the programmer decide what data needs to be saved and transported between programs. Single program systems won't need data files.

An important fact that the flowchart for the library system brings to light is that there is no way to add information to the **BOOK** or **MEMBER** files. This is revealed by the absence of any flow lines leading from a program symbol to either of the data files. This might serve one of two purposes. It might be an error in planning the system. If this is the case,the ability to write to the **BOOK** and/or **MEMBER** files would have to be added to one or more of the programs. Or, a program would have to be created for this purpose. It might indicate that no program in this system should be able to add (or delete for that matter) information from those files. These operations could belong to another system which has access to the BOOK and MEMBER files. This could be planned for security reasons. Either way, some method has to be established for adding data to the files.

SUMMARY

System flowcharts show the relationships between programs, input data, output data, and mass storage data (data files). A symbol is given to each one of these items. They are connected by a flow line when data is sent from one to another. For example, if a program makes a chart, a flow line leads from the operation symbol, which represents the program, to the document symbol, which represents the chart.

In a system flowchart, it is important to remember that the symbols do not represent devices, they represent data. If a program writes text to a printer, and then later, a table of figures to the same printer, two different document symbols would be used because the two documents represented two separate output requirements.

A system flowchart can help a program identify what functions a program should perform, decide what input and output needs to be done, and spot errors in logic.

EXERCISES

1. Write a system flowchart for the phone directory program. Because the program performs a number of functions, make a separate flowchart for each function.

2. Combine the system flowcharts created above.

3. Create a system flowchart for the following applications:

   a) Payroll system which must accept time cards, print pay checks, record tax information, etc.

   b) A University computing system which manages student academic and financial informtion.

   c) System for a business which keeps track of inventory and accounting information.

Bibliography

Aho, Alfred V.: Hopcroft, John E.: and Ullman, Jeffery D. *Data Structures and Algorithms.* Reading, Mass.: Addison-Wesley Publishing Company, 1983.

Chapin, Ned. "Flowcharting With the ANSI Standard: A Tutorial." *Computing Surveys (The Survey and Tutorial Journal of the ACM).* 2:2, 119-146.

Elliott, Ronald, E. *Problem Solving and Flowcharting.* Reston, Va.: Reston Publishing Company, 1972.

Flores, Ivan. *Computer Programming.* Englewood Cliffs, N.J.: Prentice-Hall, Inc., 1966.

Leeds, Herbert, and Weinberg, Gerald. *Computer Programming Fundamentals.* New York: McGraw-Hill Book Co., 1966.

Shooman, Martin L. *Software Engineering.* New York: McGraw-Hill, Inc., 1983.

Ullman, Jeffery, D. *Fundamental Concepts of Programming Systems.* Reading, Mass.: Addison-Wesley Publishing Company, 1976.

Index

Index